Gender & Crime

Key Approaches to Criminology

The *Key Approaches to Criminology* series aims to take advantage of the disappearance of traditional barriers between disciplines and to reflect criminology's interdisciplinary nature and focus. Books in the series offer undergraduate and postgraduate students introductions to the subject, but the aim is also to advance discussion, move debates forward, and set new agendas in the field.

Gender & Crime does just this. As Marisa Silvestri and Chris Crowther-Dowey acknowledge, second wave feminism in the 1970s and 1980s had a huge impact on criminology and criminal justice and resulted in a plethora of groundbreaking criminological texts. More recently, however, there has been a tendency to assume that 'all things are equal now', and feminist approaches to crime are all too often either limited to a single chapter in a broader textbook, or neglected altogether. This book breathes new life into existing and well-rehearsed debates about gender in three important respects. First, the fact that Silvestri and Crowther-Dowey focus on men *and* women as victims *and* offenders *and* professionals within the criminal justice system is an important and innovative feature in itself. Second, their discussion of the ways in which very recent trends, policies and practices – including new public management, penal populism, risk management and the commercialisation of crime control – may perpetuate and exacerbate inequalities between men and women, brings the gender and crime debate right up-to-date. Third, their inclusion of a human rights agenda provides a strong, unifying theme and makes this book a timely addition to the canon. Quite simply, Silvestri and Crowther-Dowey have produced a groundbreaking text which will undoubtedly stimulate new debate in this important area of criminology and criminal justice.

Yvonne Jewkes
Series Editor

Other books in the series:

Media & Crime (2004) Yvonne Jewkes (University of Leicester)

Globalization & Crime (2007) Katja Franko Aas (University of Oslo)

History & Crime (2007) Barry Godfrey (Keele University), Paul Lawrence (Open University) and Chris Williams (Open University)

Gender & Crime

Marisa Silvestri and Chris Crowther-Dowey

Los Angeles • London • New Delhi • Singapore

First published 2008

SAGE Publications Ltd
1 Oliver's Yard
55 City Road
London EC1Y 1SP

SAGE Publications Inc.
2455 Teller Road
Thousand Oaks, California 91320

SAGE Publications India Pvt Ltd
B 1/I 1 Mohan Cooperative Industrial Area
Mathura Road
New Delhi 110 044

SAGE Publications Asia-Pacific Pte Ltd
33 Pekin Street #02-01
Far East Square
Singapore 048763

Library of Congress Control Number: 2007935309

British Library Cataloguing in Publication data

A catalogue record for this book is available
from the British Library

ISBN 978-1-4129-1198-6
ISBN 978-1-4129-1199-3 (pbk)

Typeset by C&M Digitals (P) Ltd., Chennai, India
Printed in Great Britain by Cromwell Press, Trowbridge, Wiltshire
Printed on paper from sustainable resources

For Braddie and Sophie
For Libby Mae Dowey

Contents

Acknowledgments

We owe a great many thanks to a number of people during the undertaking of this book. The original concept of the book owes much to existing works on gender, crime and social justice. A great number of feminist writers have worked relentlessly to expose the ongoing gendered and discriminatory nature of social justice. These works have had an important impact on our motivations to write this book, encouraging us to be ever vigilant of claims that 'things are equal now'. We hope that this book balances realism with optimism on the issues explored.

As a joint project, we would firstly like to salute each other. Borne out of a friendship developed some years ago, working together has been an effortless project, which we have enjoyed enormously.

The completion of this book has taken somewhat longer than originally anticipated. We are grateful to everyone at SAGE with whom we have worked, but especially to Caroline Porter and Yvonne Jewkes for their patience and support over the last couple of years in seeing this book to fruition. During this time, we have both experienced much change at home and at work and have appreciated their understanding and support throughout. Thanks also to Sarah-Jayne Boyd and Louise Skelding. We are very appreciative of the challenging yet constructive comments we received from the reviewers and hope we have responded as much as possible to their recommendations. Thanks also to Amnesty International for giving permission to reproduce Biderman's Chart of Coercion in Chapter 4. Needless to say we are both responsible for any errors or omissions.

We are both indebted to a wide range of academic colleagues, friends and the many students we have taught. In particular, Marisa would like to thank Gary Fooks, Cait Beaumont, Roger Matthews, Frances Heidensohn, Chris Gifford, Robert Cook Carol Williams and Brian Clark, who have provided a constant source of intellectual support, friendship, humour and distraction when needed. Chris is grateful to Paul Senior and Matt Long for some of the ideas the three of us developed in another project, which have proved to be useful here. Lyn and Tony Cover have been great friends, sharing many good times relaxing both at home and in Rochechouart.

Last but not least, many thanks to our families. Chris would like to thank Helen for her continuing patience and love. During the final stages of this book Simon and Sally brought Libby Mae Dowey into the world, resulting in much joy and happiness to all who meet her. Just to wish the three of you all the very best in the years ahead. Marisa thanks her parents for their continuing love and support. Thanks also to her sister Antoinette and Paolo, Matteo and Luca for such a wonderful and much-needed post-book holiday. Last, but by no means least, thanks go to Stef, Braddie and Sophie. Stef, for making it all bearable through his enduring love, support and the balance that he gives; and darling Sophie and Braddie, who engender the deepest sense of sparkle and serenity.

1

Introduction

Chapter Contents

With early feminist work in British criminology focused on understanding the female offender (Smart, 1977; Heidensohn, 1985), the past 30 years or so have seen the stock of knowledge on gender and criminal justice grow exponentially. Criminologists interested in gender have taken on the challenge of making women, and more recently men, visible within the criminological enterprise. Criminology is now abundant with works considering the issue of gender, from general textbooks on gender and crime (Naffeine, 1997; Walklate, 2001) to more specific texts on women in the penal system (Carlen, 2002; Carlen and Worrall, 2004), women's and men's victimization (Newburn and Stanko, 1994; Dobash and Dobash, 2001) and the gendered nature of criminal justice organizations and those who inhabit them (Heidensohn 1992, 2003; Martin and Jurik, 1996; Brown, 1998; Brown and Heidensohn, 2000; Silvestri, 2003). With such a good range of work available, might readers be right to question our motives for writing yet another text on gender and crime? We are guided by three main motivations in writing this book. Firstly, we believe contributing to this major series by SAGE offers us an opportunity to restate the continuing significance of gender in criminology. Secondly, despite the mass of literature available, part of the impetus for this book stems from a desire to challenge the idea that the appetite for knowledge of gender and crime has been satiated. We feel that no other book currently synthesizes the material in the way that this book does. We outline both women's and men's experiences as victims, offenders and criminal justice professionals. In doing this we are calling for students of criminology to avoid empirical and conceptual complacency and for them to be aware of the evolving and ever-changing nature of the field. Lastly, we attempt to breathe new life into existing and well-rehearsed debates about gender and crime. We do so by considering the usefulness of drawing on a human rights discourse for making sense of gender, crime and criminal justice. These motivations are all underpinned by a desire to combat the growing mantra in criminal justice and broader circles that 'all things are equal now'. Indeed one of the main purposes of the book is to draw attention to the highly differentiated and complex patterns of equality and inequality. In short, for those unfamiliar with debates on gender and crime, this book will offer a comprehensive guide to some of the major debates that have influenced and shaped the study of this topic. For those already familiar with the industry of texts on gender and crime, this book will act as an *aide-mémoire* to existing debates but at the same time will make an innovative contribution to this field of enquiry.

The first part of the introduction sets out the main aims and objectives of the book and provides an overview of its overall structure. Following this, the chapter is divided into two main sections. The first section will consider the state of criminology and maps out the logic behind searching for new directions within the study of gender and crime. In doing so it will allow a greater appreciation of what has been, what currently is, and what is possible for studies on gender and crime. The second section will introduce the importance of a human rights perspective for the study of gender and crime. It is here that the book departs from traditional texts on gender and crime. The reluctance of many criminologists to take account of the significance of a human rights agenda will be outlined and its importance emphasized. We argue that academic communities have for too long clung to a very narrow conception of human rights. More specifically, we outline the feminist critique of international human rights law for failing to recognize oppressive practices against women as violations of human rights.

The decision to focus on the human rights agenda is timely for several reasons. Debates on gender and crime have rightly considered the themes of diversity, difference, discrimination and division, sometimes showing in stark terms that women's and men's lived experiences of criminal justice are highly differentiated. This conceptual point has been demonstrated through different theoretical perspectives and an expanding body of empirical work drawing on qualitative and quantitative methodologies, underpinned by competing epistemologies. Academics, policy-makers and practitioners have started to come to terms with the gendered divisions created through complex processes of differentiation. There is a mixed bag of responses and although there is some evidence that men and women today are more equal in the domain of criminal justice than their historical counterparts one, two or even three decades ago, this complex equality is muddied further by increasingly complicated forms of inequality.

The human rights agenda, at least in principle, strives towards eradicating gender differences through an emphasis on the universal characteristics of a genderless human subject. However, a closer investigation of human rights discourse shows further diversification, division and differentiation of men's and women's respective experiences of criminal justice. This book suggests that when class and race are added to the equation not only are there novel configurations in terms of relationships between men and women, but divisions amongst men and women are in some instances much sharper and more pronounced. In providing a comprehensive overview of women and men, we do outline some of the dominant explanations for women's and men's behaviours, but we should state here that the book is much more concerned with exploring how their experiences of the criminal justice system might relate to a human rights agenda. Our position is a simple one: we argue that rethinking the experiences of women and men as offenders, victims and those in control of the criminal justice system within a human rights framework will encourage a transgression of traditional debates about gender and crime.

Overview of the book and its contents

An understanding of both *femininities* and *masculinities* is a central part of this book. The book is divided into three main parts consisting of eight chapters.

A key and overarching theme of the book is the issue of control. The first part, 'Out of Control', offers an insight into the differential patterns of female and male offending behaviour, their interactions with the police, the prosecution process, the courts and the wider penal system. The second part, 'Losing Control', explores conceptions of risk, fear and victimization through an insight into women's and men's experiences of being victims of crime. The final part, 'In Control', considers the discriminatory nature of social control through an appreciation of the ways in which both the law itself and criminal justice organizations and its agents are gendered. A more detailed account of the chapters follows below.

In Chapter 2 we introduce readers to the differential patterns of female offending behaviour, charting women's participation and experiences of crime. The number of women in custody has grown at an alarming rate over recent years, rising from 1560 women in prison in 1993 to 4314 in 2007 (Home Office, 2006d). Together with the dramatic increase in the number of women in custody there has been a significant shift in describing the female offender. The emergence of the 'mean girl' (Ringrose, 2006), the 'girl gang' (Campbell, 1991; Chesney-Lind and Hagedorn, 1999; Miller, 2001), the 'ladette' (Jackson, 2006a; 2006b) and the discovery of the female perpetrator of domestic violence and sex abuse (Matravers, 1997, 2001) have all contributed to the identification of a new breed of female criminal. The female offender at the beginning of the twenty-first century is presented as one who is able and willing to participate in a culture of drinking and violence, engaging with criminal activities traditionally associated with men. In this chapter we set out what we already know about women offenders and highlight the way in which contemporary discourses about women who offend remain encased by earlier characterizations. We examine the discourses that surround the new female offender and challenge her existence, maintaining that the vast majority of women sentenced to prison are convicted of non-violent offences; they are most often sent to prison for theft and handling stolen goods.

Following the recent concern about the impact of current laws and practices on women in England and Wales, this chapter goes on to trace women's experiences and treatment as offenders through the criminal justice system. More specifically, it focuses on women's experiences of incarceration. We draw on the findings of the *Commission on Women and the Criminal Justice System* (Fawcett Society, 2004) which continues to confirm a picture in which female offenders are 'shoe-horned' into a system that is designed for men and consequently fails to meet their needs. Through a discussion of women's vulnerability before, during and after incarceration, we demonstrate that women in prison are particularly disadvantaged in their experiences. We also draw on a human rights agenda to discuss three main issues that face the female prisoner: the over-representation of women in suicide and self-harm statistics; contact with children and families; and the experience of girls in prison. In doing so we consider in more detail the relevance of Article 2: The right to life; Article 8: The right to private and family life; and the United Nations' Convention on the Rights of the Child. Our rationale for this stems from our belief that it is within this arena that the human rights agenda is relevant and has the greatest chance of making a difference.

Chapter 3 provides a descriptive overview of men's experiences as suspects and offenders through their respective contact with the criminal justice system, including the police, the courts and the penal system. Unsurprisingly it shows that the experiences of women and men are significantly different. However, unlike previous work focusing on the relationship between men and offending behaviour, the chapter focuses explicitly on the relationship between two themes. Firstly, in contrast to the 'gender blindness' of much criminological theory, the chapter critically reviews those theorizations of the cause of crime, which make conceptualizations of masculinities central to their analytical framework, focusing chiefly on structural and psychosocial schools of thought. Further, the chapter introduces the concept of human rights to the study of masculinities and crime. It is well known that men are responsible for the greater part of anti-social behaviour and crime in society, but what is missing from this understanding is an awareness of how this is related to human rights discourse. Feminists have rightly criticized human rights discourse for its propensity to sustain the privileged position of men, but this neglects the extent to which all men do not enjoy human rights in the same way. For instance, whilst male offenders from marginalized backgrounds have the same formal rights on paper, these are not always respected in practice and some men from such groups are doubly disadvantaged by their gender, as well as their ethnicity/race. It is argued that these men are potential beneficiaries of human rights values. Men are also the inhibitors of the human rights of others, especially as a result of the violence they direct towards women, an issue followed up in the chapters examining victimization.

The female victim now occupies a central place in criminological and policy agendas (Dobash and Dobash, 2001). In Chapter 4 we document the broad-based nature of women's victimization and review what we already know about the nature and extent of violence against women. Although we consider the experiences of women who have been the victims of sexual offences, for the most part the chapter focuses on the female victim of domestic violence. Despite a number of attempts to 'take domestic violence seriously' in recent years research continues to be critical of the way in which domestic violence victims are treated by the criminal justice system, with many complainants describing their experience of the legal process as a form of re-victimization (Temkin, 1997; Gregory and Lees, 1999; Jordan, 2001; Goodey, 2005). We review the official response to domestic violence through an investigation of the way in which the police service deals with victims of such crimes. We transgress existing debates within criminology by situating the issue of violence against women within a human rights framework. Cohen's (2001, 2006) work on torture and human rights has forced us to rethink the concept of 'severe pain and suffering' and has highlighted for us the inadequacy of the way in which such pain is enshrined in law. In this chapter we consider the possibility of conceiving of domestic violence as a form of torture – a clear and obvious human rights violation (Copelon, 1994). Through developing this argument we will consider the role of the state and its responsibility with respect to violence against women. Violence against women by an intimate male partner is now recognized throughout most of the world as a significant social problem and has been identified by many countries as an issue of human rights (United Nations, 1995). By situating the issue of violence against a backdrop of human rights violations, our approach goes beyond the national and encompasses a more global perspective (Cook, 1994).

In contrast to Chapter 3, which demonstrates that offending behaviour is more likely to be associated with men, Chapter 5 considers the differential experiences of men as victims in contrast to women. More than that, it investigates the relationship between victimization, masculinities and human rights. There is evidence to show that the risk of victimization is dependent on the type of crime and the gender of the victim. Take violent crime as an example. Men are much more likely to be the victim of a violent assault in a public place than their female counterparts. However, men are more likely to be perpetrators of, than victims of, an act of domestic violence occurring in a private setting. This chapter necessarily rehearses these issues but it examines them in a different way compared to much of the existing published work. It begins by considering the status of the victim in the criminal justice system in England and Wales in relation to the rights versus needs debate. This has occasioned an acknowledgement of the importance of the human rights of some victims, as well as making explicit the gender of victims. An organizing argument of this chapter is that victimizing and offending behaviour are often two sides of the same coin and many men are both victims and offenders. The final part of this chapter argues that the punitive statutory response to the anti-social behaviour of boys and young men is a form of victimization. In addition to this call for a more nuanced way of considering victimization, we suggest quite provocatively that some male victims could assume more responsibility to prevent their own victimization.

The final part of the book is concerned with those who exercise control in the criminal justice system. Each of the main criminal justice service professions originated in the nineteenth century, and in terms of gender they are very much a legacy of that period, the history books show quite clearly that each of these institutions has been dominated by men, both quantitatively and qualitatively. The criminal justice system employs hundreds of thousands of people in the Police Service, the Crown Prosecution Service, the Probation Service, the courts, the legal profession, the judiciary and in the Prison Service. Whilst women work in all of these areas it is immediately apparent from the statistics that they are not fully represented in most organizations. They are even less represented in senior positions, with only 1 woman out of 12 judges in the House of Lords; 5 women out of 43 police Chief Constables; 18 women out of 42 Chief Officers of Probation; 7 women out of 42 Chief Crown Prosecutors and 31 women out of 138 Prison Governors (Fawcett Society, 2004). Research also overwhelmingly points to a picture in which women continue to experience systematic discrimination in various ways, albeit in a less explicit form.

The final two chapters focus on the gendered nature of the criminal justice system. Chapter 6 considers the gender composition of the criminal justice professions and quantifies the number of men and women in each of the core agencies. While there is considerable variation across organizations in the sector, with higher proportions of male police officers and female probation officers respectively, it is apparent that men are concentrated in the most senior and potentially influential positions. In this chapter the concept of power is employed to understand how organizations legitimate and justify the relative dominance of male values and interests at the expense of women's interests. A case for making a more representative body of workers is unmistakably an aspect of our argument, although the workings of power and its ability to give a false impression of commitment to progressive change and to maintain a structured gender imbalance should not be underestimated.

Chapter 7 builds on the previous chapter by providing a more critical reading of women's experiences of working in criminal justice organizations. We explore the theory of gendered organizations (Acker, 1990) and draw on the police service and the legal profession as case studies within which to demonstrate the way in which criminal justice agencies and their career structures are deeply gendered at structural, cultural and individual levels. The Chapter offers an account of the various ways in which women have experienced – and continue to experience – systematic discrimination and considers more closely the issue of career progression as a key measure of gender discrimination for women working in policing and the legal profession. The chapter will map out some of the initiatives and changes that have taken place in the recruitment of women working in criminal justice organizations and speculate about the potential of a more gender-balanced and gender-aware workforce in the twenty-first century. Against the backdrop of the Equalities Act 2006 and the establishment of the Commission for Equality and Human Rights (CEHR) in 2007 we emphasize that unlawful discrimination and harassment within the workplace is an important human rights issue that needs to be addressed. The new Commission will provide a single voice on equality and human rights and take on the roles of the Equal Opportunity Commission, Commission for Racial Equality and Disability Rights Commission. In addition to its legal role in enforcing equalities legislation, the body will work to ensure that organizations and individuals have access to clear and understandable information in order to foster debate and encourage a change of culture within institutions. It will also have the role of enforcing the new 'gender equality duty'. The 'gender equality duty' requires public authorities to promote gender equality and eliminate sex discrimination. Instead of depending on individuals making complaints about sex discrimination, the duty places the legal responsibility on public authorities to take proactive steps to positively promote equality. Unlawful discrimination and harassment hold serious implications not only for criminal justice workers but also for those who come into contact with criminal justice agents, be they victims and/or offenders.

Chapter 8, the conclusion, revisits the key issues addressed in the main body of the book and summarizes its central themes, reviewing the potential theoretical and policy implications of its analysis. It also considers the usefulness of drawing on a human rights agenda for progressing existing debates on gender and crime. This chapter also rehearses a new framework, which we propose can enhance understanding of the gender and crime conundrum in future analyses. It is suggested that there are six key drivers in global crime, all having a bearing on the gender and crime debate. These drivers consist of: (1) the principles of *the new public management* (NPM), with emphases on (2) *victim-centred justice*, (3) *penal populism and public protection*, (4) the *decline of rehabilitative ideal*, (5) the *prioritization of the assessment and management of risk* and (6) the *commercialization of crime control*. While some of the observations are tentative and involve a small degree of futurology, it is hoped that these drivers will prove fruitful for forthcoming analyses of a controversy that resonates in the worlds of the academic and practitioner alike.

The state of criminology: searching for new directions

As criminology progresses into the twenty-first century, discussions about the state of its health continue to abound. The diagnosis is mixed and readings of the past, present and future states of criminology vary enormously depending on your perspective. South (1998: 222) sums these debates up well when he states that criminology 'is either in deep crisis, close to being dead and buried, or else has come through a period of conflict, resolution and consolidation, to reach a point of renewed vitality'. He concludes that criminology seems to be in a rather vigorous state of good health, producing new directions and some reflexive debate. Before giving criminology a clean bill of health, however, it might be prudent not to overstate its vigour. If we look at the indices being used to map its condition, Walters (2003) reminds us that the traditional markers, normally associated with health – in this case, the growth of criminological centres, journals, programmes and student numbers – are not necessarily evidence of a discipline in a healthy or productive state. Indeed in many cases, he argues, it may indicate the converse. Some commentators have bemoaned the lack of theoretical innovation within criminology (Rock, 1994) and others have pointed to the 'perverse' and 'deeply disturbing trends in the *content* of criminology' (Hillyard et al., 2004, original emphasis). Hillyard et al. offer an insightful discussion on the current state of the criminological research agenda. They argue that 'alongside the noise of criminology – the ceaseless chatter advocating the extension of criminal justice practices and "solutions" – there stands a series of telling, sustained silences' (Hillyard et al., 2004: 371). In particular, they note the absence of questions about power within criminological research agendas and detail the lack of attention dedicated to investigating state criminality and liability. On a more optimistic note, such characterizations fail to appreciate some of the innovative and interesting work being conducted today by newer generations in criminology. It may be that, as predicted by Heidensohn (2000), change is afoot as the fortunate generations begin to retire and new generations assume their positions. Indeed the 'Reawakening of the Criminological Imagination' was the key theme of a British Criminology Conference held at the University of Leeds in 2005.

When thinking more specifically about the issues of gender and criminology, we can see that the relationship between women, femininity and crime – and increasingly men, masculinity and crime – continues to assume an increased visibility and political significance within both criminology and the public arena. The impact of feminist perspectives is clearly observable on criminological research, policy, and practice agendas. Not only have such works assumed a greater visibility, but they have also matured within criminology. As the disciplinary boundaries become increasingly blurred in most fields, criminological works have become much more interdisciplinary in nature. If you scan the criminological literature that has emerged over recent years, it becomes fairly evident that authors of some of the more interesting work have spent considerable time searching for new vocabularies, new terms and concepts outside of the discipline. In support of this position, Heidensohn (2000: 3) notes that 'criminology has to be renewed every so often from external sources or outside visitors'. With the impact of feminism so clearly visible there is much to be proud of. Yet, not all is as good as it could be – there is no doubt that feminism and those with a gender agenda remain very much on the margins of the discipline. We concur with Heidensohn (2000) above and argue that the ability to be interdisciplinary is a key strength that provides us with new and exciting sources for the future renewal of criminology. In comparing findings from research studies over nearly three decades on various groups of women involved with the criminal justice system, Heidensohn (1994: 27) concluded that the impact of modern feminism had affected the consciousness of women. In this work, she characterizes a shift from 'being to knowing', in which women now know they are interesting, to themselves, each other and to other men. She also notes other important transitions in which women were more likely to 'resist' than 'accept' their ascribed status and to be more ready to 'voice' dissent than to maintain 'silence'. With masculinity studies still in their infancy its effects on men are harder to quantify. There is no doubt, however, that the need to understand men through an appreciation of masculinities has secured a place within criminological circles. The significant transformations that have occurred through feminist work, which will unfold in this book, are unquestionable but the extent to which mainstream criminology has acknowledged their significance is best described as providing a 'token genuflexion, rather than true respect and consideration' of gender issues (Heidensohn, 2000: 4).

In the quest for new directions, new vocabularies and new concepts, this book is underpinned by an interest in human rights. It was influenced by two events: firstly, the publication of the *Commission on Women and the Criminal Justice System* (Fawcett Society, 2004) following concern about the impact of current laws and practices on women in England and Wales; and secondly, the government's recent announcement of its intention to create a single Commission for Equality and Human Rights (CEHR) in 2007. These are important developments that give greater prominence to the issues of gender and crime, placing them within an alternative discursive framework. We feel that the discourse of human rights is uniquely placed to take on board a number of current issues in criminology. It also has the capacity to render the concerns of criminologists through a discourse of power. In doing so it seeks to make the state much more central in the quest for accountability. We think at this time it is both criminologically and politically relevant to do so. In this book the existence of power and the state are taken as a given although it is necessary to recognize that for the purposes of this book there are different state forms involved in the regulation of crime. These forms have a bearing on gendered relations in criminal justice and they are affected by the human rights agenda and/or discourses on human rights. The bulk of this book focuses on developments in criminal justice in England and Wales and to some extent the UK. What follows is an introduction to the development and growing importance of human rights in the UK together with a brief insight into some of the ways in which a human rights framework has helped to shape the arguments developed in this book.

The development and growing importance of human rights discourse

The language of human rights is becoming increasingly common currency in contemporary society with a range of individual and collective actors drawing on this body of law in a variety of ways. The concept of human rights however is not new. While the language of rights has a long history, the 'human rights project' should not be confused with the historical concept of *natural rights* because to do so would be to overlook the crucial fact that so-called 'natural rights' were not rights held solely by virtue of one's humanity. As Kallen (2004: 13) reminds us: 'Natural rights, in reality, were rights of dominant Westerners: white European men. Some 80 per cent of all human beings were excluded'. Contemporary references to human rights are those which refer to the rights that belong to every human being solely by virtue of his or her membership of human kind. In this sense human rights are frequently held to be 'universal'. The various international principles of human rights were developed in response to the world's outrage when the full account of Nazi atrocities became public knowledge. On 9 December 1948, The UN General Assembly approved the Convention on the Prevention and Punishment of the Crime of Genocide. On the very next day, 10 December 1948, the UN General Assembly adopted and proclaimed the Universal Declaration of Human Rights (UDHR). The Declaration itself goes far beyond any mere attempt to reassert all individuals' possession of the right to life as a fundamental and inalienable human right. It is a declaration that represents a statement of principles or moral guidelines for the recognition and protection of fundamental human rights across the globe (Kallen, 2004). Articles 1 and 2 of the UDHR set out the three cardinal principles of human rights – freedom, equality and dignity – as rights and freedoms to which everyone is entitled without distinction of any kind. The range of articles that follow identify particular rights and freedoms exemplifying the three central principles. The original aspirations of human rights have been perpetuated by, most importantly, the European Convention on Human Rights 1954 and the International Covenant on Civil and Economic Rights 1966, which in turn have themselves been reinforced by innumerable other declarations and conventions. Taken together these various declarations, conventions and covenants comprise the contemporary human rights doctrine and embody both the belief in the existence of a universally valid moral order and a belief in all human beings' possession of fundamental and equal moral status, enshrined within the concept of human rights. They form the centerpiece of a moral doctrine that many consider to be capable of providing the contemporary political order with what amounts to an international bill of rights (Nickel, 1992). Woodiwiss (2005) suggests that the presence of a human rights agenda is regarded by many of us in the West as symbolic in confirming our civilized condition. All in all, human rights provide an 'overarching paradigm for social equality and social justice for all of humanity, rooted in the twin foundations of human unity and cultural diversity' (Kallen, 2004: 30). For Cohen 'human rights are the last grand narrative' (Cohen cited by Halliday, 2007).

While symbolic of a 'civilized condition', the idea that human rights are universal or that they are universally enjoyed has come under increasing scrutiny. With the

Universal Declaration of Human Rights asserting that 'all human beings are born free and equal in dignity and rights', feminist groups have been vociferous in their attack on the failure of international human rights law to recognize and redress the disadvantages and injustices experienced by women. Whereas the 'rights of man' as originally conceived by the great liberal thinkers were not intended to include women, today's 'universal human rights' still overlook them as a matter of fact (Cook, 1994a). Modern human rights law owes much to the legacy of national pressure for civil and political rights at the end of the eighteenth and start of the nineteenth century. As women struggled for access to the public world during this time, men's voices were in the vanguard for political rights. The emphasis on civil and political rights reflected man's desire to regulate his relationship to the state and to set boundaries of permissible state interference in his life. Male hegemony over public life and institutions meant that rights came to be defined by men. The present hierarchy within human rights law, which gives greater attention to civil and political rights as opposed to economic, social and cultural rights, can be perceived as a manifestation of the continuing dominance men have over the process of defining the content of rights; human rights are framed in the language, needs and aspirations of men (Kallen, 2004). The exclusion of women's voices from defining the content of human rights discourse has in turn meant that human rights law has evolved along a gendered 'fault line' that distinguishes between the public and private spheres for the purpose of legal regulation (Cook, 1994). As a result, there has been a lack of understanding of the systemic nature of the subordination of women; a failure to recognize the need to characterize the subordination of women as a human rights violation; and a lack of state practice to condemn discrimination against women (Cook, 1994; Charlesworth, 1994; Fitzpatrick, 1994). Similarly minority ethnic groups, and to some extent, the working- and under-classes are subordinated. In this sense the respect for human rights has failed to be universal. It is only through women's and other oppressed groups' activism at a global level that the visibility of women and other minority groups on the human rights platform has increased.

Despite what we know about the extent and nature of violence against women, it was only formally recognized by the international community as a human rights issue after unprecedented lobbying by women's groups at the Vienna World Conference in 1993. The formal expression of this commitment can be found in the 1993 UN Declaration on the Elimination of Violence Against Women (DEVAW). This instrument has been widely welcomed as an indicator of the shift within the human rights community toward recognition of the need to address those issues that deny women their human rights. The Vienna conference not only marked an acceptance of the importance of asserting the human rights of women, but also of strengthening the enforcement mechanisms for protecting women's human rights. A number of more recent developments of the Committee on the Elimination of All Forms of Discrimination Against Women (CEDAW) are designed to enhance the effectiveness of the Women's Convention. What constitutes discrimination against women is not a point on which states readily agree. This observation is equally applicable to nation states and supranational bodies like the EU and UN. Nonetheless, the legal obligation to eliminate all forms of discrimination against women is a fundamental tenet of international human rights law. This convention moves from a sex-neutral norm that requires equal treatment, to one that recognizes the fact that the particular nature of discrimination against women is worthy of a legal response. The Women's Convention progresses beyond the earlier human rights conventions by addressing the pervasive and systemic nature of discrimination against women and identifies the need to confront the social causes of women's inequality by addressing 'all forms' of discrimination that women suffer. We will outline the significance of these developments in more detail in Chapter 4 when we consider the female victim.

Bringing rights home: cleaning up our 'own back yards'

With human rights firmly established on the statute books since 1948, some important changes have taken place in the past decade that have forced the issue of human rights firmly back onto the national and international agenda. During this time, there has been a clear shift in the way in which we think about human rights and our ability to access them. In recent years there has been a clear attempt to acknowledge citizens' human rights at a national level. The Human Rights Act (HRA) 1998 fully came into force on 2 October 2000, enabling the European Convention on Human Rights (ECHR) to be relied on directly in our domestic courts. At the beginning of the twenty-first century the discourse of human rights is no longer the reserve of those suffering international abuses. Rather, the ability to claim one's human rights is now taking place at a national and domestic level. In other words, it is becoming increasingly acceptable to draw on a human rights agenda to highlight issues within our own nation states. Not surprisingly, given the rampant and atrocious nature of some ongoing international human rights abuses throughout the world, there may be some commentators who question the need to engage with human rights on a domestic level. British citizens do after all enjoy all the benefits that come with living in a democratic state. Kallen makes a strong case for focusing on democratic states when she argues that 'If all human rights scholars shifted their attention away from democratic societies, what could well happen is that we neglect to "clean up our own back yards"'. She goes on to note that:

> It is relatively easy for people living in democratic contexts today to understand the occurrence of human right abuses when they occur in politically repressive regimes where the right to dissent is virtually non-existent and glaring social inequalities are white-washed. But how do we explain the

continuing occurrence of violations of human rights in democratic
societies whose laws and social policies are predicated upon human
rights principles of justice and equity for all citizens? (2004: xiv)

Making sense of human rights then becomes much more about understanding
how justice and equality are defined and enacted in society. In his sociological
reading of human rights, Woodiwiss (2005: xiii) neatly sums this up when he
states that the 'coverage, content, inclusions, and exclusion of rights tells us not
only who is protected against what, but also the sort of people and the aspects
of social relations that are especially valued (or not) by the governmental body
responsible for constructing, approving and enforcing the regime'. If having
access to one's human rights is about confirming our civilized condition then
focusing on the human rights of *all* citizens is an important project, offenders
included. The power of a human rights approach might lie in its capacity to provide redress for those experiencing social exclusion and who lack the power or
necessary agency to change their disadvantaged status. The extent to which
human rights legislation is capable of improving the lives of those who experience social exclusion – in this case of those who come into contact with the
criminal justice system – remains to be seen, but the sales pitch accompanying
the Human Rights Act 1998 has indeed been impressive so far. It has been
described as having the potential for being one of the most fundamental constitutional enactments since the Bill of Rights over 300 years ago (Clements and
Young, 1999). In December 1996, Jack Straw, the then Shadow Home Secretary,
and Paul Boateng MP (Straw and Boateng, 1996), produced a consultation paper,
Bringing Rights Home, which set out the Labour Party's proposals to incorporate
the Convention rights into United Kingdom law. The paper is infused with optimism, claiming that the human rights act would 'nurture a culture of understanding of rights and responsibilities at all levels in our society' and 'result in
a human rights culture developing across all countries'. In the opinion of the
Joint Committee on Human Rights (2002), the government's case was that the
Act would 'help to inaugurate a gradual transformation of civil society', create
a 'more humane society' and would work to 'deepen and widen democracy
by increasing the sense amongst individual men and women that they have a
stake in the way in which they are governed'. Others have been even more
ardent in their support. Helena Kennedy declared: 'something is happening: a different Zeitgeist, a shift in the legal tectonic plates'. Wade stated that the Act is a
'quantum leap into a new legal culture' (cited in Costigan and Thomas, 2005: 51).
Alongside this great sense of anticipation, however, there has also been much
concern over the development of human rights in Britain. Chakrabarti (2005)
notes that one of the greatest disappointments of the infancy of the Human
Rights Act lies in the way in which its values have failed to sufficiently take root

in wider society. Unlike the development of a Human Rights Commission in 1998 in Northern Ireland,[1] Britain's adoption of a rights agenda lacked the provision of a commission to advise and assist alleged victims in bringing proceedings. During the passage of the Human Rights Bill, there were many calls for a commission to be established. Baroness Amos, for example, called for a body that would:

> raise public awareness, promote good practice, scrutinise legislation, monitor police developments and their impact, provide independent advice to Parliament, and advise those who feel that their human rights have been infringed. (cited in Spencer and Bynoe, 1998)

Lester and Clapinska also emphasize the far-reaching and damaging consequences of not having a commission at the inception of the Human Rights Act. They argue that:

> [t]he time when a human rights commission was most needed was in the period following enactment of a human rights act, when a culture of respect for human rights could have been promoted, to give real meaning to the Act and to ensure that its purposes were widely understood. (2005: 170)

Attempts to develop a human rights culture in Britain have increased apace in recent years. In October 2002, the government published a consultation paper, *Equality and Diversity: Making it Happen*. The paper noted the 'complementary nature of equality and human rights', which was 'reflected in the Government's vision of a society based on fair and equal treatment for all and respect for the dignity and value of each person' (Women and Equality Unit, 2002: para 9.3). Following a series of consultation papers, the government accepted the strong case for developing a single Commission for Equality and Human Rights. While it may be somewhat premature to begin to assess its impact, what is important to note at this stage is that achieving equality is no longer simply a question of discrimination but is now one firmly associated with achieving human rights. And, this is where criminology enters the debate. For achieving one's human rights is inextricably bound up with achieving justice, an obvious and central concern for criminologists.

Human rights meets criminology

The centrality of human suffering has underpinned much of Stan Cohen's contribution to the study of deviance and control. For an excellent review of his formidable body of work see the collection of essays in honour of him by Downes et al. (2007). Through the concept of human suffering Cohen has attempted to offer a unified analytical framework for criminological inquiry. Urging criminologists to push forward an agenda of social justice, Cohen adopts a pragmatic position through what he has termed the 'voracious gods of criminology'. These gods are the broad parameters to which, according to Cohen, criminology should adhere:

> ...first, an overriding obligation to pursue honest intellectual enquiry (however sceptical, irrelevant and unrealistic); second, a political commitment to social justice, and third (and potentially conflicting with both), the pressing and immediate demands for short-term humanitarian help. We have to appease these three voracious gods. (Cohen, 1998: 122)

By reconceptualizing debates in gender and crime through a human rights lens we hope to demonstrate our commitment to these obligations.

So what can a human rights discourse offer the study of gender and crime? How can we begin to draw on these developments to improve women's and men's experiences of criminal justice? We argue that one of the key strengths of adopting a human rights framework in criminology is its ability to unify the experiences of vulnerable groups. In doing so we hope to provoke greater discussion about the location and enactment of power. To emphasize that women, for example, whether they be victims, offenders or criminal justice professionals, can be unified in their experiences renders their vulnerability and lack of power visible in a male-dominated legal and criminal justice system. It may also serve to balance up the uneven landscape of criminological knowledge in which we have seen the female victim reign over her other criminologically interesting counterparts. Those women who work as social control agents, for example, remain relatively under-researched and explored within criminology. Given the level of power that these women have achieved, there are those who may argue that they don't deserve to be drawn together under the banner of 'powerlessness' in the same way as their victimized and offending counterparts are, for in many ways, it is these women who are part of the problem, part of the repressive regimes that women experience. But, to recap, our argument is a simple one – to unify women in this way serves to expose the unequal relations that exist between women and men and emphasize the gendered nature of the criminal justice system. We are ever conscious, however, that trying to unify groups in this way may strike many as a flawed if not somewhat regressive step, particularly when theorizing about gender. For women particularly, the idea of trying to unify through a singular identity of 'womanhood' can easily be described as risking and undoing much feminist work that has already been done. To propose recourse through a human rights discourse runs counter to the main direction of feminist thinking which is moving away from such universalizing strategies. Similarly, to present men as a unitary and oppressive body is not always helpful. Some writers on masculinities are also keen to emphasize the multiple manifestations of 'manhood'.

We are also keenly aware of the complex ways that race, gender and class intersect to affect the individual experience. And, given the progressive steps that have been made in the celebration of diversity, difference and the plurality of femininity and masculinity, such a route can easily be described as a dangerous and unwarranted direction for criminology to go in. We believe that embracing a human rights perspective offers us the opportunity to attain a degree of solidarity in an existing context of diversity and difference. Recapturing a common language may provide us with a vocabulary through which to sustain pressure on governments, agencies and citizens (i.e. Garland's (2001) usage of the notion of 'responsibilization') working towards change.

The offender

The closed nature of the penal system in itself makes all those held in detention, be they women or men, particularly vulnerable to breaches of their human rights. Furthermore, prisoners often share backgrounds and characteristics, which heighten their vulnerability. The Chief Inspector of Prisons, Anne Owers, describes this dialectic when she states that:

> It is particularly the marginalised who need the protection of human rights: by definition, they may not be able to look for that protection to the democratic process, or the common consensus. And most of those in our prisons were on the margins long before they reached prison (look at the high levels of school exclusion, illiteracy, mental disorder, substance and other abuse); and may be even more so afterwards (with difficulty in securing jobs, homes, continued treatment, and even more fractured family and community ties). Prisons exclude literally: but they hold those who are, already were and will be excluded in practice. (2004: 110)

A more holistic understanding and appreciation of offenders' background prior to detention makes their vulnerability an obvious concern for criminologists. Factors such as mental health problems, educational difficulties, drug- and alcohol-related issues all pose serious concerns for those working with both female and male offenders. For those who are incarcerated, research has overwhelmingly revealed high levels of mental disorder and drug misuse and general poor health among prisoners (Carlen and Worrall, 2004). While estimates of the scale of mental disorder within the prison system vary, O'Grady (1999) estimates that about 70 per cent of inmates have personality disorders; the figure rises to 90 per cent if you include substance misuse.

The prevalence of suicide and self-harm among young inmates and women is also an ongoing and growing concern within our prisons. For many young offenders their first experience of prison custody will be on remand while they wait for their charges to be processed through court. The remand process is slow and costly. The Audit Commission found that over one third of those remanded in custody and subsequently found guilty did not receive a custodial sentence. The *Thematic Review* (HM Chief Inspector of Prisons, 1997) found that sentenced young male offenders had been on remand for an average of three months, but had spent two years on remand before being sentenced. In a study of suicide and self-harm by young people carried out by the Trust for the Study of Adolescence, young people on remand were found to be a particularly vulnerable group, being more likely than sentenced prisoners to suffer from personality and neurotic disorders, and to have had contact with mental health services before entering custody. Liebling (1995) and Lyon (2004) add further support here when they argue that young people find their experience of imprisonment more difficult than adults in every respect. Women are also over-represented in the suicide and self-harm statistics. Home Office statistics show that while less than 1 in 100 men engage in self-harm the figure for women is alarming at 1 in 6. In 1993 there was one female suicide in custody, in 2003 there were thirteen. It was specifically because of the special vulnerability of people in detention that the Northern Ireland Human Rights Commission decided to make the human rights of prisoners one of its strategic priorities. Its work highlighted an alarming number of breaches of human rights, particularly with regard to Articles 2 and 3 of the European Convention, i.e. the right to life (Article 2); and the right to freedom from torture and inhumane and degrading treatment (Article 3) (Scraton and Moore, 2004).

In claiming the authority to imprison one of its citizens, Mathiesen (2000) reminds us that the state is undertaking a responsibility for the prisoner's health, safety and physical well-being which is qualitatively greater than that owed to free citizens. Questions thus arise concerning the scope of prisoners' rights and entitlements and of the mechanisms of legal accountability. And, while prisoners may lose much when they enter prison, they also maintain and acquire some rights. In summary, they are entitled to protection from harm, and access to services which include the specific right to healthcare equivalent to that available to those outside in the community. Rule 17 states that the medical officer has responsibility for the 'care of the health, mental and physical, of the prisoners in that prison' (Reed and Lyne, 1997). Despite these basic rights there is no doubt that those in detention remain an *unpopular* and *undeserving* minority in the eyes of the general public. As we have already argued the closed nature of the penal system in itself makes those held in detention particularly vulnerable to breaches of their human rights. And, as the delivery of punishment increasingly moves to private hands, the need to be ever vigilant about what goes on behind closed doors becomes more pressing. It is through the re-framing of prisoners as people, with rights rather than privileges conditional upon good behaviour, that the human rights agenda may herald a challenge to custodial thinking, custom and practice.

The victim

We think our ability to convince readers of the usefulness of adopting a human rights approach when dealing with victims will be a less daunting task. Victims, unlike their offending counterparts, are at the outset conceived of as 'powerless' and as 'deserving' of attention. Over the past 20 years or so, the female victim in particular has slowly come to occupy centre stage in terms of visibility. One of the key issues on which this visibility has rested upon has been the victimization of women at the hands of men. This issue has variously informed feminist-inspired research agendas, analyses of criminal justice policy and practice, and feminist theorizing (Comack, 1999). Our knowledge of male victimization is also slowly gathering pace. Despite being 'deserving' of attention through their status as victims, there is still much to gain from incorporating a human rights framework when thinking about victims. For example, victimologists have for a long time drawn attention to the fact that victims do not enjoy formal rights like suspects and offenders and that the response to victims has been couched mainly in terms of needs and expectations. By conceptualizing victims' experiences of violence through a human rights lens the issue of state accountability is forced firmly onto the agenda. With regard to women, work in this area is already well underway on an international stage. Leading the feminist critique against mainstream human rights discourse for its gender blindness, rights activists have made notable progress on several fronts including critiquing the distinction between the public/private divide with respect to women's legal rights. In so doing they have held governments accountable for failing to protect women from domestic violence; led governments to condemn sexual violence against women in armed conflict; and forced governments to treat trafficking as a human rights crisis (Cook, 1993, 1994; Coomaraswamy, 1999; Coomaraswamy and Kois, 1999).

Situating the issue of violence against a backdrop of human rights violations and an international human rights agenda has also resulted in the development of a global appreciation of women's victimization, allowing differently positioned groups to unite across national boundaries. An appreciation of what goes on beyond national boundaries under the umbrella of human rights also enables us to venture into comparative criminology in a much more sophisticated way. Nelken (1994) and Mawby (1999), amongst others, have outlined the importance of developing a comparative dimension to criminology as a way of offering a reformulation of the central problems in criminological theory. It also offers us an agenda in which there are many possibilities for 'new' criminological problems and prospects. Such an approach further allows us to achieve an insight into some of the possible gendered effects of globalization. Radford and Tsutsumi (2004) argue that globalization has further influenced the scope and the nature of violence against women, bringing different and more opportunities for violence from men to women, making women and girls especially vulnerable to entrapment, exploitation and abuse.

The criminal justice professional

For those who work in the criminal justice system, we argue our position from a point of social justice. It remains undemocratic to have a criminal justice system that is dominated by men, both in numerical terms and in relation to values. We believe that a modern, democratic society requires a diverse work-force in all areas of life. It is over 30 years since implementation of the Equal Pay Act 1970 and Sex Discrimination Act 1975 outlawed discrimination in the workplace on the grounds of sex. Research continues to show that, although theoretically integrated, women still experience social closure when working in criminal justice organizations. They are subject to a broad range of discriminatory cultures and practices which can be seen in a number of areas including: pay differentials; under-representation in senior positions; ghettoization in certain areas or professions; sexual issues around maternity leave and pay; and inflexible work arrangements for those with caring responsibilities. Individuals who work within the broad range of criminal justice agencies operate within gendered environments in which organizational logics are imbued with notions of heterosexist masculinity. This has serious implications not only for those women (and some men) who exercise power but also for those service users, at the receiving end of criminal justice, either as offenders or victims. We are not suggesting that women are necessarily more competent in carrying out the functions of administering justice (although there are some studies that indicate women's transformative potential here); rather, we believe that a criminal justice machinery drawn from a more diverse background will improve its overall quality by bringing a broader range of views and experiences to criminal justice and to the culture which underpins it.

Concluding thoughts

In an article about the state of feminism and criminology, Comack (1999) offers an insightful perspective of both the problems with feminist criminology and with the solution to it. She maintains that a large part of the reason for feminists' marginalization from the mainstream discipline rests on the dualistic construction of 'women as victims' and 'men as offenders'. More specifically, she claims that feminist work continues to be sidelined through its reliance on the construction of women as victims of male violence. The consequences of thinking in such dualistic terms are far-reaching and one of its main effects is to encourage us to approach complex issues in overly simplistic ways. For feminism to move from the margins (closer) to the centre of the criminological enterprise Comack (1999: 162) points out that there needs to be a 'reconsideration and rethinking of the dualisms on which much feminist and criminological work has been premised'. At first glance, an overall reading of our work might suggest that we too are engaged in perpetuating the idea of women as victims, not only of male violence but also of a male-dominated criminal justice system. Indeed we do argue that this is sometimes the case, but we also emphasize the need to conceptualize men, as victims of a system that denies their voice and existence as men. In doing so, we are not suggesting that women and men are passive in their existence as offenders, victims or criminal justice professionals. Indeed there are numerous excellent studies that have demonstrated the active and resistant nature of those caught up in the criminal justice system. Rather, we agree with Comack's (1999) basic position but go one step further in rethinking and reconsidering the dualism that has come to characterize both women and men through their various statuses in the criminal justice system. We are proposing that *all* individuals, regardless of their status, can be perceived as potential victims and offenders at the same time. Depending on whose interpretation you are reading, women offenders, for example, can easily be perceived as epitomizing both the victim and offender. Similarly, the female victim is also criminalized by official discourse when she does not employ sufficient crime prevention strategies to protect herself. For men too, the male offender who experiences discriminatory treatment at the hands of criminal justice agents is both offender and victim simultaneously. Broadening the focus and blurring the distinctions between such dualisms as 'women as victims' and 'men as offenders' makes it possible to stand outside traditional criminal justice models and offer new insights into pressing criminological issues. In short, we are arguing that *all* individuals, regardless of their sex and status should have the right to have their basic human rights met. The realization of this principle must be based on an appreciation of the particular experiences of people in a specific time and in a specific place. From this basic premise, the book now begins.

Summary

- Gender and crime is a topic that has attracted considerable scholarly attention and this chapter acknowledges the volume of work that has been produced, especially since the 1960s. The influence of feminism on criminology was traced and we showed how this has led to a reorientation of criminological inquiry.
- The differential experiences of women and men as offenders, victims and criminal justice workers were identified as central issues and are indicative of three themes

running throughout the book: *out of control* (the offender); *losing control* (the victim); and *in control* (the practitioner).

- The distinctiveness of the approach adopted in this book was then rehearsed, specifically the inclusion of a human rights perspective. We argued that there are persistent inequalities and injustices in criminal justice policy that are gendered, and that an appreciation of human rights discourse enables us to disentangle the markedly different experiences of men and women. While human rights principles recognize the universality of human experience it can also be used to show profound gender differences.

Note

1 The Northern Ireland Human Rights Commission was set up as a result of the Belfast (Good Friday) Agreement in April 1998. It is a strictly non-party political body which strives to promote and protect the rights of all people in Northern Ireland.

2

Women as Offenders

Chapter Contents

OVERVIEW

Chapter 2 provides:

- An insight into the nature and extent of female offending.
- An analysis of the current trend to 'search for equivalence' in criminality between women and men.
- An overview of the arrival of the 'new female offender' in the form of the 'mean girl'; the 'ladette'; the female sex offender; and the female perpetrator of domestic violence.
- The impact of the 'mean girl' discourse on the punishment of girls and women.
- An exploration of women in prison and the concept of vulnerability.
- An analysis of what human rights can do for women in prison with a focus on three main issues that face the female prisoner: the over-representation of women in suicide and self-harm statistics; contact with children and families; and the experience of girls in prison. In doing so we consider in more detail the relevance of Article 2: The right to life; Article 8: The right to private and family life; and the United Nations' Convention on the Rights of the Child.

KEY TERMS

family life	ladette	search for equivalence
female offender	lean girl	vulnerablility
female sex offender	mothers in prison	women in prison
feminist criminology	punitiveness	
human rights	suicide and self-harm	

Interest in the female offender has ebbed and flowed over the past hundred years. For much of this time, she has been invisible and neglected in discussions on criminality. When she has appeared, she has been portrayed as peculiarly evil, unstable and irrational. At the beginning of the twenty-first century, the female offender is back in the limelight. In an increasingly punitive climate she has not been exempted from the 'incarceration binge' characteristic of contemporary western states (Snider, 2003). With a dramatic and alarming increase in the number of women in prison in the last decade, the female offender now occupies a central place on government and criminological agendas. Together with this sharp increase we are also being confronted with a range of new female criminal characters. The rise of the so-called 'girl gang' (Campbell, 1991; Chesney-Lind and Hagedorn, 1999; Miller, 2001; Alder and Worrall, 2004; Chesney-Lind and Irwin, 2004); the emergence of the 'mean girl' and the 'ladette' who are able and willing to participate in a culture of violence and drinking (Alder and Worrall, 2004; Worrall, 2004; Jackson, 2006a, 2006b; Ringrose, 2006); the perpetrator of domestic violence and homicide; and the discovery of the female sex abuser (Matravers, 1997, 2001) are all indicative of the female offender being back, only this time she is back with a vengeance; or so it seems.

This chapter is divided into three main parts. The first part offers an insight into the female offender. It is dedicated to detailing who the female offender is, her participation in crime and her presence in the penal system. We challenge the idea that women are becoming more criminal and concur with Worrall (2002) who argues that the search for equivalence between women's and men's participation in crime is the product of the 'backlash' of the 1990s that has been founded on the denial of the context of victimization in which women offend. The second part spends considerably more time outlining the treatment that women who offend receive as they progress through the criminal justice system. More specifically, it focuses on women's experiences of incarceration. Our rationale for this stems from our belief that it is within this arena that the human rights agenda is relevant and has the greatest chance of making a difference. In the third and final part we focus on three main issues that face the female prisoner: the over-representation of women in suicide and self-harm statistics; contact with children and families; and the experience of girls in prison. In doing so we consider in more detail the relevance of Article 2: The right to life; Article 8: The right to private and family life; and the United Nations' Convention on the Rights of the Child.

Who is the female offender?

There have been some improvements made to the availability of data on offenders. The data on female and ethnic minority offenders in particular has been more accessible since the Criminal Justice Act 1991. Section 95 of the Act required the Secretary of State to 'publish such information as he considers expedient for the purpose of enabling persons engaged in the administration of justice to avoid discrimination against any persons on the ground of race or sex or any other improper ground'. Though descriptive in nature, the publication is a useful and important source of statistical knowledge on the experiences of women and ethnic minorities as offenders, victims and criminal justice professionals. There is little doubt from the criminological literature that women's pattern of offending is different from men's. The overriding consensus within criminology remains that while women do commit a broad range of offences they commit less crime than men and are less dangerous and violent than their male counterparts (Carlen and Worrall, 1987; Immarigeon and Chesney-Lind, 1992; Heidensohn, 1996). Women are less likely to be recidivists or professional criminals, and are less likely to be involved in violent or sexual crime. Men outnumber women across all major crime categories. In 2005 between 83 and 94 per cent of offenders found guilty of burglary, robbery, drug offences, criminal damage or violence against the person were male. Although the number of offenders was relatively small, 98 per cent of those found guilty of or cautioned for sexual offences were male. Theft was the most commonly committed offence by both men and women in 2005 but, overall, men committed 70 per cent of theft-related offences. However, 55 per cent of female offenders were found guilty of or cautioned for theft and handling stolen goods compared with 32 per cent of male offenders (Home Office, 2005b). It does seem then that there is an anomaly between women's actual participation in crime statistics and their reported participation, the effects of which are explored below.

As of January 2007 there were 4314 women in prison and 74,574 men in prison. The vast majority of women sentenced to prison are convicted of non-violent offences, with women most likely to commit 'acquisitive' crimes such as shoplifting or fraud (NOMS Briefing, 2006). While the number of women in prison remains considerably lower than that of their male counterparts, when examined more closely the statistics do point to a significant trend. There has been an exponential growth in the number of women in prison. In the decade from 1995 to 2005 the women's prison population increased by 126 per cent compared with a 46 per cent increase for men (Home Office, 2006). Furthermore, the number of women in custody far outstrips the growth rate of the male prison population. Between 2001 and 2002, for example, the number of women in prison increased by 15 per cent compared with a 6 per cent increase in the number of men in prison (Home Office, 2006d). In addition to the rising number of women involved in criminal activity, the changing nature of women's offending has also been of key concern in recent years. The past decade in particular has seen a growing discourse suggesting increased gender neutrality in offending behaviour. This movement is evident in what Worrall (2002) has termed the 'search for equivalence' in offending. It is important to note here however that the search for equivalence in women's and men's offending behaviour is not new. Rather, the idea that women engage with crime in the same way as men can be seen in earlier works such as that by Pollak (1950) and Adler (1975). In *The Criminality of Women*, Pollak (1950) argued that women's crime was vastly underestimated and that women were more prominent than men in the dark figure of crime. For Pollak, women are inherently deceitful, cunning and therefore able to conceal their crimes. As evidence he points to the large dark figure of crime in abortion, theft and prostitution. Exploiting their status as helpless victims they are aided by men's besotted chivalry and so are able to 'mask' and conceal their crimes. Freda Adler (1975) also tried to make sense of the rise and changing nature of female crime throughout the 1960s and 1970s in her controversial book *Sisters in Crime*. The significance of this text will slowly unfold and our discussions serve as an important lesson to those involved in current constructions of the new female offender. Adler identified a 'new breed of female criminal' who was changing her pattern of offending to a more 'masculine' style, becoming more aggressive, more violent and unfeminine. Writing in the 1970s against a backdrop of emergent equal opportunities legislation, the link was quickly made between women's liberation and their participation in crime. Adler writes:

> Women [are] no longer indentured to the kitchen, baby carriages and bedrooms ... in the same way that women are demanding equal opportunities in legitimate fields, so a number are determined to force their way into the world of major crimes. (1975: 67)

Inherent within her argument was the idea that not only does liberation cause crime but that female criminality can be treated as an indication of the degree of liberation achieved by women. The idea that the women's movement was causing changes in women's crime became the subject of extensive media and scholarly attention (Adler, 1975; Simon, 1975; Chesney-Lind, 1989). Research overall gave little support for the hypothesis that there was a 'new female criminal' suggesting that she was more a myth than an empirical reality (Weis, 1976 cited in Chesney-Lind, 2006; Steffensmeier, 1980; Chesney-Lind, 1989). Chesney-Lind (2006: 8) perceptively describes feminist investigation during this period as a 'costly intellectual detour' as well as a 'harbinger of things to come'. The idea that women are becoming equal partners in the field of crime is once again gaining ground within media and policy circles and it seems that Pollak's (1950) and Adler's (1975) work is enjoying somewhat of a renaissance.

Current trends: the 'search for equivalence'

The search for the 'new breed of female criminal' continues into the twenty-first century. Heidensohn (2006: 7) notes that despite the fact that questions about gender, crime and justice have increased apace in various settings, the 'persistence of [these] original themes is striking'. One need only look at the headlines in recent years to see evidence of the growing unease around young women's misbehaviour in the public sphere (see Jewkes, 2004 for a good overview of the media construction of criminal women). The emergence of the so-called 'ladette' and the growth of girls' participation in bullying and gangs are evidence enough of this concern. Although the 'ladette' and the 'gang girl' refer to two distinct forms of deviance, we draw on Ringrose's (2006) concept of the 'mean girl' as an overarching term to describe and indicate women's participation in these behaviours. Characterized by binge drinking, smoking and aggressive behaviour, girls as young as thirteen are said to be indulging in the behaviour once only enjoyed by their male counterparts. A recent report in the *Guardian* newspaper notes that British girls are among the most violent in the world, with nearly one in three Scottish and English adolescents admitting to having been involved in a fight in the past year. In a survey of youngsters in 35 countries, child health experts found that Scottish and English girls ranked fifth and sixth in violence, just behind Hungary, Estonia, Lithuania and Belgium. Experts blamed the 'ladette' culture of binge drinking and drug use (*Guardian*, 24 January 2006).

The 'mean girl', the female sex offender and the female perpetrator of domestic violence

Chesney-Lind (2006) provides a good summation of the media representation of deviant women. Following a familiar pattern, stories begin with a bold and salacious headline; the story goes on to cite a range of juvenile crime experts who have spotted a disturbing nationwide pattern of teenage girls becoming more sophisticated and independent criminals. The narrative then provides graphic detail regarding the injury suffered by the victim. These forensic details are then followed by a quick review of arrest statistics showing what appear to be large increases in the number of girls arrested for violent offences. Finally, there are quotes from 'experts', usually police officers, teachers, or other social service workers, but occasionally criminologists, interpreting the narrative in ways consistent with the desired outcome: to stress that girls are getting more and more like their already demonized male counterparts and, hence, becoming more violent (Chesney-Lind and Irwin, 2004).

Writing about the 'urban delinquent gang' Hallsworth and Young (2004: 12) note that its existence has been 'sensationalised to absurdity by the tabloids and by documentary-makers hell bent on suggesting that Britain's fair streets are being over run with feral gangs'. Adding girls to the mix certainly increases the sensationalism further distorting the crime problem. The media is now awash with stories of girls' bullying behaviour (McVeigh, 2002; Talbot, 2002 cited in Ringrose, 2006). An article by Hill and Hellmore (2002) for the *Observer* newspaper titled 'Mean Girls' documents the 'insidious and sophisticated' cruelty groups of girls are exacting on one another. Ringrose (2006) further emphasizes the unprecedented media attention of the rise of the 'mean' girl who bullies, is aggressive, and is potentially violent. Her analysis of this narrative suggests that the 'mean' girl is rarely explicitly raced or classed but rather provides a more universalized discourse in which *all* girls are now increasingly conceptualized as mean and aggressive. The findings on whether or not girls' crime is on the increase remain mixed. While arrest data consistently shows dramatic increases in girls' arrests for violent crimes (e.g. arrests of girls for assault climbed an astonishing 40.9 per cent, whereas boys' arrests climbed by only 4.3 per cent in the past decade (Federal Bureau of Investigation, 2004 cited in Chesney-Lind, 2006), other data sets, particularly those relying on self-reported delinquency, show no such trend; indeed they show a decline (Chesney-Lind, 2004; Chesney-Lind and Belknap, 2004; Steffensmeier et al., 2005). Furthermore, Chesney-Lind (2006) suggests the creation of 'self-fulfilling prophecy' with dramatic effects on girls' arrests, detentions, and referrals to juvenile courts. It seems increasingly clear from this work that forces other than changes in girls' behaviour have caused shifts in their arrest (Chesney-Lind and Belknap, 2004). All in all, the desire to demonstrate that 'girls do it too' has increasingly devastating effects on girls (Chesney-Lind and Irwin, 2004; Worrall, 2004: 47; Alder and Worrall, 2004).

The search for equivalence continues with the discovery of the female sex offender and the female perpetrator of domestic violence, both of which add further fuel to the identification of the new female criminal. Matravers (1997, 2001) shows that whilst women had previously been identified as sex offenders, their involvement was constructed through discourses of passivity, normally undertaking their role as the unwilling accomplices of men. More contemporary characterizations have however focused more heavily on women's own willingness to perpetrate such acts. The high profile British cases of schoolteachers Rebecca Poole in 2006 and Amy Gerhing in 2002, both accused of committing sex acts on pupils in their care, reinforce the construction of women as sexual predators operating within an epidemic of female teacher–student sex.

Accompanying the female sex offender, the female perpetrator of domestic violence has also emerged as a new criminal player. The case of *Sun* newspaper editor Rebekah Wade – arrested for allegedly assaulting her actor husband Ross Kemp in 2005 – has made clear a number of broader societal concerns about women. The reporting of this case attracted attention and controversy about women, especially the kinds of women cited earlier in Adler's (1975) work. Known for her 'terrifying' ambition Rebekah Wade made history in 2003 by becoming the first female editor of the *Sun* – the UK's biggest selling daily paper with 10 million readers. Sadly, rather than raise the profile of men as victims, it was Rebekah Wade's successful career profile that became the prime concern of news stories. The academic field has also seen some scholars argue that women are now as violent as men (DeKeseredy et al., 1997; Miller, 2005). Research by Stets and Straus (1990) further suggests that women's violence to a male partner cannot be construed as 'self defence' because they claim that women are likely to initiate violence. A thorough search for the female perpetrator of domestic violence can be found in the work of Dobash and Dobash. Following 190 interviews with 95 couples they are critical of accounts that suggest her rise and conclude that:

> [i]ntimate violence is primarily an asymmetrical problem of men's violence to women, and women's violence does not equate to men's in terms of frequency, severity, consequences and the victim's sense of safety and well-being. (2004: 324)

Their work lends support to the work carried out by Gadd et al. (2002) on domestic abuse against men in Scotland. They reveal that one quarter of the men had not experienced violence from their partner but had misunderstood the meaning of the term 'domestic violence' and were referring, instead, to crimes in the domestic dwelling (e.g. non-domestic assaults and property crimes). Of those men who did experience some form of violence from their female partner, they were less likely than women to be repeat victims, to have been seriously injured and to have reported feeling fearful in their own home. Based on these findings, the researchers conclude that there was no need for a special agency or refuge provision for men. The consensus therefore remains that historical and contemporary evidence from many societies indicates that partner violence is overwhelmingly something perpetrated by men against women (Dobash and Dobash, 1979; Daly and Wilson, 1988; Dobash et al., 2004).

The impact of the 'mean girl' discourse

Identifying women's participation in non-traditional crimes such as violence and sexual abuse poses interesting dilemmas for those interested in the study of gender and crime. On the one hand the discourse of equivalence might act as a useful tool in unshackling women from traditional characterizations of their behaviour and their potential for criminality. Through emphasizing women's capacity to engage in a range of acts once reserved for men, the conventional idea of what it means to be a woman and of womanhood can no longer be sustained. In this way, the search for equivalence could be viewed as a positive and liberating force for women. Indeed we have already argued that there is a need to rethink the dualism that has come to characterize both women and men in the criminal justice system. Broadening the focus and blurring the distinctions between such dualisms as 'women as victims' and 'men as offenders' makes it possible to stand outside traditional criminal justice models. We certainly know a lot more about women's participation in violent crime than we previously did.

While traditional gang research almost exclusively characterized female gang members as either socially maladjusted tomboys, hopelessly trying to be 'one of the boys' (Campbell, 1991) or 'promiscuous sex objects' (Miller, 2001), more recent gang literature such as Campbell (1991), Fleisher (1998) and Miller (2001), has sought to correct the inaccurate portrayal of female gang members. These authors have immersed themselves in the lives of girls, exploring their motivations for joining and their activities in gangs more fully. Through their research, these authors emphasize that girls in gangs are more than just auxiliaries or sex objects. Indeed if we were to acknowledge and accept that women are capable of committing serious criminal acts in the same way as their male counterparts, it might follow that those who come before the courts accused of such crimes would be treated with less hostility.

An alternative reading of the search for equivalence suggests a much more dismal outcome for women. Worrall highlights the disastrous effects of such discourses when she notes that:

> [t]he 'search for equivalence' driven by a misunderstood feminist hegemony calling for the empowerment of women by making them accountable for their deeds has resulted in an inevitable increase in the numbers of women rendered punishable. (2002: 64)

In trying to make sense of the increased punitiveness directed at the criminal woman, Snider focuses her attention on how the knowledge generated about the female offender is *heard* and *interpreted* by those officials in power. In doing so she treats the:

> [k]nowledge produced by feminist and non-feminist criminologies as productive and constitutive, as an essential component of changes in the conception of the female offender and in the policies to control, discipline and punish her. (2003: 355)

Snider argues that feminist criminologists have themselves been complicit in the surge of punitiveness that criminal women receive today. She notes that a key success of feminist work has been to contribute to a discourse in which the female offender has become more 'self-aware', 'robust' and 'equipped with the languages and concepts of resistance'. Such a characterization has developed from the claim that female offending arises from female victimization. This idea has been extensively documented, debated and discussed throughout feminist criminology (Carlen, 1983; Comack, 1996; Balfour, 2000; Kendall, 2000; Pollack, 2000). Victimization discourses are now widely employed by those hoping to improve conditions for the female offender and inmate; indeed we draw on this script in order to make our own case in this book. Snider (2003: 366) notes that the victims' discourse is a useful 'tool in the kitbag of resistance' and has proved 'pivotal in the constitution of the resilient, resistant female offender'. Herein lies the problem. This knowledge has not been *heard* or *translated* into improving conditions for the female offender. On the contrary, it is this very claim that has generated massive resistance, fuelling a powerful backlash against all progressive movements, including feminism. The female offender has now been characterized as someone who no longer 'knows their place' (Snider, 2003: 356). The resulting outcome is that it is not the woman victimized by life's experience that is at the forefront of governmental intervention but rather it is the 'mean girl', in all her various forms discussed above, who has come to preoccupy government thinking as the punishable offender who deserves the increased punitiveness of the state.

The 'mean girl' phenomenon is contributing to new forms of regulation, surveillance and discipline that hold serious implications for all girls. Insightfully, Ringrose notes the differential impact of such regulation on differently positioned girls when she states that:

> [While] new technologies, therapies and educational strategies are being adopted by middle class communities, schools and parents to regulate the risks presented by the powerful mean girl, the effects of this narrative of girl-hood for those girls who lay outside the boundaries of middle-class mean-ness are quite different. New criminal categories like the anti-social behavior bans draw particular girls into growing webs of penal regulation. (2006: 412)

It is girls 'whose families and communities do not necessarily have the resources to challenge the criminalization of minor forms of youthful misbehavior' that bear the brunt of increased social control (Chesney-Lind and Irwin, 2004: 55). Not only are more women entering the criminal justice system but the move towards accepting the concept of gender neutrality in offending has resulted in the 'unmaking of "women" as a category of offender requiring any special attention at all' (Chesney-Lind and Irwin, 2004: 65). Emphasizing that women can be the same as men has effectively resulted in the denial and erasure of sex and gender from discussions. This is particularly important when thinking about policy interventions. The disastrous effects are highlighted by Worrall when she states that:

> The apparent realisation that women might deliberately sexually harm children, rather than protect them from sexual harm, justified an ideological and moral retreat by professionals and policy makers. (2002: 48)

The 'search for equivalence' in offending behaviour has been further compounded by the search for equivalence in victimization with the rise of the male victim. We are not suggesting that his existence should in any way be denied (indeed we propose greater visibility); simply that his arrival may herald important ramifications for the female offender, as Worrall observes:

> If women are no longer victims of gender-specific oppressions, such as domestic violence, rape and sexual abuse, because men are also victims of these things, then there is no need for gender-specific ways of dealing with offenders. (2002: 49)

The message then is clear. Through a discourse of gender neutrality and equivalence in offending the state can now happily rescind its obligation of treating women as a category of offenders with distinct needs. Treating women offenders as though they were men, particularly when the outcome is punitive, in the name of equal justice, amounts to nothing more than what Chesney-Lind (2006) terms 'vengeful equity'. The proclamation by Sheriff Joe Arpaio neatly sums up the concept of vengeful equity. In defending his controversial chain gang for women in Maricopa County, Arizona, he explains that:

> If women can fight for their country, and bless them for that, if they can walk a beat, if they can protect the people and arrest violators of the law, then they should have no problem with picking up trash in 120 degrees. (Kim, 1996 cited in Chesney-Lind, 2006)

Punishing the female offender

Women's experience of the criminal justice system has been the subject of much academic enquiry. To a large extent this work has primarily been concerned with scrutinizing and documenting whether women are punished differently to men. More specifically, investigations have focused on assessing whether women are the recipients of leniency or whether they are subject to a harsher form of justice than their male counterparts (Gelsthorpe and Morris, 1990; Daly, 1994; Heidensohn, 1996). In brief, it has been historically supposed that women are treated more leniently than their male counterparts; that women are less likely to be arrested, convicted and imprisoned (Simon, 1975; Harris, 1977; Nagel, 1980; Moulds, 1981; Kruttschnitt, 1984). Feminist criminologists have, however, worked hard to expose the complexity of women's experiences of criminal justice. They have highlighted the disparity between the rhetoric of leniency and the reality of practice and have portrayed a system in which women are not the recipients of chivalry protected from the full rigours of punishment. On the contrary, research has shown that women are subjected to a gendered criminal justice system, characterized by gendered organizational logics and gendered agents of power (Heidensohn, 1992, 2000; Martin and Jurik, 1996; Brown and

Heidensohn, 2000; Malleson, 2003; Silvestri, 2003; Rackley, 2007). Scholars have demonstrated that sexism is not manifest in overt disparities but operates through subtle processes that reinforce the gender roles in the discourse of law and its enforcement. So, where it may appear that women are accorded a degree of leniency, they are in fact subject to an oppressive and paternalistic form of individualized justice (Eaton, 1986; Daly, 1989, 1994). For women offenders who come before the courts there remain serious concerns that judges and magistrates are becoming harsher and more severe in their sentencing response to less serious offences leading to a steep rise in the number of women in prison. A woman convicted of theft or handling stolen goods in the Crown Court is now twice as likely to go to prison as she was in 1991. In the Magistrates' Court, the rate of increase in the use of custody for women is higher (Hedderman, 2004).

Furthermore, research has highlighted the fact that not all women are equal before the law. A number of studies have emphasized that even if chivalry is extended to women, it may not necessarily be the case that it is extended to all women. Feinmen (1980) notes that chivalry is reserved for white, middle class women. Visher (1983), Simpson (1989) and Chigwada (1999) all argue that white women enjoy a considerable advantage over black women and indeed black and white men. The study by Farrington and Morris (1983) on Cambridge city magistrates found that 'sex' had no direct influence on the severity of sentence but that a significant variable was 'marital status', with divorced and separated women experiencing harsher treatment than their married counterparts. Kruttschnitt (1984) identifies the importance of 'respectability' as a significant variable in the treatment women offenders receive. Carlen's (1983) study showed that Scottish sheriffs hated sending anyone to prison – only a 'certain type' of women end up in court, let alone prison. Carlen's evidence suggests that their sentences are made on the assessment of women as mothers, with less sympathy awarded to those women who step outside the boundaries of domesticity. Despite remaining an important and ongoing concern, measuring and assessing the differential treatment that women receive is not our main concern. Rather, we focus our attention on women's vulnerability and highlight some of the ways in which the prison experience impacts on women in a particularly damning way.

Women in prison and vulnerability

While the female prisoner may well have been overlooked and marginalized by official penal discourses for much of her incarceration, she has enjoyed a relatively high profile over the past decade. More specifically, a concern over the quality of care that women in custody receive has been the focus of various criminological, official and campaigning studies (Eaton, 1993; Carlen, 2002;

Carlen and Worrall, 2004; Fawcett Society, 2004; Home Office, 2007). The over-whelming consensus of these studies is that women in custody are particularly vulnerable on entering the criminal justice system. Furthermore it has been argued that the criminal justice system has failed to recognize the degree of deprivation that characterizes women's backgrounds or the wider consequences of custodial sentences for them and their families (Wedderburn, 2000).

Research has shown that women suffering from poor physical and mental health, the social effects of poverty, addictions and physical and sexual abuse are over-represented in the prison population (Carlen, 2002). A recent Home Office study found that 66 per cent of female prisoners were either drug dependent or reported harmful, hazardous levels of drinking in the year prior to custody. Half the women in one Home Office survey said they had experienced domestic vio-lence and the true figure is likely to be higher (cited in Fawcett Society, 2004). The same report shows that the majority of women in prison have experienced some form of abuse, and that a history of abuse is one factor amongst others contributing to the risk of offending and of a range of associated problems, including drug and alcohol problems, mental health problems and self-harm (Fawcett Society, 2004). With a higher proportion of women than men entering prison with a mental health problem, Carlen and Worrall (2004) argue that women's physical and mental healthcare needs in prison are more varied and complex than men's. In addition to suffering from poor physical and mental health before and during imprisonment, women face further disadvantage with their vulnerability extending beyond their time in custody. Whilst women have many of the same resettlement needs as men, there are additional factors relat-ing to their caring responsibilities, histories of abuse and discrimination in the labour market that further compound their vulnerability.

The various concerns generated by women in custody can be seen clearly at a governmental level. The past decade has witnessed a number of official reports aimed at addressing the specific needs of women prisoners. The publication of the wide-ranging *Thematic Review of Women in Prison in 1997* (HM Chief Inspector of Prisons, 1997) marked a turning point for official discourses on women in prison. It was published following an unannounced inspection of London's HMP Holloway by the then Chief Inspector of Prisons, Sir David Ramsbotham. The conditions of the prison at the time so appalled him that he suspended the inspection and walked out in disgust. The document covered all aspects of imprisonment and has been hailed by Lowthian (2002: 160) as 'the most thor-ough and detailed blueprint for change ever produced'. It contained clear analy-sis of the problems and set out detailed, specific recommendations for change under a range of different areas. The report was widely welcomed by many both inside and outside of the Prison Service. Following the Review there has been increasing interest within official circles to develop better practice for women offenders. The Scottish Office, for example, published *Women Offenders – A Safer*

Way: A Review of Community Disposals and the Use of Custody for Women Offenders in Scotland in 1998 (Social Work Services and Prisons Inspectorate for Scotland, 1998). For England and Wales, the Home Office (2000a) published the *Government's Strategy for Women Offenders*. The key findings of the consultation that followed fed directly into the development in 2004 (Home Office, 2004) of the Women's Offending Reduction Programme (WORP). The programme's action plan outlines two key long-term objectives: reducing women's offending and reducing the number of women in custody. The main focus of the programme is to improve community-based provision for women offenders ensuring that custody is used as a last resort for those women offenders who really need to be there because of the seriousness of their offence or for public protection. It is aimed at a range of stakeholders both within and outside the criminal justice system and is designed to ensure that their policies, interventions and services are made more appropriate to meet the needs and characteristics of women offenders. Most recently, the Corston Report (Home Office, 2007) found little improvement in the treatment of women offenders and called for a radical change in the way in which women are treated throughout the whole criminal justice system. The report emphasizes the need for a more distinct, radically different, visibly-led, strategic, proportionate, holistic and woman-centred, integrated approach to both women who offend and those at risk of offending.

Taken together, this array of official documentation provides a considerable analysis of issues and recommendations on how the state might more effectively respond to women's law breaking. At first glance, it appears that the government has finally recognized that the current methods of incarcerating women are wholly inadequate. Indeed the Comprehensive Spending Review published in July 2004 promised that the government would pilot radical new approaches to meet the specific needs of women offenders, to tackle the causes of crime and reoffending among this group and reduce the need for custody. On closer inspection, however, government policy on the female offender is riddled with contradiction. With a pressing need for more available prison places, Lyon (2004) argues that the Prison Service has responded to the need for more places for women by implementing a largely arbitrary and piecemeal process of 're-rolling' establishments – turning prisons for men into prisons for women. The Prison Service has also commissioned the building by the private sector of two new prisons for women which will create a further 800 places. Lowthian offers an insightful assessment of this decision when she notes that:

> The creation of two large new prisons represents one of the most significant barriers to reform; the resources being spent on these projects could far better have been directed into the provision of smaller units across the country, giving a better spread of places and thus enabling women to be imprisoned nearer to their home areas and local communities. (2002: 164)

More disturbingly, these developments have taken place against the backdrop of clear recommendations of both the Wedderburn Report (2000) and The Commission on Women and Criminal Justice (2004), which recommend a national network of local women's supervision, rehabilitation and support centres linked to local custodial units. With the future of women's imprisonment in flux, the final part of this chapter draws on a human rights discourse to further empha-size the plight of the female prisoner. We focus on three main issues that face the female prisoner: their over-representation in suicide and self-harm statistics; contact with their children and families; and the experience of girls in prison. In doing so, we consider the relevance of Article 2: The right to life, Article 8: The right to private and family life, and the United Nations' Convention on the Rights of the Child.

What can human rights do for women in prison?

It would be inaccurate to portray the female prisoner as devoid of any formal rights. To recap, in claiming the authority to imprison one of its citizens, the state is undertaking a responsibility for the prisoner's health, safety and physical well-being that is qualitatively greater than that owed to free citizens (Mathiesen, 2000). The Prisons Inspectorate does already rely heavily on international human rights standards in setting its 'expectations' against which it measures conditions for prisoners (HM Inspectorate of Prisons, 2004). The standards are broad-based and incorporate every aspect of prison life, including transportation and recep-tion, healthcare, education, legal rights and protection from harm. They also extend to the need to seek alternatives to custody, through preventative mea-sures, and the reintegration of prisoners into society.

While most principles apply to all prisoners, some are gender or age spe-cific, and others relate to the issue of racism or other forms of discrimination in prison (Scraton and Moore, 2004). There are some positive procedures that are designed to encourage the special status of women's rights. So far as pos-sible, men and women should be detained in separate institutions. In those institutions holding men and women 'the whole of the premises allocated to women shall be entirely separate' (United Nations, 1955: 8). In women's pris-ons there must be a special provision for pre-natal and post-natal care. Where possible, babies should be born outside prison. When babies are permitted to stay with their mothers in prison, there should be nursery provision staffed by qualified personnel (United Nations, 1955: 23). Women's prisons should also be staffed predominantly by female officers. Although it is permissible for male members of staff, such as doctors and teachers, to carry out professional duties, male members of staff should not enter the part of the prison set aside for women unless accompanied by a woman officer (United Nations, 1955: 53). Carlen and Worrall (2004) note that not all of the rights are 'absolute' and that the 'rule of law' in a civilized society limits and qualifies some of them. Indeed they argue that the Prison Service has shown a high degree of complacency about the impact of the Human Rights Act. Despite this, there are now some cases being brought which challenge prison treatment generally (under Article 3), the prison disciplinary system (under Articles 6 and 7) and restrictions on contact with families (under Article 8). The state is also obliged to ensure effective independent monitoring and inspection processes. Where there are grounds to believe that a violation of human rights has taken place, the state is under an obligation to conduct a 'prompt and impartial investigation' or ensure than an inquiry takes place (United Nations, 1999: Article 9, para 5). The United Kingdom also signed up to the *Optional Protocol to the Convention against Torture and other Cruel, Inhuman or Degrading Treatment or Punishment* adopted by the United Nations in December 2002. The object of the Protocol is:

> [t]o establish a system of regular visits undertaken by independent international and national bodies to places where people are deprived of their liberty, in order to prevent torture and other cruel, inhuman or degrading treatment or punishment. (United Nations, 2002)

Suicide and self-harm: Article 2 – The right to life

When a person is in the custody of the state, the state has a particular duty to safeguard their right to life. More specifically, the prison service claims to operate the concept of the 'healthy prison'. Drawn from international human rights principles, the prisons inspectorate uses the World Health Organization's four tests of what constitutes a healthy custodial environment to measure and assess the prison regime. In determining whether or not an establishment is 'healthy' it tests whether: prisoners are held in safety; if they are treated with respect and dignity as human beings; if they are able to engage in purposeful activity; and if they prepared for resettlement (cited in Scraton and Moore, 2004). Upholding the right to life is especially significant regarding women prisoners who are clearly over-represented in the suicide and self-harm statistics (Liebling, 1994). While women constitute 6 per cent of the prison population in England and Wales, 20 per cent of prison suicides from January to August 2004 were women (Asthana and Bright, 2004). From one female suicide in custody in 1993, the next decade saw a dramatic rise in which 14 women and girls killed themselves

MENTAL HEALTH.

while in prison (Home Office, 2003). Women on remand, who account for a quarter of the female prison population, are particularly vulnerable as they are more likely to suffer from psychosis and neurotic disorders than sentenced prisoners and are also at higher risk of committing suicide (Social Exclusion Unit, 2002). The crisis in women's prisons remains. In its third annual review of women and criminal justice the Fawcett Society (2007) reports ongoing concerns about women in prison and suicide. At the time of writing, in June 2007, five women had already taken their own lives in prison during 2007, more than in the whole of 2006.

As part of the overall development of the 'healthy prison' and following a growing concern over the level of suicide and self-harm in women's prisons, there has been an important change to the way in which the prison service perceives and deals with suicide and self-harm. With traditional explanations firmly located within models of individual pathology, recent years have seen the development of alternative theorizations. The inadequacy of prison policy to recognize or to deal with the issue of suicide and self-harm was emphasized by Her Majesty's Chief Inspector of Prisons. It states that:

> Current Prison Service policy fails to communicate the social dimensions to self-harm and self-inflicted death. It does not stress sufficiently the significance of the environment in which prisoners and staff are expected to live and work, or the importance of constructive activities in helping inmates to cope with anxiety and stress. Above all, it fails to give weight to the need to sustain people during their time in custody, the importance of relationships between inmates and between staff and inmates in providing that support. (1990: 7)

There have also been a number of important changes to the delivery of healthcare within prisons in recent years. The reform in healthcare in prisons has at its centre the principle of equivalence in standards of healthcare with that of healthcare in the community. In 1997, Her Majesty's Inspectorate of Prisons went on to favour an integration of the healthcare for prisoners with that of the National Health Service. CARAT teams (counselling, assessment, referral, advice and throughcare) now operate in all prisons, offering assessment and referral services for the high numbers of women in prison with substance abuse problems. Such developments suggest that the prison service has recognized its official obligations towards its inmates.

Recent investigations into the healthcare of women prison, however, portray a prison service working at odds with the concept of a 'healthy' environment. While prisoners retain the right to have healthcare equivalent to that available to those outside the prison, research points to an inconsistent picture within the prison estate. The quality between prisons varies considerably: some prisons provide healthcare broadly equivalent to NHS care, but many are characterized by low-quality care, with inadequately trained and professionally unsupported doctors, which fails to meet proper ethical standards (Reed and Lyne, 1997). More specifically, the worrying lack of proper detoxification programmes for women has the effect of creating unsafe environments in which women are neither held decently nor able to be effectively assessed and prepared for resettlement (HM Chief Inspector of Prisons, 2005). Lowthian (2002) also stresses the poor regimes that characterize women's prisons in England and Wales. In particular, she notes poor healthcare and hygiene standards; a lack of holistic needs-based programmes for women; an overemphasis on security and discipline over 'non-mandatory' tasks due to staff shortages; an inappropriate allocation of prisoners; and an overall inadequate standard of care due to staff shortages. It is these very conditions that have come to define the experience of imprisonment for many women.

aids with lack of mental health.

This chapter has already stressed that on entering prison women bring with them a distinctive type of vulnerability. With this in mind, Liebling (1992, 1995) emphasizes the significance of the prison environment in contributing to the risk of suicide. She notes that for certain groups of prisoners 'the situational aspects of their prison lives may be decisive' and that those most vulnerable are 'expected to undergo an experience whereby the demands made may exceed the resources available' (Liebling, 1995: 183). There is little doubt that the cumulative effects of the conditions outlined above pose serious problems for women and may well serve to increase the risk of self-harm and suicide. Findings from the Commission on Women and Criminal Justice (Fawcett Society, 2004, 2007) confirm these findings and further point to a lack of throughcare upon release back into the community. It was specifically because of the special vulnerability of people in detention that the Northern Ireland Human Rights Commission decided to make the human rights of prisoners one of its strategic priorities. Following the controversial death of 19-year-old female prisoner Annie Kelly in Northern Ireland in 2002, the highly critical HM Chief Inspector of Prisons (2003) report on Mourne House revealed that the Northern Ireland Prison Service had no dedicated policy or strategic plan for the treatment of women and girls in custody. It pointed to a number of alarming conditions, including an inappropriate level of security; a regime based on lengthy periods of lock-up offering an insufficiently busy and active day; an unhealthy balance of male staff to female prisoners; the strip-searching of women without reasons being given; and insufficient information and support for women on their first night in prison with no structured induction programme. The inspectors were especially critical of the treatment of suicidal and self-harming women, noting the inappropriate use of the main male prison hospital and punishment blocks for distressed women prisoners.

Following publication of this report, Scraton and Moore confirmed the concern about the punitive context within which physically and mentally disturbed women

CRITICISM.

↓

and girls are treated. Critical of the lack of available counselling and therapeutic pro-vision for those with mental health needs, they note:

> Holding women prisoners, particularly girl children for 28 days in bare cells with nothing to read, listen to or look at amounted to a real and serious deprivation. (Scraton and Moore, 2004: 142) ✗

Furthermore:

> [t]he use of the strip cell with no mattress, no pillow, a heavy duty blanket, a potty for a toilet to be slopped out and no in-cell access to a sink was degrading and inhumane and possibly in breach of Article 3 of the European Convention on Human Rights and of Article 3 of the Human Rights Act. (Scraton and Moore, 2004: 144)

In sum, their findings raise serious concerns about the extent to which the treatment of women and girls in custody is compliant with international human rights law and standards. Their findings point to a prison service operating a disregard for the concept of the 'healthy prison', which:

> [a]t best neglected the needs of prisoners and at worst added to the hopelessness, helplessness, and desperation experienced by many pris-oners made vulnerable through their incarceration. (Scraton and Moore, 2004: 83)

While the capacity of the prison service to uphold its duty of care to those it imprisons remains questionable, several recent landmark cases of deaths in cus-tody have forced the issue firmly within a human rights framework. When taken together, the Amin case[1] related to the death of teenager Zahid Mubarek at Feltham Young Offenders Institution in 2000; the Middleton case[2] concerning the suicide in prison of Colin Middleton in 1999; and the Sacker case[3] in which Sheena Creamer was found dead while on remand at New Hall prison in 2000, establish the important principle that deaths of people in custody should be effectively and thoroughly investigated and that the investigation should cover the measures taken to safeguard an individual's life (Scraton and Moore, 2004). In March 2004, following the inquests into the death of Colin Middleton and Sheena Creamer, the House of Lords ruled that juries in inquests into prison deaths are to be allowed to blame failings in the prison system for contributing to an inmate's suicide. Five law lords unanimously ruled that an earlier ruling virtually barring jurors from blaming shortcomings in the prison system for con-tributing to a prisoner's death no longer applied. The Human Rights Act, with its guarantee of the right to life, now meant that jurors were entitled to say not only 'by what means' a prisoner had died, but also 'in what circumstances' (Dyer, 2004). These landmark cases are pivotal in confirming the state's obligation to protect life.

Imprisoning mothers: the right to private and family life

The issue of imprisoning mothers remains high on campaign agendas. Despite their incarceration, prisoners have the 'right to a private and family life' (Article 8). In order to facilitate this, where possible, prisoners should be held in institutions reasonably near to their home. The state also has a duty to provide assistance to a prisoner's children. Further rights for the children of prisoners can be found in the broader United Nations Convention on the Rights of the Child (UNCRC). The UNCRC is important in that it emphasizes that all the rights it identifies apply to *all* children and that there should be no discrimination on the grounds of the activities or status of the child's parents. Article 9 of the Convention states that the child has a right to maintain regular contact with both parents unless it is contrary to their interests. In real terms, however, the structural configuration of women's prisons has very real and detrimental consequences for women's ability to maintain contact with their families. The small number of establishments that accommodate women means that they are, on average, more likely to be located further from their families than men are.

Currently, women prisoners are held in 19 prisons unevenly distributed throughout England, of which two are converted wings of a men's prison. There are no women's prisons in Wales. Establishments range from a high security wing of the male prison at HMP Durham, which holds the very few Category A (highest security risk) female prisoners, to a former borstal and converted country mansion at HMP East Sutton Park. Only HMP Holloway in London was built for its current purpose of incarcerating women. The relatively small number of large establishments that accommodate women means that they are, on average, more likely to be located further from their families than men. The Chief Inspector of Prisons reported that 60 per cent of women surveyed were more than 50 miles from home (HM Chief Inspector of Prisons, 2005). One of the ways in which the prison service has responded to the concept of maintaining family life has been to allow women to keep children with them in prison. For women with a child under 18 months, mother and baby units are available. The units are staffed by trained prison officers and employ professional nursery nurses and the prison accepts a duty of care towards the baby in relation to health issues.

In their work on prisons in Northern Ireland, Scraton and Moore (2004: 143) report that the right of women in prison and their children to a meaningful family life was not respected. They found that women were restricted to brief periods of unlock during which they could make telephone calls to their children, and there were no special arrangements made for family visits. Women complained that they were often only able to see their children for 45 minutes each week. It is worth reiterating here that the deleterious effects on family life of imprisoning mothers continues well after they have served their sentences and are released back into the community. With the female prisoner more likely to be the primary carer of dependent children than her male counterpart, the National Association for the Care and Resettlement of Offenders found that a significantly higher proportion of the children of female prisoners than male end up in care and for those children that are taken into care, there is an increased likelihood of them becoming offenders themselves (cited in Fawcett Society, 2004). Furthermore, Caddle and Crisp (1997) found that the children of imprisoned mothers displayed a variety of behavioural problems, including sleeping and eating problems; bed-wetting; becoming withdrawn; and problems in developing overall social skills. The dire consequences of imprisonment for women are summed up neatly by the Director of the Prison Reform Trust, Juliet Lyon when she states that:

> There is a high price to pay for overuse of custody. Imprisonment will cause a third of women to lose their homes, reduce their future chances of employment, shatter family ties and separate more than 17,000 children from their mothers. (2004)

While the establishment of mother and baby units may appear to be an attempt to address the specific vulnerability of women offenders with children, Carlen and Worrall's (2004) argument that their very existence may encourage courts to send mothers with babies to prison instead of seeking out the alternatives is perhaps a more convincing one. The very idea of imprisoning women with children, together with the current organization of the women's prison estate, hinders and indeed militates against the possibility of achieving the right for private and family life. An interesting point is raised by Carlen and Worrall (2004) when they ask what rights prisoners' children have among all this. Their answer is simple: 'not many'. There is clearly much to be gained from thinking outside of the 'penal box' (Hannah-Moffat, 2002). We have much to learn from penal systems further afield. The Ter Peel experiment in the Netherlands is often cited as a model of provision. Here, children remain with their mothers up to the age of four years but attend nurseries outside the prison on a daily basis (cited in Carlen and Worrall, 2004). In Russia, mothers of children under the age of 14 who are convicted of all but the most serious offences are routinely given suspended sentences until the child reaches 14. In Germany, women are housed under curfew with their children in units attached to prisons but outside the gates (cited in Fawcett Society, 2004).

Children: the incarceration of girls

With the United Kingdom currently locking up more young people than any other country in Europe (Howard League, 2002), the issue of children and young adults in the prison system continues to take centre stage for penal reformers. There were 3423 children in penal custody in September 2005, of whom 267 were girls. This chapter has so far emphasized prisoners' vulnerability in making its case for a human rights approach. The issue of vulnerability is ever more pressing for children who come into contact with the criminal justice system. Goldson (2002: 7) observed that children in prison can be 'innately' and/or 'structurally' vulnerable. They have more often than not suffered family breakdown, poverty, educational failure and various forms of abuse. As a result, he argues that the social circumstances of the children who inhabit our prisons are invariably 'scarred by multiple and inter-locking forms of disadvantage and misery' (Goldson, 2002: 27). A core principle of the UNCRC and other international human rights standards is that the 'best interests' of the child should be the primary consideration in all actions and interventions concerning the child (Article 3). Given their special vulnerability, children have the right to protection from harm and to have their physical integrity protected (Article 19). The detention of children should be used only as a measure of last resort and for the shortest appropriate period of time. Furthermore, every child deprived of liberty shall be treated with humanity and respect for the inherent dignity of the human persons and in a manner that takes into account the needs of person of his or her age (Article 37).

The vulnerability of girls who encounter the criminal justice system has long been a concern for academics. Research has pointed to the overly harsh treatment that girls receive throughout their interactions with the criminal justice system. Conceptualized as 'wayward' and in need of 'protection', girls are invariably harshly sanctioned for non-criminal offences and trivial misdemeanours. It is here that the criminal justice system operates a double standard. Often, girls have broken moral and not legal rules and find themselves being punished for behaviour that flaunts normative expectations (Chesney-Lind and Shelden, 1998; Phoenix, 2002, 2006). The vulnerability of girls is intensified and exacerbated on reaching prison. Unlike boys, girls are held in inappropriate establishments, where it is difficult to meet their specific needs. A report conducted by the Howard League for Penal Reform in 1997, *Lost Inside*, found that a number of girls under the age of 18 were being held alongside adult women in adult jails. The report also found that staff had little or no training in dealing with vulnerable girls. Yet the vulnerability of girls was marked: 22 per cent had self-harmed; 65 per cent had experienced family breakdown; 40 per cent had been in care; and 41 per cent reported drug or alcohol abuse. Despite the human rights principle that children have a right to family life and that contact with family is crucial in terms of children's rehabilitation, Scraton and Moore (2004) found no evidence of any appropriate and essential provision by the prison service to ensure that children and young prisoners were given as much access as possible to family and friends. It is within this context of vulnerability that 19 children killed themselves in prison in England and Wales between 1993 and 2003 (Joint Committee on Human Rights, 2003).

Following the publication of *Lost Inside*, the Howard League has challenged a number of breaches of human rights through the courts. It supported and gave evidence at a judicial review of Home Office policy concerning the holding of girls under 18 alongside adult prisoners. The court ruled that it was unlawful for the Secretary of State automatically to place children in an adult prison. In 2002 the Howard League for Penal Reform successfully challenged the prison service insistence that the protection of the Children's Act 1989 did not apply to children in prison. Since then there have been some important developments regarding the holding of girls in the penal system. In April 2004 the government announced its intention to remove girls from adult prisons and embarked on a building programme of four specialist units for detaining teenage girls. While the intention to separate girls from adult prisoners is a welcome one, to suggest that such a move will act as a remedy for dealing with the multiple problems that girls in custody face is shortsighted. The Howard League reinforces this when it argues that:

> Specialist units for girls in adult prison have been tried and failed not least because it is impossible to detach them totally from the rest of the prison. Even if physically separated from the adults, girls held in prison are still living in a punitive adult culture with high levels of self-harm, suicide, poor staff training and low staff ratios. (2004)

The message from the literature is clear – prison is no place for children.

Concluding thoughts

Our knowledge of the female offender and her experience of criminal justice has grown enormously over the past 50 years. At the beginning of the twenty-first century the female offender occupies a significant place on both criminological and policy agendas. Though no longer absent from inquiry the female offender is still subject to gross misrepresentation. We have argued that the current search for equivalence between women's and men's criminal behaviour has contributed much to the growing number of women deemed punishable. An unhealthy interest in the emergence of the 'mean girl', the female perpetrator of domestic violence and sex offences has secured a future in which *all* women risk being subjected to punishment for behaviour that contradicts normative expectations. Commentators have pointed to the current panic over girls' aggression and 'mean-ness' as related to a fear over shifting masculinities and femininities in which there are gender anxieties over girls' supposed success (Segal, 1999; McRobbie, 2004; Taft, 2004). Such arguments are reminiscent of Adler's (1975) work, suggesting a link between women's liberation, feminism and women's increasing criminality. It is girls' very success, power and adaptation in the masculine worlds of work and pleasure today that have contributed to their current status. As Ringrose writes:

> The sensationalism surrounding the shifting discourses of the vulnerable yet mean and potentially violent girl relates, therefore, to fear over girl power, the costs of girls' successes and adaptations to masculine domains, and cultural anxieties over shifting and unstable formations of gender experience and identity. (2006: 421)

Declarations of women's rising crime continue to fuel the anti-feminist backlash; disparaging it for its negative effect on women (Chesney-Lind 1980; Gelsthorpe,1989; Worrall, 2002). We would concur with Chesney-Lind (2006) when she argues that feminist criminology's agenda must consciously challenge these backlash narratives of girl and women offenders. At the same time we should be mindful of the fact that while women commit almost every kind of offence, they do so 'modestly' (Heidensohn, 1996).

The sharp rise in the number of women incarcerated over the past decade has led to an increased knowledge of women's distinct experiences of criminal justice. This is a welcome consequence and initial responses by the government were positive. The current contradictory nature of government policy on women's imprisonment however calls into question the state's original commitment to radicalizing the way in which it deals with the female offender. There is nothing concrete to suggest that the government is committed to reducing the number of women in prison. The promise by government to pilot radical new approaches to meet the specific needs of women offenders, to tackle the causes of crime and reoffending among this group and to reduce the need for custody, outlined in the Comprehensive Spending Review in 2004, has been accompanied by a expansive building programme. This failure to invest in innovative penal practice is best summed up by Lowthian (2002:164) when she states that such policies indicate 'a disregard for meaningful change and unwillingness to genuinely foster new approaches'. The Fawcett Society (2004) has also expressed its concern over the continued marginalization of women offenders in government policy noting that there is no reference to the WORP in the government's plan to create a new National Offender Management System. Indeed the only mention of women is with regard to the establishment of two large women's prisons, a move that clearly conflicts with the government's aim of reducing offending, and reducing the number of women in custody

It might also be prudent to remind ourselves here that policy does not always necessarily translate into practice easily nor does the message intended necessarily always translate with its original meaning intact. Hannah-Moffat (2002) and Hayman's (2006) accounts of failed penal reform in women's prisons in Canada illustrates this well. Despite a well-intentioned, women-centred strategy of reform Hannah-Moffat argues that a major barrier to the realization of any meaningful structural reform is its 'denial of the material and legal reality of carceral relations embodied in the prison' (Hannah-Moffat, 2002: 203). This work serves as a powerful reminder of the very real limits of reform within existing penal systems where prisoners are not perceived as deserving of their basic human rights. Mason's (2006: 182) account of the Dóchas Centre in Ireland (opened in 1999) provides a more optimistic account of gender-centred reform programmes. Overall, she concludes that 'the aspirations underlying the vision statement remained intact'. Despite this, Mason's optimism is somewhat tempered by the arrival of more stringent financial control.

While a rapidly rising prison population and a reducing budget are often used to explain the shortcomings of the penal system, the lack of appropriate care given to prisoners goes beyond financial and administrative concerns. The integration of the 'healthy prison' concept will not overcome the uneasy relationship that exists between the delivery of care within punitive containment (Sim, 1990). Moreover, as Snider reminds us:

> In a culture of punitiveness reforms will be heard in ways that reinforce rather than challenge dominant cultural themes; they will strengthen hegemonic not counter-hegemonic practices and beliefs. (2003: 368)

This chapter has provided a brief insight into some of the ways in which a human rights framework might be applied to understanding women's experience of custody. Despite its potential, there is much uncertainty about the future of the human rights agenda. The extent to which a rights-based culture will develop in Britain remains to be seen but early indications are not encouraging. Work by Costigan and Thomas (2005: 44) indicates that despite the initial anticipation among legal commentators of the deluge of work that would be generated with the advent of such law, this new avenue to recourse has resulted in a 'trickle of cases' [and that] 'going down the human rights way is often a last refuge for a lawyer who hasn't got a case, rather than the first port of call'. Sedley (2005) adds to the critique of the legal profession by pointing out that very few of those in the profession know about the actual operationalization of human rights law. More specifically, he bemoans the pedagogic shortfall within university curricula in training our future legal professionals. The implications of this are considerable. If the legal profession are not fully immersed in the potential of a human rights discourse, the public are almost certainly not. It is unlikely, then, that we will be in a position to promote, let alone protect, the human rights of offenders, who after all, remain a politically unpopular and undeserving group. But it is precisely during such times of disregard and contradiction that we should strive to keep the human rights of the offender on the agenda. To reiterate our basic position, the language of human rights offers a vocabulary for those interested in understanding the location and operation of power within a gendered criminal justice system. If approached in this way, the vulnerability of women who inhabit our prisons will become glaringly obvious. More broadly, adopting a human rights perspective offers us an opportunity to rethink and fracture our conception of the offender, and while offenders may continue to be unpopular, we might begin to conceive of them as deserving of their human rights.

Summary

- While most crime is committed by men this chapter described the extent and prevalence of female offending behaviour. It demonstrated that women are responsible for fewer offences and also that the distribution of offences is different, with women perpetrating a relatively higher proportion of crimes against property rather than crimes against the person. In other words, female offending is less serious than it is in the case of men.
- Debates about the 'search for equivalence' in the criminality of women and men were then sketched. Over recent years there has been a tendency in criminal justice policy to disregard gender and treat women offenders in the same way that men are treated. Despite the emergence of discourses highlighting the phenomenon of the 'mean girl' and women who commit domestic violence, women are far from being equal to their male counterparts, thus perpetuating more insidious forms of criminal injustice.
- The inequitable treatment of the female offender was examined with reference to human rights discourse, focusing in detail on the experiences of female prisoners. In contrast to men in prison, women and young girls who are locked up are extremely vulnerable. To be specific they are:

  o more likely to self-harm and commit suicide;
  o more likely to experience the painful and damaging consequences of being separated from their children and families.

A human rights framework offers an opportunity to create a more humane prison environment.

STUDY QUESTIONS

- Is there such a thing as the 'new female offender'?
- What are the implications of the current trend to 'search for equivalence' in women's and men's offending?
- In what ways are women offenders particularly vulnerable?
- Outline and discuss the ways in which the female offender is experiencing greater punitiveness.
- Can the human rights discourse offer anything to the female offender?

FURTHER READING

There are a number of good texts on gender and crime. These include Walklate's *Gender, Crime and Criminal Justice* (2nd edn) (2000). Though published over a decade ago now, Gelsthorpe and Morris' *Feminist Perspectives in Criminology* (1990) provides valuable insights into the differing feminist perspectives. Heidensohn and Rafter's *International Feminist Perspectives in Criminology: Engendering a Discipline* (1999) provide a more international discussion of perspectives. Heidensohn's 1996 text on *Women and Crime* continues to be an essential starting place for students wanting to review the history of criminology and the place of the female offender within it. For the more focused insight into the rise of the so-called 'new female offender' see the collection of contributions offered in Worrall's *Girls' Violence: Myths and Realities* (2004) together with Snider's excellent contribution to the *British Journal of Criminology* on 'Constituting the Punishable Woman: Atavistic Man Incarcerates Postmodern Woman' (2003). For a good overview of the problems facing women in prison see Carlen and Worrall's edited collection on *Analysing Women's Imprisonment* (2004). For an insight into new and distinctive areas for the study of gender and crime see Heidensohn's edited collection *Gender and Justice: New Concepts and Approaches* (2006).

Notes

1 R (*Amin*) v Secretary of State for the Home Department [2003] UKHL 51. The Amin case related to the death of teenager Zahid Mubarek, who in March 2000 was beaten to death by a racist prisoner sharing his cell in Feltham Young Offender Institution. Zahid Mubarek's family lawyers argued that Article 2 of the ECHR entitled the family to a public hearing and the House of Lords ruled in October 2003 that there should be a public inquiry into his death. Reporting in 2006, the inquiry castigated the prison service for a 'bewildering catalogue' of individual and 'systemic' failures. Notably, it reported a prison service plagued by institutional racism.

2 R (*Middleton*) v West Somerset Coroner and another [2004] UKHL 10. The Middleton case concerns the suicide of Colin Middleton in January 1999. The case concerned the state's procedural obligation to investigate a death possibly involving a violation of Article 2. The House of Lords ruled in March 2004 that, while not attributing criminal or civil liability, an inquest should find out 'how' the person died, not simply 'what means' but also 'in what circumstances'. Middleton's mother, who had brought the initial case, did not seek a fresh inquest, just an order that the jury's findings be publicly recorded.

3 R (*Sacker*) v West Yorkshire Coroner [2004] UKHL 11. The Sacker case relates to the death of 22-year-old Sheena Creamer, who was found dead in August 2000 while on remand at New Hall Prison. The coroner had ruled that the inquest jury could not attach a rider of 'neglect' to its verdict. The House of Lords judged in March 2004 that the inquest has been deprived of its ability to address the positive obligation of Article 2 to safeguard life and ruled that a new inquest should be held.

3

Men as Offenders

Chapter Contents

OVERVIEW

Chapter 3 provides:

- A descriptive overview of the involvement of men and boys in crime, disorder and anti-social behaviour.
- An account of the response of the criminal justice system to male offenders.
- An assessment of the reasons why boys and men are more likely to offend than girls and women.
- A summary of the main theoretical approaches developed to understand the relationship between masculinity and crime, including structural, psychosocial and discursive schools of thought.
- An analysis of the applicability of a human rights agenda in relation to men. It is argued that men may be *beneficiaries* of a rights-based agenda with reference to the over-policing of marginal men. By contrast it is suggested that the violent behaviour of men inhibits the human rights of their victims.

KEY TERMS

criminalization	gender relations	hegemonic masculinity
human rights	marginalization	masculinity/masculinities
patriarchy	psychosocial approaches	social divisions

Introduction

The previous chapter showed that prior to the 1960s it was assumed, albeit implicitly, that the offender was either a man or boy. Feminist criminologists have argued quite persuasively that 'malestream' criminology was problematic because it did not render visible the extent to which offending behaviour is gendered (see Chapters 1 and 2 of this volume; Walklate, 2004). Feminist critiques have elicited several responses from male criminologists, including a growing body of writers who have embraced the intellectual, political and practical challenges raised by feminism as well as those who are more sceptical about the essence of the case advanced by some feminists (Newburn and Stanko, 1994; Jefferson, 1997; Collier, 1998; Hall, 2002; Messerschmidt, 2004). In short, this chapter reviews some of the complex debates about men, masculinities, and offending that have been conducted over the last two decades or so. The main point is that there is an ongoing discussion where there are a number of unresolved theoretical and methodological issues within this body of work (Hood-Williams, 2001). Despite the lack of consensus in existing narratives focusing on masculinities and crime, more and more criminologists are accepting that most crimes are mainly committed by males and that for whatever reason male criminality is an indication that masculinity is, if not in crisis, deeply troubled (Jefferson, 1992, 1996a; Campbell, 1993).

In common with the previous chapter this one also considers the relevance of a human rights agenda. For instance, the HRA 1998 is a clear attempt to universalize rights, but many of the structural inequalities pre-dating 1998, or to be more accurate 2 October 2000, remain. Above all, certain groups of men continue to be marginalized, disadvantaged and excluded despite interventions in the name of human rights. Wider developments in the political economy may undermine the progressive and liberalizing tendencies of the human rights agenda through perpetuating gendered patterns of inequality. Hall (2002) sums up the desperate predicament faced by some marginal and powerless men in contemporary societies.

> Some have sunk into a general apathy that is punctuated by detonations of politically pointless interpersonal hostility (Horne and Hall, 1995), while others seek economic opportunities in those sectors of the economy where the boundary between criminal and legal commodity circulation is blurred (Hobbs, 1995; Ruggerio, 1996). Large numbers of men are engaging with criminal and quasi-legal occupations such as property theft, selling goods, drugs distribution, protection racketeering, private security and varieties of temporary, unofficial physical labour. In some areas these fields of activity are providing more opportunities than the mainstream economy (Hudson, 1986; Winlow, 2001), and here hyper-masculinities number among the gendered forms that are deeply embedded in new capital–labour relations (Taylor and Tyler, 2000) and market imperatives (Hall, 1997; Winlow, 2001).

Key themes in the study of men, masculinities and crime

This chapter is divided into three main sections. The first section on male lawbreaking and offending behaviour is quite traditional in its approach and provides a largely descriptive, although not overly statistical, overview of the involvement of men in crime and anti-social behaviour. There are two elements to this part: (i) the relationship between men, masculinities and particular types of offending (e.g. acquisitive crimes such as burglary and theft; and violent crime such as rape); (ii) the gendered dimensions of criminal justice agencies and their contact with males. In the previous chapter it was argued that more women than ever before are being brought into the criminal justice system, it is suggested here that offending is still essentially something men do more of than their female counterparts. Part two introduces the work of a number of writers on masculinity, especially the seminal work of Connell, and shows how his structural analysis has been adopted by Messerschmidt (2004). Other writers have adapted this contribution to take on board psychosocial factors (Jefferson, 1997) and the relevance of discourse (Hearn, 1998) whereas some criminologists have rejected Connell's contribution (Hall, 2002). In the third part the human rights agenda is introduced, where it is argued that men may benefit from enhanced appreciation of their human rights, a point illustrated with reference to policing and the tendency of this organization to further marginalize already marginalized men, especially in black and minority ethnic (BME) communities. Drawing on the work of Bayley (2002) human rights are equated with the principles of justice and equality, as well as fairness, freedom and dignity. It is also recognized that however marginalized some male offenders are, their behaviour inhibits the human rights of others through victimizing individuals and communities. This is explored with reference to homicide and sex offending. Crucially, this section indicates that men may be beneficiaries and inhibitors of a more fully developed human rights agenda.

Male offending and criminality – the evidence base

Given that recorded crime statistics routinely obtained by the police do not tell us the gender of the offender it makes the task of providing an accurate account of the responsibility of men for all offending behaviour problematic. It is only possible to identify the gender of an offender once they enter into the criminal justice system. The following paragraphs consider male offending, and the criminalization of men resulting from their interaction with the police service, the Magistrates' and Crown Courts, and the National Offender Management Service (NOMS); comprising therein the prison and probation services.

General offending

Men and boys are responsible for most offending behaviour, especially violent crime manifest in many different forms, ranging from warfare between nation states and power blocs such as the US/UK alliance on a global stage (Cohen, 2001), corporate crime (Beirne and Messerschmidt, 2005) to the turf wars fought on the streets of ethnically divided communities (Stenson et al., 1999). Men also occupy a dominant position in relation to women, evidenced by the extent and prevalence of domestic violence and rape and the ways in which men subordinate and exploit women in interpersonal and sexual relationships (Gadd, 2000; Hearn and Whitehead, 2006; Wykes and Welsh, 2007). In point of fact, in 2002 81 per cent of the 1.65 million 'known' offenders – or those coming to the attention of the police and courts – were men (Home Office, 2004a: 4). In terms of offence type, 34 per cent of men are found guilty or cautioned for theft and handling. Other 'popular' crimes amongst males were drug offences (21 per cent) and violence against the person (13 per cent) (Home Office, 2004a). Men are nearly four times more likely to have a conviction and seven per cent and one per cent of males and females respectively were imprisoned before reaching the age of 46 (Home Office, 2004a: 5). Interestingly, the proportions of male and female offenders culpable for indictable offences are similar. Whilst girls and young women do offend they are more likely than men to desist from crime until they reach the end of their teenage years. Male offending behaviour is likely to peak later on in the teenage years and continue into adulthood in comparison to girls (Home Office, 2004a: iii). Males are more likely to have extended criminal careers than females. The prospective longitudinal Cambridge study (West and Farrington, 1977; Farrington, 1994; Farrington et al., 2006) provides detailed evidence of this. This research focuses on 411 south London males who were born in 1953 and first studied at the age of eight in 1961. Farrington et al. (2006) reveal that:

- 41 per cent of this population had a conviction;
- the average conviction career was nine years, including five convictions for standard list offences (excluding motoring offences);
- 7 per cent of the population accounted for just over half of all convictions;
- those men convicted earliest (i.e. at the relatively youngest age) had the most convictions and longest criminal careers.

The authors of this report do raise a question about their findings, asking if they would be similar if females were considered. The fact that this question is tagged on, presumably as an afterthought, speaks volumes about the gender and crime debate.

The relationship between men and crime is also evident with regard to place and the number of males in the population (Dixon et al., 2006). For example, it is well known that crime is overwhelmingly concentrated in cities, especially urban areas with a high degree of social deprivation and a large proportion of social housing. However, deprivation does not automatically result in crime, as is demonstrated by the case of Sedgefield (the seat of a former New Labour Prime Minister (1997–2007), Tony Blair): this is an impoverished, ex-mining community with a notably low crime rate due to the low proportion of young men living in this area.

Self-report studies

The Home Office (2004a: 3) reviews a number of self-report studies where the gender of respondents was known. While such studies are not without their problems they do confirm the disproportionate involvement of males in a range of criminal acts, although they indicate that the variations may not be as profound as sometimes imagined (Graham and Bowling, 1995; Jamieson et al., 1999; Flood-Page et al., 2000). The aforementioned body of work supports the claim of Farrington et al. (2006) that those males who start to offend relatively early on in their lives are less likely to desist at a later stage in their criminal career than males who first offend when they are older.

The criminalization of men

Men are more likely to be stopped and searched and such an encounter is more likely to result in an arrest (Waddington, 1999; Reiner, 2000; Bowling et al., 2004). This observation is expanded later on in the chapter when the gendered nature of human rights discourse is scrutinized. The police are more likely to arrest men and 84 per cent of persons arrested for notifiable offences are indeed men. In the police station men are less likely to exercise their right to silence (Home Office, 2004a: 9), which means that they run the risk of been treated more harshly in the courts when they face a trial (Ashworth, 2003). There are differences when different types of offending behaviour are scrutinized. In 2003 men were arrested for the notifiable offences listed below. The figures in brackets show the percentage of offenders responsible for committing the offence who are male.

- Violence against the person (85 per cent);
- Sexual offences (96 per cent);
- Robbery (88 per cent);
- Burglary (91 per cent);
- Theft and handling stolen goods (78 per cent);
- Fraud and forgery (73 per cent);
- Criminal damage (88 per cent);
- Drug offences (86 per cent).

(Home Office, 2004a: 11)

Other Home Office studies show that males account for most violent crime (Smith and Allen, 2004) and that they are the perpetrators of domestic violence, sexual assault and stalking (Myhill and Allen, 2002a and b; Walby and Allen, 2004). This statistical evidence is supported by criminological studies, which testify to the culpability of boys and men for most burglaries (Mawby, 2001); street crimes (Hallsworth, 2005); and crimes of violence (Hearn, 1998; Stanko et al., 2002; Gadd, 2003). The causal influence of drugs (Bean, 2004; Simpson et al., 2007) and alcohol (Dingwall, 2005) on male criminality, especially in the context of the 'night-time economy' is well-documented (Winlow, 2001; Hobbs et al., 2003; Monaghan, 2004), as is the disproportionate over-representation of men amongst the population of sex offenders (Thomas, 2005). It is men who have carried out most of the media-reported shootings in run-down areas of London, Manchester, Birmingham and Nottingham (Bullock and Tilley, 2002; Povey et al., 2004). Interestingly, if we consider crime as a form of social harm Hearn's (2003) observation that some male criminologists are responsible for 'workplace bullying' does not let academics off the hook either.

Returning to the criminal justice system, overall male arrestees tend to be treated more harshly than females, demonstrated by the finding that men are more likely to be charged (60 per cent compared to 52 per cent) and therefore less likely to be cautioned. The cautioning rate for males was 27 per cent in comparison to a figure of 44 per cent for females (Home Office, 2004a: 9). While the reasons for this are complex this occurs in part because men are less likely to admit that they have offended and their arrest is more likely to result from them committing a more serious offence. Despite this, even when seriousness of offence is considered it would appear that men are less likely than women to be cautioned for indictable offences (Home Office, 2004a: iii).

Remand and mode of trial

At the next stage of the criminal justice process men are more likely to be remanded in custody, attributable to the fact that more men have previous convictions, as well as the nature of their offending behaviour (e.g. its seriousness) (Ashworth, 2003). Thus the sex of the accused is not likely to be that significant in isolation from other factors. The same observation applies to the tendency for men to be committed for trial more frequently than women (Home Office, 2004a: iii). Men remanded in custody spend more time under lock and key than women do. When it comes to the trial, for triable either-way cases men are far more likely to be committed to Crown Court for trial, although this is partly explained by the generally more serious offences committed by men (Home Office, 2004a: iii). Men (50 per cent) who are held on remand are more likely to end up in prison than women (41 per cent) (Home Office, 2004a: 15).

Sentencing and penal policy

Overall, there are 4.5 times as many men convicted in the courts for all offences in comparison to women (Home Office, 2004a: 4). Sentencing outcomes are gendered too, with men being much more likely to be given a custodial sentence for committing an indictable offence (Ashworth, 2003). Ninety-four per cent of persons given a custodial sentence in 2002 were men. A decade earlier in 1992 the equivalent figure was 96.6 per cent indicating a decline in the proportion of men in the prison population (Home Office, 2004a). Males are more likely to be received into prison for the following sentences: violence against the person; sexual offences; and burglary (Home Office, 2004a: 34). Juvenile offenders under the age of 18 are also over-represented in the custodial population with there being 2490 males compared to 117 females (Jamieson et al., 1999; Home Office, 2004a).

The above findings suggest that men are less likely to be either discharged or issued with a community-based penalty and when men are given a non-custodial sentence the outcome is more likely to be a Community Punishment Order than either a Community Rehabilitation Order or a Community Punishment and Rehabilitation Order (Home Office, 2004a: iv). It remains to be seen what happens in the long term as a result of the Criminal Justice Act 2003, the activities of the Sentencing Guidelines Council and the introduction of the generic community order (Davies et al., 2005). Generally speaking sentences for men tend to be harsher in terms of the length of the sentences they receive (Home Office, 2004a: iv). Notably, as acknowledged in the previous chapter, the number of women in prison has increased more dramatically than it has for men and there is a higher proportion of female black and minority ethnic (BME) people in prison. It is plausible that the introduction of custody minus, custody plus and intermittent custody will alter the situation by leading to further criminalization, but only time will tell (Gelsthorpe, 2006).

The perilously overcrowded prison estate of England and Wales, which as noted in the previous chapter stood at 78,888 in January 2007, comprises 74,574 males with the remaining 4314 being female. Inside the prison, in comparison to women, male offenders are much more likely to be the beneficiary of an accredited offender behaviour programme, e.g. Accredited Enhanced Thinking Skills, the now phased-out Reasoning and Rehabilitation (R&R), Think First, Controlling Anger and Learning to Manage it (CALM), and the Cognitive Skills Booster Programme, SOTP (Sex Offender Treatment Programme) (Harper and Chitty, 2005). Despite this, men in prison are not as well-educated as female offenders (Home Office, 2004a: iv). Male prisoners also experience ill health and they are more likely to have an anti-social personality disorder (Harper et al., 2004: 17) and consult a doctor more frequently than their female counterparts (Home Office, 2004a: 38). General conditions inside prison tend to be slightly poorer for men, in particular the time inmates spend on purposeful activity and the length of time they spend in their cells (Home Office, 2004a: 38). Recent theoretical work has drawn attention to the extent to which the offender management industry – including the probation and prison services – have regimes which may be oriented towards men but there is the absence of an explicit understanding of masculinity (Jewkes, 2005; Whitehead, 2005; Hearn and Whitehead, 2006).

Significantly, though, on release from prison it would seem that men have more chance of being resettled with nearly twice as many men finding employment or a training course placement than women (Home Office, 2004: v). This is only part of the story, though, and a report by the Social Exclusion Unit (2002) indicated that prisoners serving short sentences (less than 12 months) where there is no mandatory post-release support, were more likely to reoffend and be reconvicted compared to those who were serving longer sentences. For example, of those men serving up to 12 months inside prison, 62 per cent reoffended within two years of being released compared to 60 per cent for females. Those prisoners held for between one and four years were less likely to be reconvicted within two years: 55 per cent of males and 35 per cent of females. Reconviction rates more generally were the same for adult males and females respectively (Home Office, 2004a: 41). Young male offenders are at greater risk of reoffending within two years (74 per cent) confirming what criminologists know about the linkages between age and sex/gender.

The material reviewed above does not provide any surprises and confirms common sense perceptions about men and their involvement in crime and disorder. Explanations of offending behaviour have taken this for granted and there is a tacit presumption in most criminological theory that the criminal is a man or boy. Feminist critiques of the gender blindness of criminological theorizing are well known and there is no need for another rehearsal here but, in short, it has not fully come to terms with the problems posed by men (Hopkins Burke, 2005). On a more positive note, things are starting to change with some important theoretical interventions by writers on masculinity.

Theorizations of men, masculinities and crime

In this section the emergence of criminological theories focusing on men and masculinity are outlined. It considers the impact of the 'second wave' of feminism on understanding the involvement of men in crime and how some male criminologists have taken on board the 'transgression of criminology' called for by feminist scholars (Cain, 1990). The seminal work of Connell (2002) and his concept of 'gender relations' are introduced and some attempts to apply it to explain crime are then described. The scholarly outputs of men writing about the criminality of men falls into two broad categories: sociological and psychosocial. Two things need to be said about these perspectives. Firstly, at least in criminological circles, the two are not mutually exclusive and there is some articulation between them. Secondly, more has been written from a sociological perspective largely because criminology, or at least the way it is studied in Britain, has been more sociological in its conceptual and methodological orientation. Related to the latter point is the fact that one particular individual, Connell (2002), has had a major and enduring influence on thinking about men and masculinity: this macro level, materialist, and structural perspective, which is informed by a wealth of empirical evidence drawn from various areas of social life, has been the touchstone for all criminologists in this area (Jefferson, 1997). The writings of Connell are especially interesting because while he takes on board feminism he does not accept certain early radical accounts where it is evinced that male dominance and patriarchal structures are monolithic and absolute. Masculinity may be intertwined with power and authority, furthering heterosexual and specific class interests, but it can be challenged and is changeable. In short, masculinity appears in different forms in different cultural and historical contexts.

Connell has his critics (Hood-Williams, 2001; Hall, 2002) and whilst they make cogent critiques they are not able to jettison Connell's framework in its entirety and other approaches have adapted his ideas, in particular discursive (Hearn, 1998) and psychosocial approaches (Gadd and Jefferson, 2007). For the aforementioned reasons, the contribution of Connell (2002) is reviewed in some detail, followed by an exploration of one of his most sympathetic critics and occasional co-author, Messerschmidt (1993, 1997, 2000, 2004; Connell and Messerschmidt, 2005), who has made considerable inroads into a bemired area. This is followed by an overview of some other criminological work, which builds sympathetically on what Connell has done and other more sceptical accounts.

Connell – 'gender relations'

Sociological accounts of gender include variants where the focus is, on the one hand, on social identities or identity categories, namely men and women; and, on the other hand, relational approaches like that advanced by Connell (2000, 2002) in his explanation of masculinity. Perspectives relying on a notion of identity, such as biological theories, identify pre-existing and separate categories for men and women whom are polarized into dominant and dominated groups. There is a simple dichotomy where differences between men/males and women/females are naturalized. Research shows that males and females are similar in more ways than is widely acknowledged and that differences amongst males are as pronounced (Messerschmidt, 2004). A further problem with this categorical approach is that there is insufficient appreciation of power and diversity within a particular category, for instance, the homophobic violence heterosexual men direct not only towards homosexual men but heterosexual men too (Mac an Ghaill 1994, 1996). This suggests that not all men are equally dominant in social relations, opening up a wider debate about gender hierarchy and gender injustice.

For Connell, 'gender relations' are relational, occurring as a result of social interaction between men and women, rather than from the static categories of men and women. There is no attempt to explain sex and gender in terms that are reducible to bodily sex or reproduction. Rather than focusing on particular categories or types of people, 'gender relations' are based on a set of social practices belonging to a 'structuring process' creating gender regimes. For instance, the life histories of men constitute social structures. According to Connell there are hierarchical relations connecting particular gender groups who compete with each other in the pursuit of material advantage. Rather than men and women existing in separate groups they are connected through specific social mechanisms. The outcomes of these different competitive struggles are variable and not all men necessarily subordinate all women. Connell (2005: 834) therefore takes care to avoid drawing any 'universalizing claims about the category of men'. It is important to look beyond a simple opposition of males and females. Men and women and their respective varied material interests are practices carried out in many different historical, cultural and institutional contexts. Connell offers a macro level analysis of these issues showing that although there are changeable structural hierarchies and multiple masculinities men are in a dominant position overall because of something called 'hegemonic masculinity'. This concept, based on the Gramscian (Gramsci, 1971) notion of hegemony, posits that a certain form of masculinity – one amongst many – is valued more highly than others are at a particular time and place, which in turn legitimates the social domination of masculinity. Such dominance is not automatic and is achieved as part of a struggle but it serves as a touchstone towards which men position themselves. More than that there is a tendency for heterosexual women to be complicit with hegemonic masculinity, something that is more often than not achieved through persuasion rather than violence. Hegemonic masculinity is not so much about groups and interests but a socially dominant ideal of manhood. This ideal, backed up by effective authority, encourages men to see the dominant ideal of masculinity as something towards which they aspire. This task is far from straightforward because forms of hegemonic masculinity change over time in cultures and even within subcultures. Jefferson (1996a) illustrates this well in relation to risk taking amongst young men where excessive drinking, drug consumption and predatory violence are a form of *hegemonic masculinity* in a particular milieu.

In addition to 'hegemonic masculinity' Connell (1987) outlines a discussion of gender based on three main structures, which are based on Mitchell's (1971) structural model. While Mitchell wrote from the perspective of radical feminism Connell adopted and adapted her ideas to consider gender relations with particular reference to masculinity. Connell refers to three structures: power, work and cathexis.

- Power refers to authority, control, coercion and violence;
- Work refers to the division of labour and production;
- Cathexis refers to sexual and emotional relations.

In later outputs to a lesser degree he has taken on board postmodern thought, illustrated with his usage of the concept of 'symbolism' and allusions to language and sign systems. However, Connell ultimately embeds his thought in a materialist conception of the social world, which is out of kilter with post-modern thinking (Connell and Meeserschmidt, 2005).

Thus far it has been established that masculinity forms part of a hierarchical relationship in any gender regime. Crucially there are multiple masculinities rather than a singular version, but there does tend to be white-, heterosexual- and class-based dominance. The latter point is important because dominant forms of masculinity are acquiring global significance, such as the so-called 'transnational business masculinity' (Connell, 2000), which stands against gay masculinities, as well as those forms of masculinity that are marginalized in rela-tion to the social divisions of race and ethnicity as well as processes such as imperialism (Connell, 2000). Connell investigates men from different social classes and ethnic groups and men of different sexual orientations and shows that there are a multiplicity of relations between gender, class and sexuality.[1] A leitmotif running throughout Connell's work is that masculinites are negotiated as part of an ongoing struggle in relation to hegemonic masculinity – or a dom-inant type of masculinity – where masculinities are 'subordinate to, margin-alised by, or complicit with the hegemonic pattern' (Connell, 1995: 79).

Connell's work is not without weaknesses, but by drawing attention to the historical specificity of particular gender orders he shows how macro social institutions generally benefit men, resulting in the ideological legitimation of the 'global subordination of women to men' (Connell, 2005: 832), even though there is considerable variety in terms of the placement of individual men in this order. So far the complexity of Connell's thinking has been explored but there are arguably four insights that are of utility to criminologists. Firstly, Connell (2000) has consistently shown in his studies of masculinity that it is not simply a case of looking at men on the one hand and women on the other hand. Women may adopt masculinity, meaning masculinity is not something linked exclusively to men and the male body. Connell makes the point when he states that:

> Unless we subside into defining masculinity as equivalent to men, we must acknowledge that sometimes masculine conduct or masculine identity goes together with a female body. (2000: 16)

Thus criminality associated with women and girls is not unrelated to masculinities, a point made with regard to 'doing gender' in Chapter 2.

Secondly, masculinity is not static and changes over time and place. Masculinity is context-bound and influenced by prevailing institutional cultures and structures. Thirdly, gender needs to be seen as part of a relational process where there is diversity and difference not only between genders but within them too. There is no single masculinity but multiple masculinities (Whitehead, 2005). The fourth and final point relates to multiple masculinities and the consequence that there are no clear-cut and fixed identities. Despite this there are ideal types of masculinity sustaining hierarchical relations, especially patterns of male dominance. For instance, hegemonic masculinity exists because there are elite-type or powerful groups who provide moral and cultural guidance and leadership to maintain the status quo, which is buttressed if necessary by coercion. This is evidenced especially amongst the masculinities displayed by corporate, military and political elites.

Connell's (2002) work has been considered at some length, which may be rather surprising as he has not focused on crime and criminal justice at length, or in any depth. The reason for this is that, as mentioned above, Connell has produced co-authored work with Messerschmidt (1993, 2005). The latter has attempted to integrate the structural analysis of the former with the micro sociology of ethnomethodology. He shows how social action and practices are accomplished in the context of gender relations in particular social settings. Above all Messerschmidt shows that attempts to accomplish a masculine identity are a way of dealing with life and are undertaken with reference being given to idealized versions of a dominant masculinity. This ideal is, for far too many men and boys, an unobtainable aspiration in different social settings, such as at home and at work or school. Messerschmidt (1993) is concerned with recognizing a diversity of masculinities, for example by looking at youth crime and its interconnection with wider structural inequalities. He shows how masculinities are related to power and the division of labour in the context of class and race relations. In line with critical, radical and left realist criminologists Messerschmidt (1993) draws attention to those groups marginalized and excluded from labour markets, but rather than arguing that these factors push men into crime, he describes how men who cannot access economic and material resources commit crime as a method of 'doing masculinity' and the assertion of manliness. In short, what Messerschmidt has done is look at particular acts of aggression and relate them to hegemonic masculinity. Crucially, this is not a mechanical link although the pursuit of hegemony does have a causal influence (Connell and Messerschmidt, 2005: 834).

Collison (1996) deploys such reasoning in his investigation of the linkages between consumption, drugs markets and masculinities. In underclass-type communities which are awash with visual images of the affluent society, and

where the chances of obtaining wealth and material goods are all but blocked, the drugs economy is a way out. More than that, the behavioural response to these conditions sometimes involves predatory forms of masculinity, inspired at least in part by media narratives. Respect is no longer gained through hard physical labour but through the pursuit of pleasure in a chaotic environment. The physical demands of labour and the cogent images of masculinity it provides, which were so closely related in the world of work, become enmeshed with the reality of, and semi-fulfilled fantasies about, criminality in the workless society (Collison, 1996: 14).

The suggestion that crime is a form of gendered social action that creates opportunities for the maintenance of privileged forms of masculinity is shared by Byrne and Trew (2005) in their research into offender perceptions about their own behaviour and orientation towards crime. They found that a positive orientation towards crime – that is, a greater willingness to offend – was more prevalent amongst their male than female respondents.

A strength of Messerschmidt's work is that he draws attention to different offences and how different men in different classes and ethnic groups define their experiences of crime differently. For example, white working class masculinities will be markedly different to black masculinities because of their particular experiences of labour markets and other localized, context specific socio-economic and political conditions. The nature of the criminal response of these respective groups will also vary as will the nature of the masculine response, although the celebration of toughness and physical power are likely to be present. Messerschmidt has been criticized by Hood-Williams (2001) who remarked that the former is essentially a revised version of Mertonian strain theory.

Hood-Williams (2001) also argues that the concept of hegemonic masculinity covers too much by bringing in class, race and other social divisions when analysing gender. A more damaging criticism is the view that Messerschmidt presents an evaluation that is tautologous in the sense that crimes committed by men are an expression of masculinity. Related to this, not all men commit crime, which demonstrates that it is not men that are the discriminator between crime and non-crime. Finally, there is a willingness to lump together different types of crime, which are all seen as a response to a threatened sense of masculinity. For instance the theft of a mobile phone is very different to the sexual assault of a child. The concept of hegemonic masculinity has also elicited considerable criticism from Hall (2002) who suggests that hegemony refers to large scale, historical changes involving whole classes and in using this idea the focus is on a relatively narrow construction of masculinity. There are also questions about the structural determinism and restricted opportunities for change. Connell and Messerschmidt (2005) have responded to Hall and other critics with the retort that their usage of Gramsci's idea of hegemony emphasizes the 'active struggle for dominance'. Moreover, they also point out that domination is not achieved as a result of imposing force, but rather through persuasion and securing consent. Nonetheless hegemonic masculinity does incorporate subordinate masculinities and it can also fail to achieve its specific projects.

Collier (1998) has remarked that hegemonic masculinity tends to focus on the negative characteristics of masculinity – aggressiveness, a lack of emotionality, independence, non-nurturing – and their association with crime, and that it is necessary to take on board more positive features. Connell and Messerschmidt (2005: 832) reply by stating that men consent to particular ideologies of masculinity but there are 'tensions, mismatches and resistances', again strongly suggesting the potential for change and that however bleak a situation may appear there is no need to lapse into a sense of impossibilism. Masculinity is a 'configuration of practice' and it is multidimensional because it has its own crisis tendencies. They also consider the influence of 'ideals, fantasies and desires' that are linked to Freudian psychoanalysis, although this aspect is not central to Connell's voluminous outputs (Connell and Messerschmidt, 2005: 832).

Jefferson's (1997) innovative psychosocial approach, which now receives attention, draws some inspiration from psychoanalytical work and a focus on intersubjective factors.

Psychosocial and other approaches to thinking about crime and masculinities

Jefferson (1997) argues that notions of hegemonic masculinity are problematic because they are based on an assessment of a 'unitary subject' who is oversocialized as a result of the deterministic influence of social structural arrangements. To come to terms with masculinities and crime it is necessary to foreground the psyche, which has its own irreducible determinants and its own rules. Contradictory emotions in the subject create anxiety and a threat to the self which need to be handled by the psyche regardless of the class position or ethnic identity adopted by the individual man. By looking at the psyche there is an acceptance of both conscious and unconscious processes, including hidden desires. The human subject is multilayered and divided and involved in splitting and projecting different parts of their personality. For Jefferson, the key issues are how in reality men deal with their own life histories and psychic formations with regard to masculinities. This is done intersubjectively because of the centrality of 'biographically mediated difference between men' (Gadd, 2003: 333). Each man has his own highly personalized and diverse experiences and trajectories that are made intelligible by taking on board particular discursive positions to deal with or defend against a sense of anxiety and powerlessness.

The above points are illustrated in one of Jefferson's case studies, which focuses on the former world heavyweight boxing champion, Mike Tyson (Jefferson, 1996b, 1998). Tyson was imprisoned for the rape of Desiree Washington, followed by the decline of his status as a champion and his psychological disintegration. Some commentators explained Tyson's life in terms of his class (working) and race (black), but Jefferson's analysis considers the ambivalence and contradictions that Tyson's psyche had to deal with. On the surface he was a huge and powerful man, although this concealed a more troubled personality. This is apparent in Jefferson's (1996b) account of Tyson's transformation from 'A Little Fairy Boy' to a 'Complete Destroyer', which shows how the biography of this sportsman was full of contradictions. Jefferson (1996b) shows Tyson as young man who had a lisp and who lacked the physique he later acquired as a result of years of pumping iron in the gymnasium. Tyson became 'Iron Mike' by splitting-off, or rejecting, his own perceived deficiencies and projecting the resulting violent feelings toward his opponents in the ring. The victim is then blamed for the perceived weaknesses of the perpetrator. In other words, Tyson's life cannot be explained in terms of structural factors alone and intersubjective factors are important too, especially the irreducibility of the psyche, which has its own determining rules.

The psychosocial approach draws attention towards men's subjectivities and the workings of unconscious processes, a line of argument that has been elaborated by Gadd and Farrall (2004). Their research concentrates on the criminal careers and desistance literature, digging deeper to look at the 'latent or unconscious meanings embedded in offenders narratives' (Gadd and Farrall, 2004: 148). More than this they call for researchers to ascertain the meanings offenders invest into factors such as unemployment, social exclusion and drug misuse. In order to understand the criminal behaviour of men it is necessary to be aware of the unique biographies of individual men. An appreciation of men and their subjectivities shows the complex processes whereby they 'identify' and 'disidentify' themselves with particular reference points, including real figures in their lives (e.g. their father, a sibling) and 'cultural stereotypes' (Gadd and Farrall, 2004: 149), such as alcoholics and drug addicts. It is necessary, as Gadd puts it, to

> ... expose the disparity between what violent men feel, say and do, the interface of men's psychic investment in social discourses and practices. This is where changes could occur. (2000: 431)

Elsewhere Gadd (2002) questions the view that domestic violence is, as Messerschmidt (1993) insists, an example of 'accomplishing masculinity'. Rather than wife-beating being seen as a situational response by men to reassert their damaged sense of masculinity, violence is more likely to culminate in a sense of shame and guilt. Like Jefferson (1997), Gadd scrutinizes emotional and psychic complexity and attends to the dilemmas involved with 'uniting social and psychic processes, which pull in different directions'. Drawing on the account of an individual offender Gadd (2002) suggests that those men who are violent towards the significant women in their lives do not necessarily find their behaviour acceptable when they describe what they have done. While men can consciously and unconsciously invest in discourse that condones their violence there is also the issue of public condemnation. In another study, men who were violent attempted to distance themselves from identifying with 'violent, dangerous men', thus seeing themselves as different. Violent men also feel persecuted, even if this feeling cannot be expressed orally, a problem that makes difficult-to-handle emotions even more testing. Defences in the psyche allow the splitting of unwanted parts of the self, which are projected onto the victim. Basically men recognize that their behaviour is problematic and talk about changing their ways but persist with their violent behaviour. Gadd (2002) argues persuasively that the nature of the relationship between many heterosexual men have with women is based on ambivalence and contradiction where women are 'idealized' and 'denigrated'. This can be explained, in part, with reference to 'gender relations' but also the multifaceted emotions making up men's subjectivities and their tendency to 'split off' and 'reject' what they dislike or do not understand. Indeed male offenders end up blaming their female victims for their own weaknesses. Perhaps the most important insight offered by the psychosocial paradigm is that it rests on an understanding of change, so despite the presence of 'stubborn psychic investments' (Gadd, 2000: 445) men can be pushed into changing by representing violence against women in terms of 'emasculating weakness' (Gadd, 2000). The theme of change is also rehearsed in a later article by Gadd (2006), in which he draws on Benjamin's concepts of 'identification' and 'recognition'. Here he shows how a 'far-right activist' desisted from his violent past when he recognized that the hostility projected onto his victims was a part of himself that had been projected onto the victim and that this part was also in need of being reclaimed.

The psychosocial perspective has faced criticism, not least from Hood-Williams (2001) who posits that psychic processes are not sexually differentiated or if they are it is far from straightforward. An alternative way of looking at this dilemma is to ask if there is anything in the psyche that is masculine or should researchers consider masculinity as a presentational or performative phenomenon. Furthermore, the psyche is 'fictional' and a series of 'enactments' inasmuch as masculinity is what the psyche deals with, not what psyches are. In sum,

> Masculinity must be understood phenomenologically, that it is not the exclusive property of men, that it has no essential underpinning in sex or in the intrinsic character of what is to count as masculine (Hood-Williams, 2001: 53).

Whitehead (2005; see also Hearn and Whitehead, 2006) is also critical of Connell and Messerschmidt but retains a strong sociological focus, resisting the call for a psychosocial explanation like Jefferson's. Whitehead (2005) is interested in what men share in common as a category such as an involvement in domestic violence and sexual offending. He is critical of Connell's over-concentration on relations between men and women at the expense of men in relation to other men. He concedes that recognition of masculinity in the plural (i.e. masculinities) has cast some light on the diversity of men's identities and experiences but suggests that this leaves a gap, specifically those patterns of behaviour men share in common and women do not. More than that he refers to behaviours that men share regardless of their race and class. Whitehead argues that the idea of 'manhood' captures the masculinity of all men regardless of their class, ethnicity and sexual orientation. The mythical figure of the Hero, albeit manifesting itself in various forms, is an ideal form of masculinity. Men do not display manliness at all times if at all, for example at work and in the context of family life. The qualities of heroism are reserved for those occasions where men encounter conflict with other men. Not surprisingly men may sense masculine anxiety or the complete collapse of their self-identity. Men, especially young men, are constantly adjusting their perceptions and behaviour in line with an unobtainable 'Ideal Masculine Self'. A result of this may be the onset of panic and an irrational overreaction to certain social cues, hence man-on-man violence in pubs and on the street. An illuminating insight granted by Whitehead (2005: 411) is that an individual man may 'demonstrate their masculinity by two categories of violence to other men: violence which includes victims in the category "man" as worthy rivals and violence which excludes victims from the category "man" as unworthy of being there. The latter category is likely to include gay men and men from minority ethnic groups'.

This brief overview of debates about masculinity and crime all hold to the view that male behaviour is problematic. It has also shown that feminists have argued that criminology is male-centred and the work reviewed above continues to focus on males; however this body of work is informed by the feminist critique of malestream criminology. The work of Connell has been particularly influential, especially his study of gender relations. Connell's structural analysis focuses on three structures: power, work and cathexis to demonstrate the development of something he calls 'hegemonic masculinity'. This shows how male power is applied in different social settings to maintain masculine dominance and to marginalize subordinate masculinities. Messerschmidt has drawn on Connell's work to show how men do masculinity in relation to crime. Structural accounts of men, masculinities and crime are not without their limitations and Jefferson (1997) and Gadd (2002) have suggested that a psychosocial perspective is also important, not least because it argues that masculinity is shaped by the psyches and not just social structural forces and processes. More than that it attempts to theorize masculinities in a form that is recognizable by men.

Men, masculinities and crime – towards a human rights perspective

Relatively recent writing by a disparate group of social scientists in response to feminist scholars and their respective problematizations of the relationship between men, crime and criminology are to be welcomed, even though they have not fundamentally reoriented the directions taken by criminological theorists and state-funded research agendas. Correspondingly, the main question continues to be largely hidden although those who have made a contribution have laudably brought to the fore key questions about the men, masculinities and criminality. Much of the work has revisited classical debates in social science about the relative significance of structure and agency or accounts attaching relative primacy on the one hand, to societal, political, economic influences on crime, and on the other hand, to individual and psychosocial influences. Although students of criminology now have a more sophisticated evidence base to think about men as offenders it is still not clear why men are so inherently crime-prone and why their behaviour causes so much harm and suffering in an increasingly troubled and insecure world. We do not have any answers to this perplexing question and are grateful for the insight gained from the writers discussed in the previous section. However, as made clear in Chapters 1 and 2 there are other ways of seeing the gender and crime debate.

In this part of the chapter, issue is taken with the notion of human rights, which has the potential to create a universalistic discourse about crime and public policy. Since the passing into law of the Human Rights Act 1998, which came into full effect on 2 October 2000, there has been considerable debate about its impact on the criminal justice system. Without trying to oversimplify what has happened in the early twentieth century it would appear that there has been general compliance with the HRA, and that most legislation pre-dating it conformed with its principles anyway (Norrie, 2001; Department for Constitutional Affairs, 2006; Human Rights Watch, 2006). The main exception to this rule is the government and its counter-terrorism legislation, demonstrated by the controversies surrounding the detention of foreign nationals under the Anti-Terrorism, Crime and Security Act 2001 (Martin, 2006). The House of Lords decided that the detention of suspects on the grounds of their nationality or immigration status was incompatible with Article 14. The previous chapter showed how an appreciation of human rights discourse exposes a range of injustices relating to female offenders. This chapter attempts a similar exercise for male offenders, focusing in particular on the police.

The Human Rights Act 1998 and other related legislation does not openly mention gender, although it is arguably gendered in a way that favours male interests, at least if a macro level analysis is adopted. The evidence presented elsewhere in this book shows quite clearly that women in general, and female offenders in particular, continue to be disadvantaged despite the aspirations of human rights legislators. Men and those subjects accomplishing a range of masculinities may appear, at least on the surface, to benefit from having their rights shored up, but a closer inspection of males who offend indicates a more complex situation.

Male offenders and human rights discourse:
threats and opportunities

The human rights agenda and the discourses surrounding it offer an opportunity for criminologists to consider the diverse experiences of men as offenders and suspects. Ideally we would like to focus on this issue in a similar fashion to the previous chapter, but it is our argument that a symmetrical approach is not the most appropriate method of appraising the situation of men and their masculinities. It is argued that the status of the male offender can be studied from two perspectives; either as a *potential beneficiary* of human rights values or as an *inhibitor* of the human rights of others.[2] Although this is a binary approach some men are likely to be both inhibitors and beneficiaries of any emancipatory discourses, such as human rights. The notion that men may be beneficiaries refers to the experiences of relatively marginalized and powerless masculinities that would benefit from an enhancement of their human rights. The observation about inhibitors is a more tentative attempt to come to terms with the fact that male offending behaviour seriously compromises the human rights of individuals and communities and calls for the 'responsibilization' (Garland, 2001) of some men to address this. The remainder of this section considers these perspectives in turn, focusing mainly on the former; before that, though, it is necessary to restate explicitly in concrete terms the reasons why human rights are important for coming to terms with men, masculinities and offending.

In accord with our earlier statements the following points are at stake, in particular our adoption of a human rights framework that observes the three principles of freedom, equality and dignity. Faulkner (2007: 137) and his characterization of a 'classical' view of the offender underpin this:

> ...as a person empowered by free will, entitled to dignity and respect as a human being capable of change and improvement. It found expression in the European Convention on Human Rights, incorporated into domestic law by the Human Rights Act 1998. How it is interpreted and applied will change over time – the Convention is to be regarded as a living instrument – but the values are permanent and not to be set aside because the 'world has changed'.

These important touchstones are there as a moral imperative to ensure that the equal status of each and every human being – however distasteful or heinous the acts of some men may be – is not only recognized but also protected. We argue that all social relationships in which male offenders and suspects participate need to be based on an appreciation of justice and equality, two core values that compliment the human rights agenda. This is far from straightforward, however, because human rights are based on unity and diversity, which can create tensions in attempting to establish equal rights for all. In principle, human rights discourse may be used to unify the experiences of vulnerable groups (i.e. offenders) but in practice criminal justice is gendered in complex ways and there are profound inequalities existing amongst male offenders, relating to wider social divisions, principally ethnicity, class and age.

In the past, human rights discourse has focused mainly on the international violations and it would be possible to continue this tradition with a discussion of masculinities in the context of warfare and militarism, although in this chapter we seize the post-1998 opportunity to consider human rights in a domestic setting, specifically the criminal justice system in the UK. It is also shown that the human rights agenda is premised on the transformation of civil society through the so-called 'civil renewal' agenda and by deepening and widening democracy.

It is necessary to restate one of our introductory observations, namely that human rights are inextricably linked with civil and political rights and a preoccupation with the public sphere. It is now a truism in socio-legal studies and political science that the prioritization of these considerations reflects patriarchal, or at the very least masculine, interests at the expense of women. Also neglected are the economic, social and cultural rights which have impacted the most on women although these factors also have consequences for our understanding of the human rights of men who offend. This is the stuff of citizenship and the need for reciprocal rights and obligations or responsibilities. It is argued that when it comes to men the application of human rights discourse leads to a certain moral and political ambiguity, which is unique to men. In the forthcoming paragraphs a similar case to the one in the previous chapter will be made to show that certain unitary categories of male offenders are not treated equitably and that their freedom and dignity are compromised. This is not to say that specific articles and principles of the Human Rights Act are routinely contravened, rather some vulnerable men and their masculinities are marginalized and subordinated due to their powerlessness and their lack of appreciable economic, social and cultural rights. Consequently, these men are denied equal access to resources and an experience of justice that is compatible with our broader understanding of human rights. In short, there is a justice and equity shortfall for some male offenders resulting in them being marginalized, devalued and denigrated. Such men may be conceived of as *potential beneficiaries* of human rights.

Men as beneficiaries *of human rights discourse*

Many male offenders are marginalized or kept away from the centre of society, not only at a macro level but also in terms of the communities and the families to which they may or may not belong. It is such men who may be *potential beneficiaries* of a radical human rights agenda that moves beyond the legalistic discourse of the 1998 Act and other conventions. Many men in prison are denied a voice, partly because they are disenfranchised but also because many have been deprived of an adequate education, and indeed some men lack basic literacy and numeracy skills. The mental health of many men in prison is poor and the minds of far too many who are locked up are addled as a result of drug and alcohol misuse. Many men arrive in prison with very little in terms of socio-economic status or cultural capital and they leave with even less (Senior, 2002). The prison estate is not only full of Bauman's (1998) 'flawed consumers', but damaged and disturbed people who are further dehumanized by a punitive system. Research shows that these problems are much worse for some male BME, especially African-Caribbean, prisoners as a result of their experiences of wider structural inequalities and institutionalized racism (Bowling and Phillips, 2002). The issue of imprisonment has been examined in depth already and the observations about Article 2 ('The right to life') and Article 8 ('The right to family and private life') apply to male prisoners too, albeit in different ways. The next section of the chapter takes us to the start of the criminal justice system where offenders meet the police in their capacity as gatekeepers. Based on an observation made by Jefferson nearly 20 years ago it is argued that police powers are applied more readily against particular groups:

> ...in which sections of male, especially male, especially black youth and militant dissidents of all kinds – pickets, demonstrators, etc. – figure prominently with whom the preferred negotiated approach – the 'unwritten system of tacit negotiation' – has never been properly established or has broken down. This breakdown may be fairly temporary, in the case of say a particular industrial dispute, or, in the case of some highly alienated groups – Afro-Caribbean youths, for example – apparently irrevocable. (1990: 41)

To capture developments in the first decade of the twenty-first century this paragraph needs reworking to take stock of the emergence of different conflicts and groups, although the presence of gender and ethnicity remain central to police accountability and legitimacy. It is shown that the structuring of masculinities by the police service in its approach to stop and search may result in the denial of human rights, but more crucially, drawing on the work of Bayley (2002), we show how recognition of human rights standards can enhance the experiences of male suspects and offenders. In short, our argument is that an explicit formulation of human rights discourse in Bayley's terms can address many of the injustices affecting marginalized masculinities.

Introducing human rights – the police and discrimination against marginalized men

The police service is charged with many responsibilities, including the prevention and detection of crime and disorder amongst an expanding remit. Both of these activities, but especially the latter, necessarily involve some compromise of the rights and civil liberties of individual citizens and the police from time to time represent a threat to the rights of some groups of marginal men, especially socially excluded and discriminated against masculinities. There is recognition of the need for a balance, though. As Smith (2002: 12) puts it, there is a perpetual 'search for a balance between the demands of the general interests of the community and the protection of individual human rights'. Thus police officers cannot undertake crime fighting without some limits to what they may do: citizens do have fundamental human rights that need to be protected and safeguarded if only to avoid the wrongful conviction of the innocent. This has been achieved by the Police and Criminal Evidence Act (PACE) 1984 and the Human Rights Act 1998. Taking the latter as an example, Articles 2 and 3 protect persons from having their life taken away from them (Article 2) and from torture and inhuman or degrading punishment or treatment (Article 3). These are absolute rights. Article 5 is a limited right that ensures the right to liberty and security. It pertains to the police power to detain a person and the fact that the police need to have sufficient reasons for detaining a suspect, reasons that need to be made transparent to the suspect. Another limited right is Article 6 or The right to a fair trial. This is arguably more closely related to what takes place in the courts, although the police in their gate-keeping capacity do influence developments that occur later on in the criminal justice process. A study of sentencing policy and practice in a sample of West Midlands courts, for instance, evidences some gendered and racialized discrimination which was partly explained in terms of police activities prior to the prosecution process (Hood, 1992). Citizens are given a qualified right to privacy under Article 8 meaning that any surveillance of a person needs to be proportionate. Article 11 refers to the freedom of the individual to associate and assemble with other persons to march or demonstrate.

A key article, at least for the purposes of this chapter, is Article 14 where it is asserted that the individual should be free from discrimination. Significantly, this article actually refers to sex and gender, as well as other variables like race/ethnicity, age and religion. However, Article 14 is not free-standing and must necessarily be set alongside other Articles such as 5 (Liberty and security) and 8 (Privacy). This can be seen in relation to stop and search where the use

of discretion and selective law enforcement is rife (Choongh, 1997); for example, black people were six times more likely to be stopped and searched than
white people. Asians were two times more likely to experience this aspect of
policing than whites (Home Office, 2006c: viii). According to critics, 'stop and
search powers allow unjustified interference with Article 5 and, in the way they
are used, breach Article 14 as well' (Wadham and Modi, 2004: 222).

Several other studies expressed concern about the use of stop and search,
especially the finding that officers do not always observe the 'reasonable suspicion' requirement found in the legislation.

> Reasonable suspicion can never be supported on the basis of personal fac-
> tors alone without reliable or supporting intelligence or information or some
> specific behaviour by the person concerned. For example, a person's race,
> age, appearance, or the fact that the person is known to have a previous
> conviction, cannot be used alone or in combination with each other as the
> reason for searching that person. Reasonable suspicion cannot be based
> on generalizations or stereotypical images of certain groups or categories
> of people as more likely to be involved in criminal activity.

Most crucially the studies above found that the powers of stop and search were
used disproportionately against black people, principally males (Bowling and
Foster, 2002; Sanders and Young, 2003).

Bayley (2002) has written a provocative article, calling police scholars to
consider the role of the police in response to interpersonal violent crimes motivated by hatred on the grounds of race, ethnicity and religion. The issue of gender is not an explicit element of his essay yet criminological research shows quite
clearly that men mainly carry out this type of offending. More than that, Bayley's
ideas are applicable for addressing the policing of marginalized masculinities. The
concept of fairness, based on recognition of human rights standards is applied in
order that the police can formulate accountable, transparent or open and effective
interventions. As Bayley (2002: 90) puts it, 'the police need to become a minority
group themselves – a minority group dedicated to equality and citizenship'.

In the context of England and Wales Bayley's thoughts are related to diversity,
an agenda that requires the police to be open and fair in their treatment of suspects and offenders. The police are not equipped to deal with the subjectivities
or structural location of violent men. However, they can perform their duties in
such a way that their actions are underpinned by the values of justice and
equality. The realization of such an aspiration is not easy, especially amongst
men in marginalized positions where there is a history of discrimination sustained by the state and political elites.

Bayley draws inspiration from the Patten Commission in Northern Ireland, which
was convened in 1998 to set up a post-Good Friday police system. Patten concluded
that a human rights-based approach should be central to police activity. Whilst the

Troubles in Northern Ireland at that time are beyond the remit of this chapter, Bayley shows the importance of the police for maintaining human rights and a respect for diversity in multi-ethnic societies. Clearly this is a political issue and the police cannot aspire to achieve this end without the total commitment of central government. Under New Labour, for example, attempts were made to deepen and widen democracy but the human rights of some men have been threatened. In the aftermath of 9/11 and 7/7 Muslim communities have increasingly been placed under surveillance and the stop and search powers of the police have been deployed against young Asian men. The activities of the police are articulated with the war on Iraq and the Bush–Blair axis and the powerful influence of military and political masculinities where human rights abuses are considered at best secondary, if not irrelevant, in a 'war on terror'. The structured masculinities of state actors, including the politicians and senior police officers, tap into and project public anxieties onto an 'enemy within'. Crowther (2000) notes that in the past this was young black men in the inner cities whereas since 2001 it has been young Asian men (Webster, 2007).

A strength of Bayley's (2002: 85) piece is that he situates human rights in relation to discourses about citizenship and the police who perform a highly visible role in demonstrating that rights are real and evenly distributed. The rights of suspects can be protected in several ways. Firstly, police leaders must demonstrate their commitment to human rights, not only of the general public but also of suspects. Officers who infringe human rights need to face disciplinary measures, based on a code of conduct, to give off an unequivocal message that discrimination will not be tolerated. This needs to be underpinned by robust diversity training. If things go wrong there needs to be a clear mechanism for remedying failed policies and initiatives.

Unfortunately, there are impediments to these goals, not least the point that the preservation of human rights is out of kilter with the crime control model outlined by Packer (1968), which has been prioritized all too often in many modern societies (Bowling et al., 2004). Having said this, police research shows that the use of hard policing styles can be counterproductive because it alienates marginal sub-cultural groups.

The effectiveness of the police is dependent on recognition of universal needs although specific communities have their own needs and these need to be considered at the expense of the slavish observance of narrow performance regimes imposed by central government. To counter any human rights deficit experienced by some excluded and marginalized masculinities there is a clear need for consultation. Furthermore, to ensure that policing is compatible with a human rights benchmark it is necessary to make efforts to ensure resources are allocated fairly and effectively with a focus on transparency and accountability. To achieve this:

- Police operations must be lawful and not political;
- The rule of law needs to be visible and free from political interference;

- Operational strategies need to be evaluated;
- Allegations about police misconduct need to be investigated;
- There should be independent civilian review of complaints against the police;
- Recruitment must reflect diversity;
- Covert intelligence should be regulated in line with the European Convention on Human Rights;
- Civilian familiarization of policing must occur, either through observing police operations or by attending police civilian training academies.

(Bayley, 2002)

Although we have made a case for protecting the rights of suspects and offenders this needs to be balanced by recognizing the harm caused by these individuals, especially the harm experienced by victims of violence.

Men as inhibitors of human rights discourse

In contrast to our consideration of the female offender in Chapter 2 we argue that it would also make sense to consider the orientation of men with regard to human rights discourse from a markedly different standpoint, namely as *inhibitors*. The fact that men commit most murders (Dorling, 2005) and that they are responsible for most sex offending, including paedophilia (Thomas, 2005) shows the type of suffering they cause. It is the crimes of men that are most likely to compromise the human rights of others. The New Labour mantra that with rights comes responsibilities may be taken as an invitation to men to assume personal responsibility for the victimization they cause, particularly of women and children, and arguably the community more generally. In the next chapter a persuasive case is made to show the parallels between domestic violence and torture. To be more precise, how male violence (including domestic and sexual forms) undermines the freedom and dignity of women and children (see Articles 2, 3, 4 and 5). More generally, the social and economic costs of male crime and anti-social behaviour can have an indirect effect on other economic and social rights because of the drain their actions have on the increasingly finite resources available for the delivery of crime prevention and public policy. By adopting this stance we make both a political case and a pedagogical case for bringing about change in men to ensure they respect the human rights of others. For example, while men and masculinities are characterized by difference and diversity there is the potential for a common language to be developed, which gives equal respect to the freedom and dignity of all citizens. Some of the insights offered by the psychosocial approach may be instructive here, in the sense that individuals have the capacity to recognize a need to change although there are 'stubborn psychic investments' (Gadd, 2003). At a macro level there is also the

'subordination and marginalization of some masculinities that are not able to or committed to conforming nor complying with hegemonic patterns' (Connell, 1995: 79).

Concluding thoughts

This chapter has demonstrated that the statement that men and boys are responsible for the bulk of offending behaviour has the status of a truism in criminological
debate. Considerable advances have been made in terms of theorizing the relationship between men and criminality although some confusion and ambivalence still
remain in terms of causality. The introduction of an appreciation of human rights
discourse has been used as part of an attempt to come to terms with male offending behaviour. Despite the claims to universality underpinning human rights
rhetoric, gender is still a vital determinant of differential experiences when it comes
to suspects and offenders. By drawing attention to a diversity of configurations of
masculinites relating to both men/boys and women/girls some of the masculinities
routinely accomplished by some offenders are subordinated and rendered inferior.
The outcome is that all citizens have human rights but that these are compromised
by public policy and political economic conditions (Crowther, 2000; Hall, 2002).

With the exception of certain forms of theft – in particular shoplifting and
offences relating to prostitution – the disproportionate involvement of the male
sex is very pronounced. Most anti-social behaviour on street corners and outside
shops is linked with groups of teenage boys. In the chapter on males as victims
it is argued that some of these boys are, in effect, the victims of over-punitive
criminalization by statutory agencies and vocal citizens belonging to 'middle
England' and so-called 'respectable' society. Acquisitive crimes such as burglary
and the theft of and from motor vehicles tend to be carried out by boys and men,
many of whom misuse drugs. Similarly, more violent offences including street
robberies committed in predominantly urban areas, as well as interpersonal
violence committed both in public places as well as the private sphere, are all
inextricably associated with men. The position is remarkably similar for those
individuals committing crime in the suites of the commercial and industrial
sectors. Even the majority of perpetrators of crime in virtual environments tend
to be men, demonstrated by a disparate group of offences such as Internet paedophilia and carousel fraudsters (sic) (Yar, 2006). On those occasions when the
police confront groups of protestors either rioting in socially excluded communities or as part of a new social movement (i.e. anti-capitalism/globalization
marches) the people they face tend to belong to the male sex.

The first part of this chapter reviewed what we know about offending behaviour and confirmed this picture. It should be noted that crime statistics are socially
constructed, sometimes telling us more about the behaviour of those producing

the data, and that this information does not necessarily shed much light on the dark figure of crime (e.g. those offences that do not come to the attention of the police service or Home Office statisticians). Despite this observation it would be fair to say that notwithstanding this caveat there is not a hidden reserve of hitherto unknown female offending and that the disproportionate involvement of men in crime and disorder is a reflection of some kind of underlying reality. However, the conventional methods of measuring the correlation between offending behaviour and sex are not without problems. The methods used to render visible gender in relation to offending is based on a physical marker of difference, which in the last analysis is based on differentiation on the grounds of genitalia. Officials responsible for compiling Home Office figures, for example, are not troubled by the deficiencies of looking at sexual difference in this way, nor is there any discernible concern with the concept of gender, especially debates about the problems with collapsing gender into sex. This point is of theoretical significance and was examined in more detail in the second part of the chapter.

Criminology has rightly been criticized for its taken-for-granted sexism and although the field of study has not been redefined as such by feminist critiques there has been a partial reorientation of its subject matter. It would be fair to say, though, that some scholars have been more responsive to the criticisms made by 'second wave' feminism than others. Whilst most theoretical criminologists have not denied the problem of sexism inherent to criminological theory in many instances they continue to think in a way that is to all intents and purposes 'gender blind' and essentially androcentric.

Scholars who have started to take seriously the relationship between gender and crime invariably start with a reference to the work of Connell (2002), although many writers question some of his conceptual assumptions (Hood-Williams, 2001; Whitehead, 2005; Jefferson, 2002). Connell's structural analysis of gender relations shows how men, in relation to women, produce dominant forms of masculinity or masculinites. Messerschmidt (2005) has drawn on Connell's work, combined curiously with ethnomethodology, to show how offenders accomplish masculinities with reference to class and race. Jefferson (2002; see also Gadd, 2000) has approached this work sympathetically but has argued that it is also necessary to consider the contribution of certain strands of psychology and psychoanalysis, resulting in a psychosocial perspective. Rather than reading off masculinities from the structural location of offenders, it is necessary to consider the rigidity of psychic identities to understand the particular masculinities they present and their relationship with mainly violent criminality. Criminological theory has certainly been enriched by this growing body of work and other material has reflected on the practical consequences of such insights for working with male offenders (Gadd, 2004; Whitehead, 2005). These different explanations of masculinities and crime are all persuasive but the question remains, 'Why is it that not all men offend?', despite seemingly sharing similar psychological and sociological characteristics. This chapter has not been able to answer this question and has taken a detour by considering the linkages between different masculinities in relation to human rights discourse where an attempt has been made to universalize and equalize the outcomes of human experience.

Recent reviews of the anticipated impact of the Human Rights Act 1998 have been 'sceptical' and academic and the state evaluations have concluded that the predicted avalanche of appeals in criminal law cases have not materialized (Norrie, 2001; Department for Constitutional Affairs, 2006; Human Rights Watch, 2006). This chapter suggests that the masculinities accomplished by certain male offenders make their human rights more vulnerable. An involvement in crime – or increasingly for some offenders a potential involvement in crime – places people in vulnerable positions as they enter into the criminal justice process, where their human rights are likely to be jeopardized. The use of stop and search and its resultant criminalization of African-Caribbean and – increasingly in the post 9/11 and 7/7 universe – Asian men, makes their human rights more vulnerable. However, some male offenders also place victims in a situation where their human rights are fragile or in extreme cases nullified.

Summary

- This chapter described the distribution, extent and prevalence of male crime. It is clear that men commit most offences, especially violent crime; they are over-represented in most categories of crime in comparison to their female counterparts.
- Men experience criminal justice agencies such as the police, courts and correctional agencies in different ways than women do. Inevitably more men come into contact with the criminal justice system although they are treated in a gender-neutral way in the sense that masculinity is not problematized. It is shown that current arrangements are not explicitly designed for men yet they effectively deal with the problems caused by, and the needs of, men.
- A question running throughout this chapter is 'Why do people commit crime?' This dilemma has preoccupied theorists since the development of criminology and traditionally the discipline has been gender-blind in its reply. Drawing on the work of writers who have taken seriously the issue of masculinities and crime we reviewed the contribution of two schools of thought: the structural and the psychosocial. Both approaches provide persuasive accounts of different aspects of the male-crime debate, although there are other possible interpretations.
- We argued that human rights discourse provides a potentially complimentary approach to come to terms with the crime and disorder of men. It was argued that men routinely inhibit the human rights of their victims and that they need to assume a greater degree of personal responsibility for their harmful actions. However, there are inequalities existing between men and some masculinities are marginalized, resulting in criminalization and over-policing. This latter group of men may potentially benefit from a human rights-based approach that highlights the salience of equality, fairness and justice.

STUDY QUESTIONS

- Account for the different nature of male and female offending behaviour.
- Assess the relevance of the concept of hegemonic masculinity for explaining the crime and disorder of men.
- Evaluate the contribution that the psychosocial approach can make to our comprehension of male crime and anti-social behaviour.
- Outline and analyse the different ways in which the human rights of male offenders may be threatened.
- Critically assess the usefulness of the distinction between men as beneficiaries and men as inhibitors of human rights in relation to the crimes of men.

FURTHER READING

A useful starting point is Chapter 2 in Walklate's *Gender, Crime and Criminal Justice* (2004). Though published over a decade ago now, the special issue of the *British Journal of Criminology* published in 1996 (volume 36, issue 3) introduces the field and although much work has since been done this captures the main currents of the debate. This should be read alongside Jefferson's 'Masculinities and Crimes', in Maguire et al.'s *The Oxford Handbook of Criminology* (2nd edn) (1997). For the structural approach developed out of Connell's contribution, a good entry into the field is Connell and Messerschmidt's 'Hegemonic Masculinity: Rethinking the Concept' (2005), in *Gender and Society* 19(6): 829–59. This should be followed up by reading Messerschmidt's *Masculinities and Crime: Critique and Reconceptualization of Theory* (1993). For an introduction to psychosocial approaches see Gadd's and Jefferson *Psychosocial Criminology: An Introduction* (2007). For a more accessible and lively overview the topics covered in this field see the relevant articles in the autumn 2003 issue (no. 53) of *Criminal Justice Matters*, a magazine published by the Centre for Crime and Justice Studies.

Notes

1 Given Hood-Williams' (2001: 41) insightful observations about the 'et cetera clause' any consideration of the linkages between different structures and social divisions is fraught with difficulties and would require more attention than is feasible in a book of this size.

2 These are not mutually exclusive categories and are separated here for heuristic purposes.

4

Women as Victims

Chapter Contents

OVERVIEW

Chapter 4 provides:

- A review of the growing prominence of the female victim.
- An outline of the broad-based nature of women's victimization.
- A critical review of the changing official response to domestic violence, with a particular focus on changes in law and in the police service.
- A discussion on the problem of attrition in rape and domestic violence cases.
- A consideration of the influence of early victimological studies on the contemporary treatment of domestic violence victims.
- A re-conceptualization of domestic violence as a human rights violation.
- An in-depth discussion on the similarities of the experiences of domestic violence and official victims of torture.
- A critical discussion of state responsibility and accountability with respect to violence against women.

KEY TERMS

attrition	no-criming	torture
domestic violence	rape	victim precipitation
extra legal factors	secondary victimization	
human rights	state accountability	

There has been considerable innovation and reform for the victims of crime in recent years. With a growing body of research into 'victimology' and a New Labour government determined to put the victim at the heart of the criminal justice system, we have seen a demonstrable commitment to increasing the prominence of the victim in criminal justice proceedings (Home Office, 2006e). The Domestic Violence, Crime and Victims Act 2004 has cemented the ascendancy of the female victim. The drive to recognize victims' needs has resulted in an array of measures including: the establishment of criminal injuries compensation; the introduction of the Victim's Charter; a significant increase in public funding for Victim Support; a Victims' Commissioner; and a Victims' Advisory Panel. Within this climate of reform, it is the female victim who has enjoyed the greatest benefits of such an increased profile. One of the key issues on which

this visibility has rested has been men's violence against women. This issue has informed feminist-inspired research agendas, analyses of criminal justice policy and practice, and feminist theorizing. The impact of feminist research has succeeded in naming the abuse and violence in women's lives and, in the process, has assisted in transforming the problem from a private issue to a public one (Comack, 1999).

The chapter is divided into three main parts. The first part reviews the growing prominence of the female victim. Here we document the broad-based nature of women's victimization and review what we already know about the nature and extent of violence against women. While gender-based violence incorporates a wide range of behaviours we focus predominantly on domestic violence against women in this chapter. In focusing on the violence perpetrated by men against women, we do not deny the fact that women can and do perpetrate violence against their intimate male partners. Chapter 2 provided an insight into some of the studies that support this notion. We do, however, maintain that partner violence is overwhelmingly perpetrated by men against women (Dobash and Dobash, 1979, 1992; Daly and Wilson, 1988; Dobash et al., 2004). Given that our knowledge of this issue has become global, we will endeavour to offer a picture that goes beyond national boundaries. Despite considerable attempts to 'take domestic violence seriously', research has been critical of the way in which domestic violence victims are treated by the criminal justice system, with many complainants describing their experience of the legal process as a form of secondary victimization (Temkin, 1997; Gregory and Lees, 1999; Goodey, 2005). The second part of the chapter critically reviews the official response to domestic violence. We focus our attention on the police service as gatekeepers of the criminal justice system. In doing so we consider the influence that early victimological studies, in particular, the notion of 'victim precipitation', have had on the treatment of victims of domestic violence. The third and final part of this chapter transgresses existing debates within criminology concerning violence against women and situates the issue of violence against women within a human rights framework. The issue of victim rights is still a contentious area of debate (Mawby and Walklate, 1994) and though the statutory response to victims has increased, Rock (2007: 39) reminds us that 'no formal rights have been ceded directly to the victim'. In this chapter we consider the possibility of conceiving of domestic violence as a form of torture – a clear and obvious human rights violation. Violence against women by an intimate male partner is now recognized throughout most of the world as a significant social problem and has been identified by many countries as a human rights issue (United Nations, 1995). Through developing this argument we will consider the role of the state and its responsibility with respect to violence against women.

Gendering the victim: the extent and nature of violence against women

Our knowledge of women's victimization in Britain has vastly increased over the past few decades. This has, for the most part, been as a direct result of feminist activism. Since the 1970s feminist work has actively campaigned to transform the issue of violence against women from a 'private trouble' into a 'public issue' (Hamner and Maynard, 1987; Hester et al., 1996). Although we focus our attention on domestic violence in this chapter women experience various forms of victimization. The Declaration on the Elimination of Violence against Women (DEVAW) adopted by the United Nations General Assembly in 1993 defines violence against women as:

> [a]ny act of gender-based violence that results in, or is likely to result in physical, sexual or psychological harm or suffering to women, including threats of such acts, coercion or arbitrary deprivation of liberty, whether occurring in public or private life.

The definition has allowed for a broad-based interpretation of gender-based violence, including: domestic violence (murder, rape and battery by husbands or other male partners); genital mutilation (female circumcision); forced pregnancy; forced abortion and forced sterilization; gender-based violence by police and security forces, including torture of detained women; gender-based violence against women during armed conflict; gender-based violence against women refugees and asylum seekers; violence associated with prostitution and pornography and violence in the workplace, including sexual harassment (Fitzpatrick, 1994: 533). In recent years the definition has been expanded to include more structural forms of gender-based violence. Certain cultural practices, like son-preference, dowry customs and virginity tests, for example, are highlighted as denigrating or objectifying women (Bloch and Rao, 2002; Edwards, 2007).

While the manifestation of violence against women may differ depending on the economic, social and cultural context, research indicates that the phenomenon is universal and contributes enormously to women's subordination world-wide. In countries where reliable large-scale studies on gender violence are available, between 10 and 70 per cent of women report that they have been physically abused by an intimate partner in their lifetime (World Health Organization, 2002). A recent report by UNIFEM (2003) claims that globally, one in three women will be raped, beaten or coerced into sex or otherwise abused in her lifetime. In 2002, the Council of Europe declared violence against women a public health emergency citing it as a major cause of death and disability for women 16 to 44 years of age. In Australia, Canada, Israel, South Africa and the United States, 40–70 per cent of female murder victims were killed by their partners (Krug et al., 2002). Female genital mutilation affects an estimated 130 million women and girls. Violence against women also takes the form of other harmful practices – such as child marriage, honour killings, acid burning, dowry-related violence, and widow inheritance and cleansing (Watts and Zimmerman, 2002). Forced prostitution, trafficking for sex and sex tourism appear to be growing problems (Radford and Tsutsumi, 2004). Each year, an estimated 800,000 people are trafficked across borders – 80 per cent of them women and girls. Most of them end up trapped in the commercial sex trade. Reports of trafficking in women come from nearly every world region. The greatest number of victims are believed to come from Asia (about 250,000 per year), the former Soviet Union (about 100,000), and from Central and Eastern Europe (about 175,000). An estimated 100,000 trafficked women have come from Latin America and the Caribbean, with more than 50,000 from Africa (cited in UNPFA, 2005).

In Britain we know that one in four women will be sexually assaulted at some point in their lives and that two women a week are killed by violent partners (Fawcett Society, 2004). Drawing on British Crime Survey 2005/6 data Nicholas et al. (2007) show that the risk of being a victim of domestic violence is three times higher for women than for men. The risk of being involved in a violent incident caused by a stranger however remains substantially greater for men than for women, with men being three times more likely than women to suffer this form of attack. The problem of women's multiple victimization is emphasized by Finney (2006) who notes that 50 per cent of women who had experienced one or more incidents of any intimate violence since the age of 16 had experienced more than one type in that time. Although the vast majority of these (30 per cent of all victims) had experienced two forms, four per cent of female victims had experienced four. The relationship between the perpetrator and victim has been at the centre of much discussion about women's victimization. With official sources emphasizing the significance of the 'stranger' as a key perpetrator of violence against women, feminist work has worked hard to challenge and combat this notion. Walby and Allen (2004) report that whilst it may be true that less serious sexual assault is most likely to be committed by a stranger (62 per cent) serious sexual assault is most likely to be committed by a partner (51 per cent) with one in five female victims reporting that a current partner, boyfriend or girlfriend had been an offender (19 per cent). The victim–offender relationship was more evenly spread for stalking with 33 per cent of female stalking victims reporting a partner; 34 per cent someone known to the victim other than a partner or family member; and 42 per cent reporting a stranger as an offender.

With sexual offences often at the heart of much theorization about women's victimization the issue of rape and sex crime in general has provoked fierce debate among commentators and researchers. In particular, feminist critics have long argued that official crime statistics and generic crime surveys tend to underestimate the true extent of rape (Chambers and Miller, 1983; Temkin, 1987; Lees and Gregory, 1993; Lees, 1996; Harris and Grace, 1999; Kelly, 2002). The relationship between rape, sexual victimization and the law has also historically generated much debate, particularly in relation to the questions of rape within marriage and of the unequal application of rape laws between men and women. The 1990s saw two major changes relating to the law on rape. In 1991, rape within marriage became illegal within the common law system and this was placed into statute in the Criminal Justice and Public Order Act 1994. The second major change, also made within the 1994 Act, acknowledged that a man could also be a victim of rape. Findings from Myhill and Allen (2002a) show that rape is the crime that women fear more than any other. It estimates that in England and Wales around 47,000 women are victims of rape/attempted rape and that there are around 190,000 incidents of serious sexual assault in a year. They go on to estimate that approximately three-quarters of a million women have been raped on at least one occasion since the age of 16. As with domestic violence above, in the vast majority of rapes the victim knows the perpetrator, with the most common group of perpetrators being husbands and partners. Women are most likely to be sexually attacked by men they know in some way, most often partners (32 per cent) or acquaintances (22 per cent). Current partners (at the time of the attack) were responsible for 45 per cent of rapes reported to the survey and 'strangers' were only responsible for 8 per cent of rapes. The importance of the relationship between the perpetrator and the victim will become clearer as we outline the problem of attrition in crimes against women.

The effects of violence against women

The effects of violence against women are substantial. Women's extraordinary and increased fear of crime has been pointed out as a key consequence of their experience of domestic violence. Under the auspices of the Home Office and what has now been called 'administrative criminology', the 1980s and 1990s saw the construction of women's fear of crime as an 'illogical' and 'irrational' response to the reality of their experience (Young, 1986). Such an approach argued that while young men reported being the least fearful, they were in fact statistically more likely to be victimized than women. Feminist writers have explained this paradox easily as an effect of domestic violence. They have argued that given the prevalence rates for violence against women, it should come as no surprise that women report feeling less safe than men. Women live with a consequence of being 'at risk' of violence which is not experienced in the same way by men. Stanko sums up the way in which women's experiences of domestic violence impact on their general feelings of safety and danger when she notes that:

> Women's lives rest upon a continuum of unsafety. This does not mean that all women occupy the same position in relation to safety and violence.... Somehow, though, as all women reach adulthood, they share a common awareness of their particular vulnerability. Learning the strategies for survival is a continuous lesson about what it means to be female. (1990: 85)

As a result, women's fear of crime is both logical and rational.

A number of works have also detailed an extensive list of health consequences of violence against women. Severe injuries, including broken bones, fractures, burns and lacerations; as well as pregnancy and long-term mental health problems are all evident in relation to assaults by partners (McWilliams and McKiernan, 1993; Williamson, 2000; Krug et al., 2002). Rape and sexual assault may also result in women acquiring sexually transmitted infections, including HIV and hepatitis (World Health Organization, 2002). Sexual assault is also linked to a range of gynaecological complications, including vaginal infection, bleeding, recurrent urinary tract infections, and chronic pelvic pain (Golding, 1996). Violence against women during pregnancy has been associated with miscarriage, premature birth, low birth weight, foetal injury and maternal death (Johnson et al., 2003). Women who have experienced physical violence also report significant mental health difficulties (Williamson, 2000; Carlson et al., 2003).

Commentators have also pointed to the devastating impact of violence on children. The Royal College of Psychiatrists (2004) report that in relationships where there is domestic violence, children witness about three-quarters of the abusive incidents. They also note that children in such households are frequently at risk of physical, sexual and emotional abuse themselves. With three-quarters of children in Britain on the child protection register living in households where domestic violence occurs (Department of Health, 2002) the link between child physical abuse and domestic violence is high, with estimates ranging between 30 and 66 per cent (Hester, 2000; Humphreys and Thiara, 2002).

Others have emphasized the importance of demonstrating the impact of domestic violence to society in economic terms. Walby (2004) has produced a comprehensive and wide-ranging analysis of the current cost of domestic violence in Britain. Centred on the year 2001, she estimates the cost of domestic violence for one year in England and Wales to total £23 billion. Broken down, this amounts to £3.1 billion in costs to the state; £1.3 billion to employers; and £17 billion in the cost of human and emotional suffering. In this current trend toward greater state efficiency, taking an economic, cost–benefit perspective may prove to be a more effective language for communicating with the state (Crisp and Stanko, 2001; Yodanis et al., 2000).

The police response to victims of violence

There has been a focused and determined effort in recent years by criminal justice and related agencies to 'take domestic violence seriously'. Significant
changes in policies and practices have occurred world-wide, but particularly in
Britain, the United States, Canada and Australia (Dobash and Dobash, 1992,
2004; Stubbs, 1994; Mullender, 1996; Schneider, 2002). At a policy level the
police service of the twenty-first century has done much to transform the way
in which it polices domestic violence and protects its victims. Before we outline
some of these changes, we give an account of how things were before such a
determined effort. Our motivation here is threefold. Firstly, it will provide an
important backdrop to understanding how criminal justice agencies have historically dealt with and conceived of women as victims of violence. Secondly, it
will allow us to demonstrate that a change in policy does not necessarily translate into a change in practice. Thirdly, such an insight will better enable us to
speculate about the efficacy of new initiatives to combat domestic violence.

Feminist academics and community activists have worked relentlessly to
expose the inadequate and unjust treatment that victims have received at the
hands of a gendered criminal justice system (Faragher, 1985; Edwards, 1989;
Stanko, 1989, 1995; Bourlet, 1990; Mullender, 1996; Temkin, 1997). The police
service in particular has been at the centre of much criticism from a number of
sources, including official bodies, such as the Women's National Commission,
the Equal Opportunities Commission and Her Majesty's Inspectorate of
Constabulary. A good starting place can be found in Radford and Stanko's (1991:
192) observation that in 1984 Sir Kenneth Newman, the then Metropolitan
Police Commissioner, attempted to shed police responsibility for domestic violence along with stray dogs, considering them to be 'rubbish' work and non-
police matters. The idea that policing domestic violence is not 'real' police work
has been an enduring criticism levelled against the police service. Studies on the
organizational culture of policing have made some important observations here
about how the police perceive themselves and the work that they do.
Characterized by a 'cult of masculinity' the damaging effects of such a culture
has now been extensively documented (Cain, 1973; Manning, 1977, 1989;
Reiner, 1978, 1992; Holdaway, 1983; Smith and Gray, 1983; Feinman, 1986;
Fielding, 1988; Young, 1991; Heidensohn, 1992; Anderson et al., 1993; Fielding,
1994; Chan, 1997; Waddington, 1999). We return to these debates in our final
two chapters but suffice to say here that the police culture is one that is hostile
to women and continues to have a strong influence in defining and structuring
policing and police work. Understanding how the police perceive themselves
and their role goes some way to accounting for their inadequate response to victims of male violence. Silvestri (2003) argues that through encouraging the
imagery and mythology of 'street cop' masculinity to pervade organizational

processes, the police organization and its officers continue to subscribe to a crime-fighting mission, as opposed to of more a crime prevention, peace-keeping model. Police work continues to be imagined in its mythological form where the crime-fighting role is routinely constructed, negotiated, and reconstructed. It is within this crime-fighting model that victims of domestic violence feel the brunt of inadequate and poor policing. Working within a crime-fighting model the role of policing and protection is played out in the public and not the private sphere but by its very nature much domestic violence takes place behind closed doors in the private sphere. Violence then is easily constructed as a 'private matter', something that goes on within families, and hence not the responsibility of public policing but rather the responsibility of social services, whose role it is to mediate rather than enforce the law.

While debates about what the police role is and should be continue to plague the police organization and academics, Waddington (1999: 177) best sums up the police reality when he states that the 'occupational self-image of the police as crime-fighters is not just a distortion of what they do, it is virtually a collective delusion'. Domestic violence accounts for nearly a quarter of all recorded violent crime in England and Wales and the police service in the UK receives a domestic assistance call every minute. The resulting outcome of such a distorted view of the police role is that incidents of domestic violence are not taken seriously and are seen as civil rather than criminal matters (Faragher, 1985; Hamner and Maynard, 1987; Edwards, 1989; Radford and Stanko, 1989; Stanko, 1989, 1995; McConville et al., 1991).

The attrition of domestic violence and rape cases within the criminal justice system has been of growing concern to both academics and practitioners. Attrition refers to the process whereby cases drop out of the criminal justice system at one of a number of potential points of exit from that system. Gregory and Lees identify four major points in the judicial process at which domestic violence cases are excluded. They write:

> The first occurs when a case is 'no-crimed' by the police, the second when the police fail to refer a case to the Crown Prosecution Service, the third when the CPS decides not to proceed or reduce the charge to a less serious offence, and the last when the court dismisses the case or the jury finds the defendant 'not guilty'. (1999)

We take the first two stages of police involvement to elaborate our discussion on the treatment of victims. It is important to remember that much of police work is discretionary (Sanders, 1993; Newburn, 2003; Sanders and Young, 2003). The role of discretion in relation to the front-line officer who attends a domestic incident is of paramount importance in understanding the underenforcement of the law in these cases. The discretionary power that police officers have in carrying out their duties means that 'arrest is never the *automatic* outcome of any police involvement' (Walklate, 2001: 133). Rather, commentators have pointed to the ways in which police officers' own attitudes and prejudices about women have a profound impact on the way in which that discretion is used. Studies have emphasized the persistence of 'no-criming' and 'downgrading' as key features in the policing of domestic violence and rape. Edwards (1989) reports that of the 93 cases of domestic violence in her study, 83 per cent were subsequently 'no crimed'. In sum, she found that the police tended to avoid making arrests and referred victims on to other agencies. By doing this police were able to divert cases away from criminalization whilst simultaneously minimizing their role in the process. A key element of 'no-criming' rests on the police assumption that women complainants often make false allegations and waste police time (Stanko, 1989). In addition to no-criming, the process of reclassification has done much to downgrade the crimes of domestic violence to less serious offences. Gregory and Lees (1999) found substantial evidence of the reclassification of offences in cases of rape, sexual assault and domestic violence. These findings are replicated and further reinforced by the more recent findings of the Fawcett Society (2004), which found that charges in domestic violence cases are routinely downgraded to a lesser offence, or dropped completely, sometimes without the woman's consent or knowledge. The effects of such practices have resulted in inadequate recording practices obscuring the true picture of the extent and nature of domestic violence.

Attrition in rape

While rape is not strictly the focus of this chapter, it does fall into the broader concept of violence against women and the criminal justice response to it shares much in common with that shown to the victims of domestic violence. Research points to an alarmingly high rate of attrition for rape cases. While more and more men are being reported to the police for rape, the proportion that are convicted for rape has been steadily falling (Chambers and Miller, 1983; Smith, 1989; Lees and Gregory, 1993; Harris and Grace, 1999; HMCPSI and HMIC, 2002; Lea, et al., 2003). Phillips and Brown (1998) report that this offence has the lowest conviction rate of all serious crime. Home Office figures on reported rape cases show an ongoing decline in the conviction rate for England and Wales, putting it at an all time low of 5.6 per cent in 2005. The figure becomes conceptually greater if we acknowledge that the majority of women who are raped do not report the incident to the police. Myhill and Allen (2002) found that only two in ten women who have been raped reported the incident to the police. Comparative analysis also noted that the high rape attrition rate is not confined to England and Wales but is echoed to different extents across Europe (Kelly and Regan, 2001).

A recent report by Her Majesty's Crown Prosecution Inspectorate (HPCPSI, 2007) on the investigation and prosecution of rape offences provides a further damning attack on both police and prosecutors for failing rape victims by wrongly recording many cases as 'no crime' and dropping others prematurely without following possible lines of investigation, often due to sexist and insensitive treatment. Of a sample of 752 rape reports in 2005 looked at by the inspection team, 179 were 'no-crimed', of which 57 should have been recorded as crimes. Among the eight police areas studied, the rate of no-criming varied hugely – from 4 per cent to 47 per cent. There are also significant variations in the treatment of rape across the country. The number of rapes reported to police that end in a conviction depends on a 'postcode lottery' which sees convictions fluctuating between 1 per cent and 14 per cent depending on where you live. The conviction rate in Gloucestershire for example is less than 1 per cent of reported cases compared with 13.8 per cent in Northamptonshire. Access to victim services such as rape crisis centres, sexual assault referral centres and specialist domestic violence courts is also uneven across the country (Fawcett Society, 2004). With conviction rates so low, Rake (2005) argues that there appears to be a 'near licence to rape'.

The significance of the police organization in this process of attrition is emphasized by Kelly et al.'s (2005) finding that the highest proportion of rape cases in the UK are lost at the earliest stages, with between half and two-thirds dropping out at the investigative stage. In a literature review on rape cases for the Crown Prosecution Service (CPS) and Police Inspectorates, Kelly (2002: 27) notes that since the CPS do not interview witnesses prior to trial, decisions about continuing a rape case are made in reliance on police statements and the police assessment of the complainant's credibility. As a result, 'there is a danger of stereotypes and subjectivity entering the process'. We have already established that police officers have considerable discretion in how they choose to deal with situations. Police officers' decision to charge is not restricted to judgement of guilt or innocence of the assailant, nor to the legal seriousness of a sexual and domestic assault but to a range of extra legal factors (Berk and Loseke, 1981; Waaland and Keeley, 1985; Stewart and Madden, 1997). Officers draw on their own internal belief systems, their own attitudes, prejudices and 'common sense' notions concerning violence against women (Edwards, 1989; Ferraro, 1989; Stanko, 1989). In this way, the 'moral' perspective takes dominance over the 'legal' perspective in the policing of such crimes. Here, not all women are equal in the eyes of the law and the concept of 'deservedness' is key to understanding which cases go on to secure a conviction. For the most part, factors that have been identified as pertinent to the process of attrition include the age of the victim, the relationship between the complainant and the suspect, and the degree of violence used. Cases where a conviction is secured tend to involve young single women attacked by a stranger and physically injured during the attack (Grace et al., 1992). While this 'ideal victim' scenario does have the possibility of being played out in the crime of rape (although this is a serious distortion of who rape victims are); victims of domestic violence, whose experience of violence takes place with intimates within a familial frame, have little chance of demonstrating their deservedness to authorities.

Blaming victims

The idea that women play a part in their own victimization owes as much to the legacy of early victimological studies as it does to the so-called 'cult of masculinity' in policing. Early concern with the victim can be found in the work of Mendelsohn (1937) and Von Hentig (1948). In trying to understand the relationship between the victim and the offender, the victim was treated as a central and key participant in a crime. Victims were classified and typologies constructed according to the nature of their involvement in the criminal act. Whilst neither of these writers intended to suggest that there was such a thing as being a 'born victim' they were nevertheless searching for ways of differentiating the potential victim from the non-victim. These early works challenged conceptions of the victim as passive actors and focused both on those characteristics of victims which precipitated their suffering and on the relationship between victim and offender (Zedner, 1994). Mendelsohn (1937) drew particular attention to the part played by victims in precipitating crimes of violence, for example through provocation. Studying the role of the victim as co-precipitator of the crime continued in the empirical studies of Wolfgang (1958) and Schafer (1968). The issue of victim precipitation has been the subject of much criticism, particularly from feminist researchers, who argue that by focusing on the victim's involvement, attention is diverted from the structural causes of women's victimization. Perhaps the most controversial application of 'victim precipitation' is Amir's *Patterns of Forcible Rape* (1971). In his study, Amir argued that of the 646 forcible rapes recorded by the police in Philadelphia, 19 per cent were victim-precipitated. His work has attracted considerable criticism both on methodological and ideological grounds for providing a problematic and partial picture of women's experiences (see Zedner, 1994 for a good review of the problems). In short, one of the key problems of Amir's approach is that it conflates an analysis of the dynamics of crime with the attribution of responsibility to the victim. In doing so, it seems to suggest 'that victims of assault have no one except themselves to blame if they deliberately walk in dark alleys after dark' (Anttila, 1974: 7 cited in Zedner 1994: 1210). Despite the intention to make the victim more visible in the criminal act, the tendency of such studies has resulted in a shift in the way in which responsibility and blame are accorded, with women being 'blamed' for their own victimization (Morris, 1987; Walklate, 1989). Research has indicated that the police view victims of domestic violence as being responsible for the crimes committed against them. Victims are blamed because they are seen as provoking the violence which could be avoided by being more accommodating to their assailants (Hart, 1993). The belief amongst some criminal justice professionals that many complainants are false further places unreasonable requirements on complainants to demonstrate that they are 'real' and 'deserving' victims (Kelly et al., 2005). The notion that victims by their provoking behaviour trigger their victimization by male victimizers – and in fact deserve to be victimized – is part of the patriarchal mindset that is at the root of many of such crimes.

'Taking domestic violence seriously'

A policy response

Following such sustained criticism, the 1990s saw the Home Office, together with the police service, respond to such criticisms with a package of reforms, pushing for greater multi-agency working and more positive policing (Home Office, 1990). A collection of Home Office circulars have worked incrementally towards shifting the issue of domestic violence and the treatment of its victims to a more central position in the policing remit. Home Office circular 69/1986 was advisory in nature, reminding officers of the seriousness of domestic violence and of existing legislation. Home Office circular 60/1990 was more forceful in its approach. It encouraged the development of policy documents and clear strategies for dealing with domestic violence incidents; an interventionist approach based on the presumption of arrest when an offence has been committed; a recording for domestic incidents which reflects procedures for other violent crimes; and the establishment of dedicated units or specialist officers to deal with domestic violence incidents. Home Office circular 19/2000 further reinforced the seriousness of domestic violence to police organizations but more specifically bound the quality of policing of domestic violence to the measurement of Best Value performance indicators (Home Office, 2000b). Many forces in Britain now have Sexual Offence Squads, Family Protection Units and Domestic Violence Units (DVUs) staffed by specialist officers (Bourlet, 1990; Farrell and Buckley, 1999). Tackling violence against women became a key part of the multi-million pound government Crime Reduction Programme in 1998 with the Violence against Women Initiative.

The new millennium has also brought with it a greater push towards acknowledging the incidence of violence against women. The Sexual Offences Act 2003 builds on an extensive range of policy interventions nationally and locally over the past decade, aiming to reduce the incidence of sexual and domestic violence and improve the treatment of victims by the criminal justice system. The government promised further action in its *Safety and Justice* report (Home Office, 2003) setting out an agenda for tackling domestic violence through the strands of prevention, protection, justice and support. Further measures include the Domestic Violence, Crime and Victims Act 2004 which sees an increase in protection, support and rights of victims and witnesses, giving the police and other agencies the tools to address domestic violence crimes. The *Domestic Violence National Action Plan* (Home Office, 2005c) further aims to reduce the prevalence of domestic violence, increase victim reporting to the police, improve support for victims and bring more perpetrators to justice. While much progress has been made and there is much to be optimistic about, evaluations of these initiatives show mixed findings. In some areas, there is evidence of improvements in police practice. Hanmer and Saunders (1990), for example, reported greater satisfaction with police treatment after the introduction of DVUs in West Yorkshire, and Morley and Mullender (1994) found that women generally preferred dealing with non-uniformed DVU officers. Mooney (1993) found that women who had sought help from the police since the implementation of the new policies were more satisfied with the treatment they received than were women who had been to the police prior to the policy changes. Radford and Gill (2006) also offer an encouraging overview of the various improvements within the criminal justice system. They note that domestic violence has become a key priority in policing plans and local crime reduction strategies; that key agencies such as the Crown Prosecution Service have reviewed and overhauled their policy on domestic violence, moving towards a more proactive approach to gathering evidence for prosecution; that specialist domestic violence courts have been established; that refuges have received funding related more to need, through the 'Supporting People' provisions; and that there has been a growth in specialist services to provide outreach, advocacy and victim support, in services to work with domestic violence perpetrators, and in supervised contact services for children.

More critically, Harris and Grace (1999) suggest that the passage of time has done little to improve things. An evaluation of domestic violence units by Cromack (1995), based on research in Hull, found little evidence of improvement in police practice since new policies had been introduced. Officers surveyed in this study still thought it a waste of time to prepare documentation if the victim was uncertain as to whether to proceed; the arrest of offenders was generally avoided; officers found it hard to comprehend why women stayed in violent relationships; and little awareness was demonstrated in how to monitor and follow-up repeat victimization. The overall conclusion was of:

> [a]n underlying police culture that tends towards the belief that domestic violence is a private family matter and more appropriately a subject for the civil law. (Cromack, 1995: 197)

Such views are echoed in Plotnikoff and Woolfson's (1998) study which found an overall lack of progress in the policing of domestic violence. They note that the problems related:

> [l]ess to structure than to the status of domestic violence work within forces, the level of commitment of headquarters and divisional commanders, the clarity with which responsibilities were defined and the effectiveness of management arrangements.

They document the persistence of outdated attitudes to domestic violence including a perception that it did not constitute core police business. More significantly, they note the lack of motivation and direction at leadership level as pivotal in ensuring the marginalization of both domestic violence and the work of domestic violence officers. The murder of Banaz Mahmod, a young Kurdish Muslim woman killed by her father and uncle in 2006, has once again forced us to consider the quality of policing in the private sphere. In recent years the police service in Britain has increasingly been forced to confront the problems of 'forced marriage', 'honour' killings and 'female genital mutilation'. In 2003 the Metropolitan Police set up a strategic task force to tackle the issue. A specialist unit was given the task of researching 'honour' crimes and 100 murder files spanning the last decade were re-opened in an effort to find common links. At that time Andy Baker, head of the serious crime directorate of the Metropolitan Police, said that 'police had been unaware and ignorant of crimes that were going on' and admitted that 'honour' killing was not on the police radar. Four years on and it seems that the police service still seem to lack a basic knowledge of the phenomenon. In the Mahmod case a police officer dismissed her claims that her father and uncle were trying to kill her as 'melodramatic' (*The Times*, 19 June 2007). The revelation that a number of police officers had failed to take seriously Miss Mahmod's cries for help points to a fundamental misunderstanding and ignorance of the practice of 'honour' killing.

To sum up briefly, there is ample evidence to suggest that at a policy and institutional level criminal justice agencies have gone some way towards 'taking domestic violence seriously'. The concern however continues to focus on the extent to which changes in policy have been translated into changes in practice. While policing priorities may have shifted or at least become redefined (Edwards, 1989) the translation of policy into practice has been less successful (Grace, 1995). In reviewing the work of the government on tackling domestic violence, the Fawcett Society (2007) reports that little progress has been made on introducing a strategic and integrated approach to ending violence against women.

An international response

On a global level, significant inroads have been made in the fight against violence against women. Eliminating violence against women has become a key concern for the international community. Critical of the way in which international human rights law has ignored and marginalized the concerns of women, feminist activists have lobbied hard to place the issue of violence against women on a human rights platform. The issue was formally recognized by the international community as a human rights issue at the Vienna World Conference in 1993. The formal expression of this commitment can be found in the 1993 UN Declaration on the Elimination of Violence Against Women (DEVAW). This instrument has been widely welcomed as an indicator of the shift within the human rights community toward recognition of the need to address those issues that deny women their human rights. The Vienna conference marked an acceptance of the importance of asserting the human rights of women. Further developments have gone on to strengthen and progress women's voices at an international level, from the meeting of the UN Fourth World Conference on Women in Beijing in 1995 to the UN General Assembly in 1999 and to the Security Council in 2000.

While feminist activists have done much to ensure that domestic violence is on the global agenda, developments within the international human rights community remain slow. In making sense of this lack of progress, Kallen (2004) adopts a historical perspective. She argues that modern human rights law owes much to the legacy of national pressure for civil and political rights at the end of the eighteenth and nineteenth century. As women struggled for access to the public world during this time men's voices were at the forefront for political rights. The emphasis on civil and political rights reflected man's desire to regulate his relationship to the state and to set boundaries of permissible state interference in his life. Male hegemony over public life and institutions meant that rights came to be defined by men. In this way the present hierarchy within human rights law, which gives greater attention to civil and political rights as opposed to economic, social and cultural rights, can be perceived as a manifestation of the continuing dominance men have over the process of defining the content of rights. The exclusion of women's voices from defining the content of human rights discourse has in turn meant that human rights law has evolved along what Cook (1994) has termed a 'gendered fault line' that distinguishes between the public and private spheres for the purpose of legal regulation. For the most part this has emphasized the way in which human rights law privileges the public world leaving the private sphere of home and family outside the scope of legal regulation. Roth (1994) on the other hand has argued that while human rights law does attempt to regulate the private sphere, it has simply failed to do so in respect of issues that particularly touch women's lives. This point of difference does not concern us here, in either case the consensus appears to be that the human rights community has not taken women's issues seriously. Roth (1994) argues that traditional human rights groups such as Amnesty International and Human Rights Watch have been unwilling to focus on violations of women's rights. Borne out of a concern with the victims of politically motivated abuse and on violations by the state, the female victim who experienced abuse at the hands of her husband or partner within a private setting (that is, the family) did not therefore assume any real significance on campaign agendas. Roth (1994) points to a narrow reading of the broad language of the International Covenant on Civil and Political Rights (the Covenant) as a key cause of this neglect. He argues that while the Covenant does not explicitly establish a state's duty to combat private violence, its broad language is fully compatible with this duty. For Roth, the powerful and expansive guarantees provided in Article 6 (1): 'Every human being has the inherent right to life'; Article 7: 'No one shall be subjected to torture or to cruel, inhuman or degrading treatment'; and Article 1: 'Everyone has the right to ... security of person', all have obvious and potential relevance for the fight against domestic violence and could be read as imposing a duty on the state to address both official and private violence. In this next section we transgress existing debates about the domestic violence victim by offering an alternative discursive framework within which to present domestic violence – a framework of 'torture'.

Reconceptualizing domestic violence as torture

In 1975 the United Nations (UN) General Assembly unanimously approved the Declaration on the Protection of All Persons from Being Subjected to Torture and Other Cruel, Inhuman or Degrading Treatment or Punishment. Member nations agreed to eliminate torture. Article 3 made clear: 'No State may permit or tolerate torture or other cruel, inhuman or degrading treatment or punishment'. Though the practice of torture remains ever-present in contemporary society, it is simultaneously universally condemned as one of the most heinous forms of violence against humanity. Article 1 of the United Nations Torture Convention defines torture as:

> Any act by which severe pain or suffering, whether physical or mental, is intentionally inflicted on a person for such purposes as obtaining from him or a third person information or a confession, punishing him for an act that he or a third person has committed or is suspected of having committed, or intimidating or coercing him or a third person, or for any reason based on discrimination of any kind, when such pain or suffering is inflicted by or at the instigation of or with the consent or acquiescence of a public official or other person acting in an official capacity. It does not include pain or suffering arising only from, inherent in or incidental to lawful sanctions' (United Nations, 1993)

Despite the knowledge we have of the global violence that women face, intimate violence remains on the margins and is still considered different, less severe, and less deserving of national and international condemnation and sanction than officially inflicted violence. In this section we draw heavily on the work of Rhonda Copelon in making our case. Copelon's basic starting point is that:

> [g]ender-based violence is no less grave than other forms of inhumane and subordinating official violence, which have been prohibited by treaty and customary law and recognized by the international community as *jus cogens*[1], or peremptory norms that bind universally and can never be violated. (Copelon, 1994: 117).

From such a position she ably demonstrates the commonalities that exist between officially defined torture and domestic violence. By focusing on the infliction of severe pain and suffering and the intentionality and purpose of that infliction (both elements of Article 1) we also hope to convince readers of the need to associate the acts of domestic violence and torture more closely.

Administering and feeling pain

When discussing the concept of pain we refer to both its physical and psychological components. The infliction of physical pain is common in the practice of torture. Common methods of physical torture and ill treatment reported by Amnesty International and Human Rights Watch include electric shocks; rape and sexual abuse in custody; suspension of the body; beatings; suffocation; mock execution or threat of death, prolonged solitary confinement; and sleep and sensory deprivation. The powerful effects of inflicting such brutal physical pain are obvious and we need not outline them here except to note that the body is weakened and essentially destroyed. A more critical appreciation of the suffering experienced by the victims of torture requires us to transgress the traditional concept of physical pain toward an understanding of more insidious forms of torture that do not involve overt physical brutality. While all forms of physical torture are likely to have psychological aspects and consequences some forms of torture are primarily psychological in nature. Copelon argues that the destruction of one's sense of self can easily be accomplished through methods that passively as well as actively attack the body. She notes:

> Fear is instilled through threats to kill, mutilate, or torture the person, or family members or friends. Torturers use subtle methods to break the prisoner's will: isolation, arbitrary and unpredictable punishments, intermittent

rewards, and the alternation of active and passive brutality with kindness in order to undermine the prisoner's morale. (1994: 124)

In this way, we can begin to understand torture as a context and process of domination and not simply a set of brutal acts. It is through understanding the relationship between the abuser and the abused as one founded upon domination that we can begin to make the connection between the more traditional victims of torture and the victimization that women experience in a domestic setting. Like officially defined torture, domestic violence commonly involves some form of escalating, physical brutality. Victims are subjected to verbal insult, sexual denigration, and abuse. The methods used against women in intimate violence resemble many of the common methods of torture, and include beating with hands or objects, biting, spitting, punching, kicking, slashing, stabbing, strangling, scalding, burning and attempted drowning. The suffering caused to women as a consequence of living in a battering relationship is profound and includes physical and mental pain and suffering, disfigurement, temporary and permanent disabilities, maiming, and death (Copelon, 1994). Women's lives and that of their loved ones are threatened and they are made to fear the loss of their children. Walker (1979) describes women's experiences through the context of a 'cycle of violence'. The cycle begins with a phase of 'tension building' and limited physical violence. In these early stages, victims are occasionally showered with apologies, promises and kindness. Increased and escalating forms of violence soon return to then be followed again by remorse and intensive care-giving. The phases then restart and become worse over time unless there is intervention.

A key feature in the enactment of torture is the eliciting of information through interrogation. Scarry (1985: 38) argues that the pain of torture is almost always accompanied by the 'Question'. Consisting of questions, statements, insults, and orders, the interrogation is 'internal to the structure of torture, exists there because of its intimate connections to and interactions with physical pain'. While the content of the interrogation may appear meaningless, its commission is essential to the torturer's self-justification and a tool in the destruction of the victim (Scarry, 1985). In this way the eliciting of information demonstrates the power dynamic between the torturer and the victim, with the torturer maintaining control and the victim powerless. Like torture, Copelon (1994) argues that domestic violence is both physical and verbal. Whether precipitated by rage, jealousy, or a real or feared loss of control, domestic violence has its own interrogation-type questions, accusations, insults and orders: 'Where were you today?; 'Who were you with'; 'Why is the house dirty?' are all fairly typical forms of interrogation that those in abusive relationships face. The goal of such interrogation is not to elicit the truth necessarily, but rather to instil a sense of dread, humiliation and submission in the victim. As Copelon (1994: 131) writes:

What the confession is to torture, the explanation, the accounting for oneself, the apology, the begging is to domestic violence. In both contexts, the victim/survivor seeks to stop or avert the pain, to protect others from harm, and to pacify the aggressor. (1994: 131)

To clarify our position further, we draw on the work of Biderman to demonstrate the relationship between the abuser and the abused. Biderman developed his Chart of Coercion following a study conducted in the 1950s after the release of US prisoners of the Korean War. His chart shows the methods used by captors to brainwash prisoners and force compliance. We draw on his work to explore the dynamics for violence against women. The following chart identifies the methods and purpose of control used by abusers and considers the anticipated result on those at the receiving end. The first and second columns are taken directly from Biderman's Chart of Coercion; they show the stages of coercion and the general methods and intentions of the captor. The third and fourth columns have been adapted to account for the actions of the domestic violence abuser and the effects on those in an abusive relationship, that is, the victims of violence.

Biderman's Chart of Coercion as it relates to domestic violence

Biderman's stages of coercion	Captor's actions	Domestic violence abuser's actions	Victim's response
Isolation	Deprives victim of all social support for the ability to resist. Develops an intense concern with self. Makes victim dependent upon the interrogator.	The abuser deliberately isolates the partner from friends and family. The abuser controls the victim's time and physical environment. The abuser controls finances.	Having been deprived of social support with friends and family, the abused initiates total dependence on abuser.
Monopolization of perception	Fixes attention upon immediate predicament; fosters introspection. Eliminates stimuli competing with those controlled by captor. Frustrates all actions not consistent with compliance.	Sabotages or disables the victim's opportunity to work or have interests outside the home or relationship. Makes her responsible for meeting abuser's wants and needs. Becomes abusive or violent when she does something abuser doesn't want her to do.	The abused loses self-esteem and doubts her abilities and becomes consumed by introspective thoughts. Her attention becomes focused on how to keep abuser from becoming angry and how to avoid problems.

(Continued)

Biderman's stages of coercion	Captor's actions	Domestic violence abuser's actions	Victim's response
Induced physical and mental exhaustion	Weakens physical and mental ability to resist.	Makes her do most or all of the work at home. Prolongs the extent and length of arguments or assaults. Discourages and disrupts sleep patterns.	The abused becomes physically and emotionally too weak to resist or challenge. She also loses the ability to reason rationally.
Threats	Cultivates anxiety and despair.	Abuser makes partner fearful of what could happen. Makes threats to take children or not support them; hurt or kill her and loved ones; damage her reputation. The abuser shows unpredictable responses with drastic mood changes or sudden emotional outbursts.	The abused despairs of any change in the situation. She displays anxiety about every action performed, remains hypervigilant about abuser's mood changes. She shows symptoms of escalating depression.
Occasional indulgences	Provides positive motivation for compliance. Hinders adjustment to deprivation.	Abuser may behave like the person they originally fell in love with. Abuser promises or appears to change, to be loving or supportive, buys gifts, promises to start counselling, or apologizes.	The abused believes they have finally reached the accepted standard and that the pattern of abuse will stop. They then begin to doubt that the abuse really happened. In turn they become reliant on the abuser for further praise.
Demonstrating 'omnipotence'	Suggests futility of resistance.	Abuser reminds the victim of her dependency, suggesting that she has nowhere to go and no-one to turn to for support.	The abused accepts powerlessness. Accepts the pattern of behaviour by the abuser as normal.

(Continued)

Biderman's stages of coercion	Captor's actions	Domestic violence abuser's actions	Victim's response
Degradation	Makes cost of resistance appear more damaging to self-esteem than capitulation. Reduces prisoner to 'animal level' concerns.	Abuser uses a range of degrading behaviour including verbal assaults, berating, belittling, criticizing, name-calling, screaming, threatening, excessive blaming, sarcasm and humiliation toward the victim. Abused is forced to do things which feel degrading to her.	Over time this type of abuse erodes the abused's self-confidence and self-worth. The victim feels disgraced and humiliated and loses all will to resist.
Enforcing trivial demands	Develops habit compliance.	Abuser places unreasonable demands on victim to meet his needs. It could be a demand for constant attention or frequent sex.	The abused accepts habit of compliance, dependency and learns helplessness.

Source: The chart is originally from an Amnesty International publication entitled *Report of Torture* (1975) depicting the brainwashing of prisoners of war.

To sum up our argument so far, we have argued that the official torturer and the perpetrator of domestic violence much in common both in terms of their mindset and in the modus operandi used to carry out their acts. Indeed the domestic abuser may operate with even fewer external constraints than the official torturer. All too often, absent cultural condemnation, ineffective community intervention, and access to responsive law enforcement has resulted in a situation where there is no system of review and denunciation by the state (Copelon, 1994). We now turn our attention to the role of the criminal justice system in protecting women from violence.

The role of the criminal justice system in protecting women

With a widening network of international obligations through state adherence to multilateral human rights conventions, the role of the state in protecting women from violence has come under close scrutiny in recent years. While states have gone some way to recognizing their responsibility for violations that take place in the public sphere, the extent to which the state assumes responsibility or accountability for behaviour within the private sphere remains a point of contention. Despite taking a more active role in tackling domestic violence, Cook (1994) notes that states are likely to contest both their legal responsibility and their accountability for such wrongs. While anyone can commit a common crime, only a state and its agents can commit a human rights violation under international law. Non-state actors are not generally accountable under international human rights law, but the state may sometimes be held responsible for related human rights violations (Roth, 1994). Since the perpetrators of domestic violence are by definition private, they cannot be treated as appropriate subjects of international human rights law unless the state can in some sense be held responsible. In turn, those abuses committed by private actors within the private sphere do not attract the attention and shame of the human rights community. In what ways then can we hold the state responsible for the domestic violence that women experience? Roth (1994) offers an interesting reading of state accountability in which he argues that the state can be held responsible under international human rights law for both its *inaction* and its *action* (emphasis added). He writes:

> The state's abdication of its duty to protect citizens from crimes of violence amounts to a tacit endorsement of that violence. That complicity provides the requisite governmental dimension to consider the violence as a human rights issue – this is state responsibility by omission rather than commission (Roth, 1994: 329–30).

In other words, when the state makes little or no effort to stop a certain form of private violence, it is in effect tacitly condoning that violence. In turn, this 'complicity transforms what would otherwise be wholly private conduct into a constructive act of the state' (Roth, 1994). In this way the theory of liability by omission can be used to treat the state's systematic failure to confront domestic violence against women as a human rights issue. Given the changes in Britain outlined above we are unable to find the British state complicit in violence against women. And, while there may be various nation states that do continue to omit such crimes from its policy and legislative agendas, Britain's position is far from this. On the contrary, as noted earlier on in the chapter, Britain has a well-developed raft of policy and law, aimed directly at tackling such crime. Herein lies the paradox. Despite this mounting range of policy and law, violence against women in Britain remains rife, rape convictions are at an all-time low and the research presented above continues to represent damning evidence of the way in which women are treated by criminal justice agencies. With the potential explanation of governmental complicity now exploded, how else are we to hold the state to account for such forms of violence?

Pushing the boundaries of government accountability

In making the state responsible for domestic violence perhaps we should be asking if it is enough that the state outlaws the practice of domestic violence or if it is enough that those responsible for its regulation make the occasional arrest, launch a periodic prosecution, or secure the occasional conviction. Human rights advocates would argue that such efforts are not enough for a state to avoid being held complicit in domestic violence. Roth asks:

> When does a state's failure to stop private violence constitute a human rights violation, as opposed to a mere policy failure? (1994: 331)

Roth (1994) develops his argument about state accountability further when he notes that where a state is doing the bare minimum in combating domestic violence to escape charges of complicity, a discrimination-based theory of liability allows insistence on greater diligence as a matter of international human rights law. The demand can be made that a state's effort to combat domestic violence be at least on a par with its efforts to fight comparable forms of violent crime. In other words, when a state moves beyond the stage of obvious complicity, which Britain has, a discrimination-based theory of state responsibility permits an additional argument: a state can be said to condone a particular form of violence because it pays inadequate attention to prevent it in relation to comparable forms of violence. The textual basis for a discrimination-based theory of liability can be found in several provisions of the Covenant. Article 2(1) for example, states that:

> [e]ach State Party to the present Covenant undertakes to respect and to ensure to all individuals within its territory and subject to its jurisdiction that rights recognised in the present Covenant, without distinction of any kind, such as race, colour, sex, language, religion, political or other opinion, national or social origin, property, birth or other status.

Article 26 states that:

> All persons are equal before the law and are entitled without any discrimination to the equal protection of the law. In this respect, the law shall prohibit any discrimination and guarantee to all persons equal and effective protection against discrimination on any ground such as race, colour, sex, language, religion, political or other opinion, national or social origin, property, birth or other status.

The basis of these provisions requires that whatever efforts a state makes to combat private violence; it must do so in a non-discriminatory way. Whatever level of resources a state decides to devote to enforcing criminal laws against private acts of violence, it must ensure that crimes against women receive at least as thorough an investigation and as vigorous a prosecution as crimes against men. Taking this line of reasoning to its logical conclusion suggests that if less attention and less rigour is adopted in the regulation of domestic violence than other comparable acts of violence, this could constitute not only a violation of the anti-discrimination provision of the Covenant but could also provide evidence of the complicity needed to make out a substantive violation (Roth, 1994). In the case of Britain, applying this theory of discrimination requires us to establish that the lack of policing and resulting lack of prosecution is due to a prohibited form of discrimination. As Roth (1994: 336) writes:

> It is necessary to show that these cases of non-prosecution are not aberrational – that they reflect a pattern that is fairly attributable to the state rather than to the exceptional behaviour of isolated functionaries.

It is here that we can perhaps begin to contextualize the position of the British state and its criminal justice system. There have been a number of welcome changes in the regulation of domestic violence and substantial inroads have been made to secure greater protection for its victims. At a policy level, at least, there is much to be cheerful about and we certainly cannot hold the state responsible for its inaction towards the victims of male violence. Yet, despite the optimism brought about through changes in policy, we urge a more cautious reading of change in which we draw attention to the continued disjuncture that exists between policy and practice. This chapter has provided substantial evidence of the discriminatory way in which the various forms of violence against women are policed. The worrying extent of 'no-criming' and 'downgrading', together with the dominance of the 'moral' perspective when dealing with crimes against women, indicate that the policing of the private sphere does not receive the same degree of rigour as those crimes policed in the public sphere. Research has also shown us that the problems of policing are not those that reside with individual rogue officers or of 'isolated functionaries' as noted by Roth (1994) above. Rather, gender discrimination is something best described as a systemic condition and the gendered nature of the criminal justice system can be felt at structural, cultural and individual levels.

Concluding thoughts

While the administration of justice to the public and the private spheres remains a contested issue there is little doubt that the issue of violence against women has now become a recognizable one. Our increased knowledge of the female victim has had an undeniably positive impact on exposing the reality of many women's lives. As a result a number of significant and positive transformations in various areas have taken place including community support, public policy, social services and civil and criminal law and law enforcement. At a more micro level, women's consciousness, language and awareness has also dramatically increased. More women throughout the world now understand and speak about their right to live free of violence. At the same time, we have demonstrated that change at a policy level does not easily translate in practice. Given the effort that has been directed at improving the victim's experience of the criminal justice system, research continues to report inadequate redress for victims of violence. We urge those working with domestic violence victims not to become complacent about the extent to which domestic violence is being tackled. To restate Kallen's point, made earlier in the introduction:

> It is relatively easy for people living in democratic contexts today to understand the occurrence of human right abuses when they occur in politically repressive regimes where the right to dissent is virtually non-existent and glaring social inequalities are white-washed. But how do we explain the continuing occurrence of violations of human rights in democratic societies whose laws and social policies are predicated upon human rights principles of justice and equity for all citizens? (2004)

Indeed it seems that things are set to get worse. Radford and Tsutsumi (2004) argue that globalization has brought with it *different* and *more* opportunities for increased violence against women.

With systems now in place to police the perpetrators of violence and protect its victims, it is all too easy to give up the fight for improved services. We encourage a more critical dialogue between researchers and criminal justice agencies to make sense of the ongoing inadequacy of protection to victims. The resistance shown by the various criminal justice agencies to the policing of domestic violence has much to do with the gendered nature of criminal justice organizations, their work and their workers. Despite a discourse of organizational change, the police service and its agents remain firmly rooted within a crime-fighting model (Silvestri, 2003). The criminal justice system and its agents all work within clearly defined 'gender schemes' which set the boundaries of what is considered appropriate and inappropriate behaviour for men and women (Kelly et al., 2005). Given that criminal justice work remains an overwhelmingly male activity, it is invariably men's attitudes about women that count here. More specifically and in relation to the police organization, with only 22 per cent being policewomen, much of the mandate for policing violence against women rests in the hands and minds of men. We discuss the implications of this in greater detail in Chapters 6 and 7 of this book, but suffice to say here that gender remains a crucial division in and a defining feature of the criminal justice system. We are under no illusion that making the state more responsible and accountable for violence against women will end its practice; far from it. Violence against women is complex and has its roots in the structural relationships of power, domination, and privilege between men and women in society. Drawing on a theory of non-discrimination, however, is a useful first step in emphasizing the seriousness of such acts and will encourage a challenge to the traditional rules of state responsibility.

Summary

- The discovery of victims of crime is closely related to an interest in the victimization of women and the propensity to associate men with offenders and women with the status of victim.
- The experiences of female victims are outlined in detail and it is apparent that women are particularly vulnerable to violent victimization at the hands of men in the private sphere.
- We explored the phenomenon of domestic violence and sexually motivated violence – specifically rape – both of which impact most on women. Changing definitions and responses to these types of victimization were charted and we considered the effectiveness of legislative changes on police policy and practice. Female victims of these crimes are under-protected by criminal justice agencies, demonstrated most tellingly by the high attrition rate, or the low number of offences that result in a successful conviction of an offender.
- This chapter also develops an argument stating that domestic violence is a fundamental violation of human rights. Drawing on Biderman's chart of coercion it is suggested that this type of victimization is a form of torture. Governments across the world need to recognize this to guarantee that the rights and dignity of victims are safeguarded and actively promoted. This aspiration is dependent on the power and dominance of male interests in crime and public policy being successfully confronted.

STUDY QUESTIONS

- To what extent has criminology acknowledged the female victim?
- Outline the ways in which the criminal justice system is said to be 'taking domestic violence seriously'.
- Critically discuss the problem of attrition with regard to sexual offences and violence against women.
- Critically debate some of the dilemmas and tensions that police officers may face when policing the private sphere.
- Outline the role of the state in relation to domestic violence victims and think about how we can make the state more accountable for such crimes.
- What do victims of domestic violence and official torture victims share in common? Is there anything to be gained from reconceptualizing violence against women in such terms?

FURTHER READING

Developed from a broader concern with victims, Mawby and Walklate's, *Critical Victimology* (1994) and Goodey's *Victims and Victimology: Research, Policy and Practice* (2005) both provide up-to-date and critical overviews of the rise of the victim in criminological agendas. Various studies commissioned by the Home Office listed in the chapter provide important sources of knowledge on the prevalence and nature of women's victimization by domestic and sexual assault. These include those by: Kelly (2002); Myhill Allen (2002a, 2000b); Walby and Allen (2004); Kelly et al. (2005); and Finney (2006). There are a great number of academic works on women's victimization. Hester et al.'s *Women, Violence and Male Power* (1996) remains an important text. Lees' *Carnal Knowledge: Rape on Trial* (1996) is a seminal text on the problematic nature of dealing with rape. Gregory and Lees' *Policing Sexual Assault* (1999) is a useful text for achieving a good overview of the regulation of crimes against women. It also provides good insight into the complainants' view of the criminal justice system. For an international insight into women's victimization see Krug et al.'s *World Report on Violence and Health* (2002). Cook's *Human Rights: Women* (1994) offers a good collection of national and international contributions. Copelon and Roth's contribution in this text offers an opportunity to engage with understanding domestic violence and torture.

Note

1 A peremptory norm (also called *jus cogens*, Latin for 'compelling law') is a fundamental principle of international law considered to have acceptance among the international community of states as a whole. Unlike ordinary customary law that has traditionally required consent and allows the alteration of its obligations between states through treaties, peremptory norms cannot be violated by any state.

5

Men as Victims

Chapter Contents

OVERVIW

Chapter 5 provides:

- An audit of the patterns of victimization experienced by men.
- An outline of the needs of male victims and the services they receive.
- A critical review of explanations of the causes of male victimization.
- A consideration of the need to think about the links between victim and offender statuses.
- An in-depth account of the victimization of young boys involved in anti-social behaviour.
- A call for male victims to take more responsibility for their victimization by recognizing the risk factors attached to their behaviour.

KEY TERMS

anti-social behaviour	homophobic violence	responsibilization
criminalization	interpersonal violence	the rights and needs of victims
fear of crime	respect agenda	

Introduction

In the previous chapter we outlined the extent and prevalence of the victimization of women by men, describing domestic violence as a form of torture. We also demonstrated that while individual men perpetrate such violence across nation states, their law enforcement apparatus is often complicit in privileging and sustaining violent masculinities. Finally, the case for adopting a human rights framework was outlined based on the premise that violent men do not give due respect to the human rights of their victims. This chapter turns to the male victim to account for the gendering of his treatment and experiences at different stages of the criminal justice process. A cursory glance at recent books on victimology show the higher profile of the female victim in academic and public policy debate, which has occurred largely as a result of the influence of feminism on victimology and the victim's movement more generally (Spalek, 2006). Indeed some commentators have posited that victimology is almost synonymous with the female victim (Walklate, 2004; Goodey, 2005). In contrast to mainstream criminology where the concern is with the male offender, the study of victims has until relatively recently neglected the victimization of males.

The reasons why the male victim has been disregarded are complex although we suggest there are three main reasons. The first is that socially and culturally constructed ideas about masculinities do not entertain the idea that men can be victims and as Goodey (1997) observes, 'boys don't cry', thus denying their vulnerability and emotionality. Secondly, most male victims are the *victims* of other men, especially with regard to interpersonal violence, and in some ways male-on-male victimization is normalized. Thirdly, the discovery of male victims of female violence is an issue that has attracted the attention of researchers but is something that is seldom talked about without a degree of ambivalence.

Key debates

In order that we can develop an understanding of men as victims this chapter consists of three main strands, which although overlapping are rehearsed in discrete sections for the purpose of elucidation. The opening and longest section considers the knowledge base relating to the phenomenon of male victimization, focusing in particular on interpersonal violence. In line with the previous chapter it is suggested that this type of offending behaviour illustrates most starkly the gendered nature of victimization and that gender is less obviously relevant for other types of crime, principally property offences. Because this book is about gender and crime the focus is mainly on men although it is necessary to avoid reifying masculinities above other social divisions because it is intertwined in myriad ways with ethnicity, age, sexuality and social class.[1] The salience of masculinities in relation to the services victims receive is then rehearsed, showing how the criminal justice system in England and Wales has been oriented towards victims' needs despite the word 'rights' being in circulation. Secondly, there is a brief review of prevailing explanations of male victimization in light of victimological and masculinities research. A key point emerging from this section is that the distinction between victims and offenders is not hard and fast. Therefore when we consider boys and men there is a clear need to recognize the intricate linkages between complex patterns of exclusion that marginalize men both as victims and offenders, although spelling out the significance of the former at more length. Thirdly, we utilize human rights discourse to provide an alternative way of conceptualizing the victimization of men. We argue very briefly that some male victims need to be 'responsibilized' (Garland, 2001), the attainment of which can reduce risk of violent victimization for some men. Another way of deepening our appreciation of the potential application of human rights discourse is by focusing on how the state has on some occasions unfairly and unjustly criminalized – and victimized – the anti-social behaviour of boys and young men. We realize that this is a provocative standpoint though one that is consistent with a human rights agenda and accepted definitions of the crime victim, such as that promulgated by the United Nations (UN):

> Victims means persons who, individually or collectively, have suffered harm, including physical or mental injury, emotional suffering, economic loss, or substantial impairment of their fundamental rights, through acts or omissions that are in violation of criminal laws, including those proscribing abuse of power. (United Nations, 1998 cited in Goodey, 2005: 10)

It is our contention that under New Labour crime policy involved the mobilization of political power that criminalized boys through the partial violation of Articles 6, 7 and 14 of the Human Rights Act 1998. More than that, this links with wider developments involving the subordination of concerns about the mental and emotional well-being of young people in general, but especially boys, to the goals of crime reduction and penal populism.

Men as victims of crime – the knowledge base

It is worth returning to the point that official statistics often reflect police priorities and information about victims can often be limited, something known as the 'dark figure of crime' (Coleman and Moynihan, 1996). Also, it is ironic that the state-funded administrative criminology, which now dominates research agendas, maintains hegemonic masculinities that are not studied systematically in terms of their gendered identities either structurally or psychosocially. To start coming to terms with male victimization there are various sources of data although the British Crime Survey is that which is most widely used. There are a plethora of other more localized studies that have taken seriously the victimization of men. However, there are fewer studies of this type in comparison to female victims. An important lesson that can be learnt from studies of crime victims is that clearly any person – regardless of their gender – may become a victim of offences against the person, offences against property and offences against public order. Having said this gender is more conspicuous with regard to certain types of crime than others. Taking offences against property such as burglary and theft as an example there is not necessarily a discernible gender pattern and alternative explanatory factors are more significant. There are some snippets of data showing that 18 per cent of young men lose earnings as a result of being burgled compared to 11 per cent of all burglary victims, for example, but they are just that, snippets (Dixon et al., 2006: 30). Victims of burglary consist of both men and women and other demographics such as socio-economic status, housing type and the lack of capable guardians are more accurate indicators of the likelihood of victimization (Davies et al., 2007). This is demonstrated in unequivocal terms by the most innovative research examining the extent and prevalence of burglary where repeat or multiple victimization is studied. A search of the repeat victimization and burglary literature resulted in no hits when searching for the words men, women, male and female (Pease, 1998). Naturally the situation is different with regard to domestic violence.

If our attention switches to crimes against the person there is an altogether different story. According to the Home Office (2004a: 43) British Crime Survey (BCS) data examining violent crime – including domestic violence, mugging and other violence by strangers and acquaintances – describes a situation that is very much gendered. Overall, young men experience the greatest risk of becoming a victim of violent crime (Levi with Maguire, 2002; Maguire, 2002; Stanko, 2002; Walker et al., 2006). The 2002–3 survey showed that 5.3 per cent of males and 2.9 per cent of females were the victim of a violent crime within a 12-month period prior to them being interviewed. The 2004–5 BCS shows young men aged between 16–24 to be most at risk and 15.1 per cent of males and 6.9 per cent of females respectively reported that they had been a victim of a violent crime in the year before being surveyed. This is in contrast to a figure of 3.6 per cent for all adults. Staying with young people, 29 per cent of males aged 10–15 were a victim of violent crime compared to 18 per cent of females. Like offending behaviour the risk of becoming a victim reduces as men age (Hird, 2006: 16).

The aforementioned points are made at a very high level of generality so the category of violent crime needs to be deconstructed carefully. This reveals a situation that is perplexing if factors such as different types of violent crime (e.g. rape, robbery), age, and victim–offender relationships, to name but a few, are considered. The nature of the relationship between the victim and offender is very significant, with male victims stating that they were more likely to be the victim of stranger violence than their female counterparts. For example, 75 per cent of male victims know the offender, compared to 90 per cent of female victims. A similar proportion of males and females reported that they were a victim of mugging, but there is a more even distribution than for other violent crimes. Mugging is a form of robbery and according to 2001–2 British Crime Survey data 67 per cent of incidents of robbery involve a male victim and a quarter of all victims of this crime are males aged 14–17 years (Home Office, 2004a: 44). Half of male victims know their attacker whereas for females the equivalent figure is one third. If specific sub-categories of victimization are acknowledged, such as mobile phone theft, in 2000–1 77 per cent of 550,000 crimes involved a male victim and male perpetrator (Harrington and Mayhew, 2001). The motive for mugging/robbery is more likely to be economic where violence is deployed to facilitate the seizure of desirable goods, so while victims' gender would appear to be significant it is meaningful in ways that are different to the motives behind sexual and domestic violence. For domestic violence, where the more likely motivation is power and control over another individual, the economic factors behind an offence are less apparent, though not irrelevant.

Turning to domestic violence, figures gathered for the year 2004–5 show that the risk of a woman becoming a victim is – at 0.7 per cent – higher than it is for men (0.2 per cent) (Hird, 2006: 16). The difference is perhaps not as pronounced as students often initially think, which supports Karmen's (2004: 26) observation that '...in some couples the presumed victim offender relationship is reversed: the woman is the aggressor and the man the injured party'. This dimension of the offender–victim relationship has been largely 'hidden' until relatively recent times (Cook, 1997; Grady). Just to corroborate our observations in the previous chapter, Mirrlees-Black (1999 cited in Home Office, 2004a: 143) found that men experienced 27 per cent of incidents of domestic violence. Those aged under 25 and people experiencing financial difficulties are particularly at risk. Interestingly it was found that 4.2 per cent of both males and females said that they were attacked either by their current partner or ex-partner in the last year. Indeed ex-partners are at a relatively high risk of abuse. Slightly fewer men (4.9 per cent) than women (5.9 per cent) experienced a physical assault or frightening threat (Mirrlees-Black, 1999). Even though 'battered husbands' are – just like women – slapped, kicked, bitten and have objects thrown at them, they are less likely to be injured by their partner and even less likely to suffer frightening threats (Karmen, 2004: 246). Given that domestic violence consists of the diverse acts just listed it would seem that the cumulative nature of domestic violence is reflected by this finding in the sense that men are likely to be less fearful of their violent partners than female victims. The fact that women are between three and four more times likely to be victimized on a repeat basis; are more likely to be upset and frightened in their day-to-day lives; and are more likely to seek medical help relating to domestic assaults, also adds weight to this supposition (Home Office, 2004a). Mirrlees-Black (1999: 62) offers a cautionary caveat, suggesting that men may express less fear due to 'shame, embarrassment or machismo'. If a longitudinal perspective is observed it is clear that that men are less likely to be physically assaulted in a domestic relationship (15 per cent men compared to 23 per cent women) or experience a frightening threat (17 per cent males compared to 26 per cent females) (Home Office, 2004a: 43–4).

Despite the points made in the above paragraph other researchers have evaluated the 'unmet needs' of those men who are victims of domestic violence (Gadd et al., 2002). Interviews were conducted with 44 men out of the 90 who reported to the Scottish Crime Survey that they were the victim of domestic violence, and although the qualitative interviews involved some reinterpretation of their responses in the questionnaire, interviewers noted a tendency to downplay or, as Cook (1997: 91) put it, *deny* to varying degrees what had happened. Following closer investigation it also seems that male victims are also perpetrators, although this may sometimes be seen as an act of retaliation. This illustrates the importance of the perception of the victim. While there were 'harrowing' accounts of serious violence comparable to those routinely described by women there are clear gender variances. On the whole, and echoing the research findings cited above, in contrast with women, men are less likely to be victimized on a repeat basis and their injuries are of a less serious nature. Consistent with the latter point men (one out of three) are less likely to recognize their abuse than women (four out of five) are, but like men in England and Wales, the men in Scotland reported that they are less fearful of potential abuse and the impact of this form of violence is less severe regarding their general health and well-being. Crucially, the long-term control and intimidation violent men exert over victimized women is not as evident and while men suffer from the equivalent of 'battered woman syndrome' they are less likely to be 'immobilized' by a sense of helplessness and perception that there is no other option (Wallace, 1998: 151). Men are not, in our view, subjected to the torture sketched in our narrative on women as victims. To this, Gadd et al. (2002) add that male victims are financially better off, in full-time employment and less likely to live in rented accommodation, which is in contrast to the predicament of many female victims.

There are other studies of male victims of domestic violence. George and Yarwood (2004) refer to a survey carried out for an episode of *Dispatches* (a television programme) broadcast in 1998 that measured the diverse experiences men have of domestic violence. Half of the 100 interviewees said that they remained in a violent relationship because of a concern for the welfare of their children. Later research undertaken in 2001 by a private consultancy, Dewar Research, focused on the qualitative nature of female-on-male domestic violence. It was found that some men tolerated abuse so they can protect their children and also due to apprehension about the involvement of criminal justice agencies taking their children into care (George and Yarwood, 2004: 12).

Another type of interpersonal violence where there are gender differences is sexual violence, which may or may not include domestic violence. Males are less likely to experience indecent assault (including buggery) committed by a stranger (27 per cent compared with to 37 per cent of females) and 70 per cent of male victims of this type of offence were aged 16 years and under; for females the equivalent figure is about a half. Fewer men than women are raped and in 2002–3 for example, Home Office figures showed that the police recorded 11,441 rapes of females compared to 825 (6.5 per cent) male rapes (Home Office, 2004a: 45). An equivalent figure did not exist before the Criminal Justice and Public Order Act 1994 when male rape was first made a statutory offence, the first case being upheld in 1995. Prior to that, 'the unwanted penetration of the male body was not considered as problematic as the unwanted penetration of the female body' (Graham, 2006: 201).

Research co-authored by the HMCSPI and HMIC (2002) reviewing 1741 crime reports of rape taken from 10 police forces provides some pertinent information about victims of male rape. In its study it showed that 7 per cent of victims were male, adding that between 1996 and March 2001 there was an 'enhanced reporting rate' of 192.5 per cent as more men reported their victimization.

The rather limited research literature scrutinizing the policing and prosecution of male rape shows that relatively few suspected rapists are actually detected but interestingly the percentage of detections is slightly higher for male victims (37 per cent) than it is for female victims (36 per cent) (Home Office, 2004a: 45). The other study referred to above demonstrates that there is also a gender specific difference if conviction rates are taken into consideration because 37.5 per cent of suspects accused of male rape are convicted compared to 21.8 per cent of suspects accused of female rape (HMCPSI and HMIC, 2002: 36).

O'Donnell's (2004) work has focused on the act of male rape that has been evidenced inside prison, an environment characterized by 'rampant homophobia'. Rather like in the outside world the perpetrators of male rape are, at least in their own eyes, heterosexual, and their violently aggressive behaviour is seen not as a homosexual act but rather as a way of asserting dominance over a passive victim. The motivations behind the offender's actions and the experiences of the victim are similar to the rape of women carried out by heterosexual men, although in a prison setting rape is one stage in an ongoing process and is a '... form of persistent sexual slavery' resulting in the long term control of the victim. The victims of this crime are emasculated and labelled as 'girls', 'pansies' and 'fairies' (O'Donnell, 2004: 243). While rape is a form of sex offending it is the victim who is subjected to degradation and humiliation and in contrast to other sex offenders, in particular paedophiles and predatory rapists, the prison rapist is likely to have a high status amongst other men.

Researchers have also evaluated gendered patterns of victimization in relation to 'intimate violence', which includes partner abuse that is not sexually motivated; family abuse that is not sexually motivated; sexual assault; and stalking. It is shown that, like female victims of sexual assault, the perpetrator is more often than not known to the male victim: 83 per cent of males compared to 89 per cent of females (Jansson, 2007: 56). Thus the dynamics of interpersonal violence are gendered. Taking the issue of victim–offender relationships further, women are more likely to be assaulted by a stranger (63 per cent) than men (51 per cent), indicating that men are more likely to know the offender. For serious sexual assault, more male victims (65 per cent) know the perpetrator than do females (40 per cent) either as a friend or acquaintance. A partner or ex-partner is more likely to victimize a man (36 per cent) than a woman (54 per cent) and strangers are more likely to victimize a male (17 per cent) than a female (11 per cent) victim (Jansson, 2007: 60). However, these statistics are rather limited due to the relatively small numbers of male victims.

Other pertinent findings are that victims may experience more than one type of intimate violence although men were less prone to this than women (Finney, 2006). Men are also less likely to be victimized by multiple offenders (i.e. be stalked and sexually assaulted by different perpetrators) (Jansson, 2007: 60). Men are also less likely than women to be the victims of non-sexual forms of family abuse (9 per cent and 12 per cent respectively) and are less likely to receive a non-sexual threat/use of physical force by a family member (7 per cent of women and 5 per cent of men). Earlier on we referred to the concept of repeat victimization and its disregard of gender in relation to burglary. The 2005–6 BCS takes into account the relative risks men and women are exposed to in relation to intimate violence, although having said that 33 per cent of men have experienced two types of victimization in their adult lives (Jansson, 2007: 58).

We know that altogether men face a higher risk of becoming a victim of violent crime but to avoid reifying masculinity other variables may account for this, including marital status (being married reduces the risk for men and women), whereas frequency of visits to pubs and living in rented property increases the risks for both men and women (Jansson, 2007: 61–2).

Another form of sexually motivated victimization is homophobic violence, a variant of 'hate crime', which consists of verbal abuse, damage to property as well as threatened and actual physical assaults. Such violence is an expression of intolerant attitudes towards gay and homosexual people or individuals that are perceived to be of this sexual orientation. This crime is the materialization of heterosexist ideologies which promulgate heterosexuality as the preferred sexual norm and deny and calumniate any behaviour or identities that are non-heterosexual (Herek and Berrill, 1992). Heterosexism is similar to racism and other ideologies that legitimate oppression and it is sustained and reproduced by state institutions as well as in civil society. Thus the heterosexual norm is hegemonic masculinity whereas homosexuality is marginalized and subordinated. Given that such assumptions are embedded in the social structure it is not altogether surprising that homosexuals are subject to exclusionary processes in some areas of economic, social and political life, a sense of exclusion that may be exacerbated by a fear of homophobic hate crime.

Dixon et al. (2006: 15) demonstrate that two-thirds of gay men have been the victim of a homophobic crime. Reviewing Metropolitan Police Service figures gathered between January and June 2001, Stanko (2002: 34) shows that for every female victim of this type of crime there were seven male victims. Of the incidents reported to police three out of five received no physical injuries and in two-thirds of cases the victim had no prior relationship with the perpetrator. Over half of the offences (53 per cent) occurred in the vicinity of or in the home of the victim, with 17 per cent being reported as occurring on the street. Another study carried out in Edinburgh showed that 50 per cent of gay men had experienced harassment with one in four men becoming the victim of violent crime (four times the national average for heterosexual men) (Morrison and Mackay, 2000 cited in Stanko, 2002: 34). Stonewall show that young gay men under 18 are especially vulnerable and:

> ... 48 per cent experienced violence, 61 per cent reported being harassed and 90 per cent said they had experienced verbal abuse because of their sexuality.[2] (2005 cited in Dixon et al., 2006: 15)

Other studies have utilized qualitative interviews, such as data released by an Australian civil rights pressure group, Gays and Lesbians Against Discrimination (GLAD), operating in the state of Victoria (cited in Mason and Tomsen, 1997). This showed a high prevalence of victimization of homosexual people with 69 per cent of men reporting an incident of abuse or violence based on the perpetrator's perception about their victim's sexual orientation.

What about other violent crimes, such as murder? Drawing on an analysis of data gathered between January 1981 and December 2000 looking at 13,140 victims of murder in Britain, Dorling states that:

> ...the rate [of murder] for men, at 17 per million per year is roughly twice that for women (at nine per million per year). The single age group with the highest murder rate are boys under the age of one (40 per million per year) and then men aged 21 (38 per million per year). A quarter of all murders are of men aged between 17 and 32. A man's chance of being murdered doubles between the age of 10 and 14, doubles again between 14 and 15, 15 and 16, 16 and 19 and then does not halve again until age 46 and again by age 71 to be roughly the same then as it stood at age 15. (2005: 27)

The above quotation shows indubitably that the gender of homicide victims is relevant and in the region of up to 70 per cent of known victims are male. Most victims know their killer and circumstances resulting in a fatality are unsurprisingly often emotionally charged (Innes, 2003). According to figures covering 1995–2000 on most occasions the victims of homicide are men (68 per cent) (Francis et al., 2004: 9). This figure is remarkably consistent and in 2005–6, for instance, 67 per cent of murder victims were male (498: the equivalent figure for females was 248)[3] (Coleman and Read, 2007: 7). The modus operandi used to kill men and women varies with more men being killed by a blunt instrument. This method accounts for 28 per cent of all victims, but if gender is considered then 31 per cent male victims are killed in this way compared to females (23 per cent). This suggests that male victims are subjected to more physical force, an observation supported by the finding that the second most common method of homicide experienced by males is hitting and kicking (18 per cent). The second most common cause of death in cases involving females is asphyxiation (17 per cent) (Coleman and Read, 2007: 8). An earlier study showed that 3 per cent of male victims were murdered in this way (Home Office, 2004a: 45). Given the frequent 'moral panics' about gun-related killings it is perhaps surprising that in 2005–6 there were 50 victims murdered in this way (the lowest number in seven years), but perhaps less surprising that 8 per cent of male victims (n=39) and 4 per cent of female victims (n=11) met their demise in this way (Coleman and Read, 2007: 8). There is an association between shootings carried out by BME males, especially young black men: between 1995–9 in 32 per cent of incidents where either the suspect or victim was black a firearm was used. In cases of so-called black-on-black male crime a firearm was evident on 27 per cent of occasions (Brookman and Maguire, 2003: 34).

The nature of the relationship conjoining the victim and perpetrator is also gendered and early American research into homicide victims illustrates that the killer of male victims is most likely to be a close friend/acquaintance (49.7 per cent). The most popular victim–offender relationship for female victims is a close family member (51.9 per cent) (Wolfgang, 1966). According to one calculation, in 60–67 per cent of all cases a male victim is killed by another male, and females account for the deaths of men in under 10 per cent of cases (Stanko, 2002; Coleman and Read, 2007). Brookman and Maguire (2003: 33) claim that approximately half of all homicides are male-on-male and that in 40 per cent of incidents death results from a fight or feud between two previously unrelated persons. A link between this type of 'fair fight' has been found in Victorian England, suggesting that male-on-male violence is a persistent feature of social life, although the cultural motivations and modus operandi will change (D'Cruze, 2000). In 36 per cent of such episodes there is no recorded motive. Other Home Office data (Coleman and Read, 2007: 9) shows that men are less likely to know the suspect(s) at the time of death: 38 per cent of men compared to 54 per cent women. Within this category men are much less likely to be murdered by a partner, ex-partner or lover: 12 per cent of males and 61 per cent of females. It follows therefore that men are more likely to be murdered as a result of the act of a stranger or a relatively superficial acquaintance. In 2005–6 44 per cent of males died in this way compared to 33 per cent of females, although the female figure is distorted by the events of 7/7 and the statistic for females is typically 27 per cent: the percentage for men is unchanged (Coleman and Read, 2007).

Brookman and Maguire (2003) cite evidence showing that victims of homicide have other factors in common. As well as being predominantly male they tend to occupy a relatively lowly socio-economic status, with 40 per cent of victims being unemployed and of the remainder a significant proportion are employed in unskilled manual jobs. Indeed Dorling (2005) offers a compelling account that exposes the close mapping of murder rates and structurally generated inequalities. This demonstrates that male victims are similar to male offenders, reinforcing a point made throughout this chapter about the inextricable links between men and their identities as victims and victimizers. Amongst the victims of infant homicide, a higher number of boys are victimized and between 1995–9 102 boys were murdered compared to 70 girls (Brookman and Maguire, 2003: 17–18). There are other lifestyle and situational factors connected with an increased risk of victimization, particularly alcohol consumption, which is an issue for 50 per cent of victims, including not only those murdered in public houses but also in or in close proximity to their homes (Brookman and Maguire, 2003).

In addition to actually becoming a victim of crime in concrete terms fear of crime, which is essentially being worried about becoming a victim, is also gendered. Research into the fear of crime indicates that even accounting for macho attitudes men are less fearful of victimization (see Hale, 1996) although on the basis of using an innovative methodological device, known as the 'lie scale' Sutton and Farrall (2004: 221) surmise quite persuasively that because of a 'macho concealment of fear' men are actually more afraid than women. This scale is able to sift out the effect of men giving socially desirable responses – answers that conform with prevailing forms of 'hegemonic masculinity' – when they are questioned about their fearfulness. They observe that there are considerable variations between crime types and that men are able to justify to themselves a fear of assault. As Sutton and Farrall put it:

> ...masculinity may be compatible with a fear of assault, in so far as being masculine may entail asserting oneself and not shrinking from the possibility of violence. This ideology may be expressed along the following lines: 'I don't back down from a fight and I'm prepared to defend my honour. Because of this I am at risk of becoming assaulted'. If one is at risk of assault because of this masculine code then it may be 'excusable' to fear assault. (2004: 220)

Given such attitudes we can anticipate that the unwillingness of men to become victims may push them into offending. This theme is followed up after statutory response to victims has been discussed.

The criminal justice response to male victims

Once a victim of crime has been recognized or acknowledged what does society do in response to this experience and their particular needs? Unlike the offender who is drawn into the criminal justice system and who enjoys various rights to safeguard them from any abuses of power by statutory agencies like the police and the courts, victims have no rights and the kind of response they receive is something of a lottery (Ashworth, 2003). Unfortunately from time to time victims of crime may be victimized again by the criminal justice system. The police may disbelieve a victim or a victim may have their character assassinated in the courtroom. This is known as 'secondary victimization' (Zedner, 2002). There have been various criticisms directed at this tendency, resulting in fundamental reforms and gradually the enhanced status of crime victims.

Since the early 1990s successive British governments have introduced so-called Victims' Charters in 1990 and 1996 (Home Office, 2001), followed by the Victims' Code of Practice, coming into effect in 2004 with the passing into law of the Domestic Violence, Crime and Victims Act 2004. First the charters and then the code have raised the profile of crime victims. The outcome is not the distribution of rights to victims, like those possessed by offenders, but as noted earlier on they can now expect a better quality of service and some additional support throughout the criminal justice sector. The police have to provide more information and support. In the courts victims can also expect to be kept informed of their cases, and special arrangements may be made for vulnerable witnesses and victims who are testifying in court. Child victims may be allowed to give their evidence by live video-link. Even the probation service, traditionally an offender oriented agency, now undertakes victim contact work, particularly focusing on the victims of violent crime (Home Office, 2005b).

As a result of the above, victims may not be centre stage but they are now entitled to basic support in the form of information and in some instances this may be backed up with services.

The aforementioned changes have been welcomed by many organizations campaigning on behalf of victims as well as by victims. However, it is quite clear that the delivery of services and support to victims is uneven and lacking equity. This is partly explained by the fact that the victim does not have formal rights and therefore has limited scope for questioning the treatment they may receive. There is more to it than that though, as a distinction is frequently drawn between two types of victim: on the one hand there is the 'deserving' victim; and on the other hand, a victim who is designated 'undeserving' (Mawby and Walklate, 1994). This differentiation of victims is based on the personal characteristics of the victim and any putative relationship this may have to their victimization. Early victimologists (Von Hentig, 1948) adopted the concept 'victim precipitation' to explain how some victims brought about their own victimization. If any evidence of this was found then the victim would be deemed 'undeserving'. Another example is the treatment received by victims of rape in the courtroom. A woman who was a sex worker with a drug misuse problem is much more likely to be cast as an 'undeserving' victim, in contrast to another victim who is an educated professional woman, who is well-spoken and gives the impression of coming from an affluent background. The latter is more likely to be characterized as 'respectable' and subsequently a 'deserving' victim (Zedner, 2002).

Let us now consider the relevance of the above points for understanding male victimization.

While men are more likely to consider that the rights of the accused are respected by criminal justice authorities they have less confidence in the criminal justice system in general than women and most crucially male victims are less satisfied with the effectiveness of the police response than their female counterparts (Allen et al., 2006).

The HMCSPI and HMIC (2002) study found that the police were struggling to come to terms with the investigation of male rape with regard to a relatively new group of crime victims although the constabularies involved in the study had all made a concerted effort to encourage male victims to come forward and report their experiences. A number of possible reasons were given for the reluctance of male victims to report their victimization to the police. Some did not know that what they had experienced was a criminal offence whereas some victims who did know were reluctant to tell the police because of a fear of being disbelieved or anxiety about their own sexuality and/or the views of a third party about their sexuality. Female victims of rape express similar worries although male victims seem to be much more worried about how their sexuality is perceived, reflecting cultural attitudes about rape and male sexuality (Graham, 2006). There is notable under-reporting of homophobic violence due to a lack of trust and confidence in the police and a perception that the police may end up charging the complainant with a 'gay' offence. There are also anxieties about retribution and possible outing, as well as an acceptance of violent victimization as normal (Dixon et al., 2006: 15).

George and Yarwood (2004: 9) show that male victims of domestic violence are not always taken seriously by the police who may be sceptical about the veracity of the reported incident. It is not surprising therefore that they remark that '... current policies thus generally do not appear to deal at all with the large extent of female violence or abuse against male partners' (George and Yarwood, 2004). Such a finding is not out of kilter with the kind of attitudes female victims experienced when they contacted the police and it would appear that the police could take heed from the lessons they learnt. What is more, on some occasions the male victim was treated by officers as if they were the perpetrators, resulting in the police threatening to arrest them for breach of the peace. Men reporting abuse or violence experience prejudicial and discriminatory treatment not just from the police, but the courts and other agencies as well. This is apparent from the police response to emergency calls and the finding that 35 per cent of respondents said that the police did not take much notice of the information they received (George and Yarwood, 2004: 12). Due to this, such victims were reluctant to report their experiences and this reluctance influenced wider reporting to friends or family due to a fear of being mocked, embarrassed and disbelieved (Karmen, 2004: 247). An obvious consequence of this is gross under-reporting of this type of victimization. Gadd et al. (2002) also argue that the response to male victims of domestic violence needs to pay attention to the difficulty of distinguishing victims and perpetrators. Above all, though, recognition of the fact that men have different needs to women and that different types of service needs to be provided is imperative. Having said that, the lack of hostels and other voluntary sector provision for men is a notable gap in service provision. In 2006 the Home Office (www.crimereduc-tion.gov.uk/domesticviolence57.htm (accessed 15 February 2006)) did launch a media-led campaign to raise awareness about all forms of DV, including that experienced by men. It called for victims, as well as their friends and family, to report their victimization.

Explaining patterns of male victimization: masculinities and the fluidity of victim–offender statuses

Victimology is renowned for some of its more controversial theories about the factors and processes leading to victimization. Mendelsohn (1956) is amongst the founders of this field of study and his typology of victims claims that vic-tims of crime are to some degree responsible for what happens to them and in actual fact provoke their own victimization. Research published by the Institute for Public Policy Research makes this point about the 'huge numbers' of young males who are victims of violent crime, stating that:

> ... some of these victims may not have been entirely blameless – they may well have unreasonably provoked the offender. ... In England and Wales together these figures suggest that nearly 450,000 young men were attacked by a stranger in 2004–5 (GAD, 2005). Lifestyle undoubtedly plays a part here: people who visit a pub at least three times a week are more than twice as likely to be victims of violent crime as those who never go (Nicholas et al., 2005). (Dixon et al., 2006: 16)

Clearly, this problematically reduces the responsibility of the offender and appor-tions more blame to the victim yet it requires us to take seriously the fact relation-ships do exist between the victim and their assailant and that associations arise to varying degrees on the basis of mutual consent. Another pioneer is Von Hentig (1948) whom, as noted in the chapter on women as victims, referred to the 'acti-vating sufferer', again drawing the victim into an equation that makes them to some degree responsible for their fate. Similarly, Schafer (1968) suggested that a victim may behave negligently, thus provoking or precipitating his own victimization. The adoption of these perspectives produces a number of well-rehearsed pitfalls although what we know about the dynamics surrounding male-on-male homicide prevent us from jettisoning them absolutely. Having said that the lifestyle approach, which concentrates on the routine activities of people, reveals that certain choices of leisure activity, as well as occupation type or housing tenure, for example, increase the risk of victimization.

It is almost a truism, although one that is not always acknowledged in all accounts of victimization, that many victims are also offenders and that this is related to masculine identities. The linkage of these two statuses is explored by Winlow and Hall (2006) who describe a state of affairs in the 'post-industrial pleasure dome' where men need to demonstrate a capacity for violence as well as recognizing the perennial threat of victimization to their 'social status and psychic security'. Interestingly, in this work the men involved do not exclusively belong to underclass populations and many are employed, albeit under economically insecure conditions. Men engage in an internal dialogue where they are characterized simultaneously as potential victims as well as 'victors'. Indeed victimization is perversely sometimes perceived as part of an initiation ritual leading a person into manhood. Being beaten up, for instance, is just part of 'growing up' and actually *toughens up* some individuals. Victimhood is never far away and men need to show that they can take violence but in doing so this must avoid 'excessive damage or humiliation' to their social and psychological status (Winlow and Hall, 2006: 158–9). In a *habitus* where violence is accepted as the norm and a near inevitability, men must accept their predicament with stoicism and 'fortitude'. Consequently, they position themselves in order that they can avoid humiliation, a pose maintained by an emphasis on physicality, survival, honour and respect. Violence is therefore used defensively to control a status that is dependent on the vilification of victimization. There is a reluctance to report violence, especially if the physical condition of a victim shows that they came off worse. The hazard of violent victimization is just an aspect of the fun and entertainment sought in the liminal spaces belonging to a burgeoning night-time economy. Overall, when the different interpretative strands are synthesized we are left with an impression of victims with:

> ... stoical, fatalistic and reactionary attitudes to violence [and] a deeply entrenched and highly productive form of 'survivalism' that infuses the localised culture and the habitus of its male members. (Winlow and Hall, 2006: 161)

Reilly et al. (2004) describe the relationship between victims and offenders, which is especially glaring in situations of serious armed conflict, such as the situation in Northern Ireland where it was difficult to distinguish and separate the involvement of young men as victims and offenders. In referring to the inevitability and ubiquity of violence and the fluidity of offender–victim status, Reilly et al. express this in stark terms:

> All discussions generated consensus that in Northern Ireland, and more generally, violence is a major factor in the lives of young men. One discussion generated a list of groups of people they associated with violence, including paramilitaries, skinheads, bullies, Hoods (local gang members), Combat 18, the Klu Klux Klan, and the police. Violence was mentioned in relation to a lot of contexts such as school, clubs and bars, the street, the home, drugs and alcohol, domestic violence, sectarian violence, kneecappings, shootings, and riots. In all discussions there was complete acceptance that whether as victim or perpetrator, violence was an issue that all young men must negotiate. (2004: 474)

Both of the accounts reviewed above are interesting inasmuch as they are both tainted with a fatalistic acceptance of the threat and actual reality of violent victimization.

Male victims and their human rights: a critical framework

The section before last shows that there is a commitment on the part of criminal justice agencies to respond to the rights and needs of victims of crime and that this orientation is based on an assumption that the rights of victims are partly met by adopting more punitive and exclusionary practices towards the offender (Spalek, 2006). We have already acknowledged an inherent problem with this type of approach, specifically the fluidity of victim and offender identities, especially amongst men and boys. We argue that this dilemma is clearly exposed when the policy response to the victims is considered with reference to the:

(a) responsibilization of victims;
(b) the anti-social behaviour of predominantly excluded youthful masculinities.

'Responsibilizing' male victims

The point we wish to make here follows up our observations in the chapter on male offenders that argued that the behaviour of some men inhibits the human rights of others. Here we suggest that men who engage in behaviour that runs a high risk of victimization, in particular alcohol misuse, needs to be challenged. The reasoning behind this claim is that men who offend when drinking are also more likely to be victimized at the same or other times. In other words, certain lifestyle choices are intimately related to victimization, especially regular visits to pubs. Avoidance of risk situations or changing certain elements of personal lifestyle can limit those situations where human rights are compromised. More importantly, refraining from heavy drinking will reduce the costs of the response to this type of behaviour, freeing up more resources for responding to the human rights and needs of a wider range of crime victims. Clearly there are powerful vested interests and a modicum of 'hypocrisy', especially in the night-time economy that would need convincing, but this may be a fruitful way of reducing some gendered forms of victimization that impact most on men (Hobbs et al., 2005).

Anti-social behaviour (ASB) and masculinities

Senior (2005) has remarked that the government was conflating essentially the sub-criminal conduct constituting ASB with the global threat of terrorism and serious and organized crime. In line with a left realist approach, we do not wish to minimize or trivialize the degrees of anxiety and suffering caused to communities, rather that the disproportionately punitive ethos underpinning crime policy in this area treads perilously close to disregarding the rights of children, in particular boys who are responsible for most incidents of ASB (Lea, 2002). This admittedly controversial argument is based on the premise that the legislative and policy framework in place for responding to ASB can result in powerful state actors and agencies victimizing vulnerable masculinities.

Below is a brief history of the origins of ASB and its main characteristics, followed by a contextualization of this phenomenon in New Labour's youth and criminal justice policy (1997–2007). The principal strategies implemented to tackle ASB are then sketched, including anti-social behaviour orders (ASBOs), dispersal orders, parenting contracts and parenting orders. This is followed by an evaluation of the antipathetic nature of these policies towards the human rights of the insecure and precarious masculinities of the young.

The origins and definitions of ASB

ASB is not exclusively about young boys in particular or youth in general but under New Labour the connection is axiomatic. ASB includes a range of general issues such as: criminal and sub-criminal behaviour; disorder and incivilities; community safety/public protection; fear of crime; and quality of life issues, as well as, more specifically, drinking; vandalism; noise (i.e. nuisance neighbours and 'neighbours/families from hell'); threatening behaviour; joy-riding; violence; racial harassment; dropping litter; and verbal abuse. These problems are not new and have been around in one form or another in all societies, although the frames used to think about and respond to them are contextually specific (Pearson, 1983). In the nineteenth century ASB was more likely to be associated with fears about social revolution whereas in the early twenty-first century there is an underlying concern with the perceived moral and behavioural deficiencies of the young (Waiton, 2001). In 2000 the Home Office-funded British Crime Survey identified drug dealing/misuse, litter, teenagers hanging around (rude or abusive behaviour) and disputes between neighbours (especially on low-income housing estates). Even the aforementioned behaviours refer to many different activities. For example, ASB related to drinking may occur in subways and public parks in the daytime, but outside pubs and clubs in the context of the night-time economy. In short ASB refers to a diversity of behaviours.

In the 1990s, the term ASB was used to focus on behaviour in relation to housing, but this definition was broadened to encompass a variety of civil disobediences and criminal activities. ASBOs, for example, were used as a measure to tackle prostitution, racial abuse, verbal abuse, criminal damage and vandalism, graffiti, noise nuisance, threatening behaviour in groups, begging, kerb crawling, throwing missiles, assault and vehicle crime (www.renewal.net). Whitehead et al., in attempting to produce a universal definition of ASB, said that:

> ASB is defined in relation to the harm caused to others. ... ASB is also
> defined by categories of behaviours or activities, some of which directly
> harm people, others of which damage property and some of which are
> simply a nuisance (Whitehead et al., 2003: v).

They also highlighted the diversity of definitions in use: 'Most definitions of ASB involve some overlap with definitions of crime. Some indeed include all crimes' (Whitehead et al., 2003: v). They therefore conclude that 'Given the difficulties of definition ... it is hardly surprising that measurement of the extent of ASB presents considerable difficulties' (Whitehead et al., 2003: v).

Concern about ASB and young people is inextricably linked to the agenda of the previous Conservative government of the mid-1990s, mainly the response to the Jamie Bulger case. In 1993 two young boys abducted Jamie Bulger, a toddler, in a shopping centre in Bootle, Merseyside, and later on they murdered him beside some railway tracks. The crime itself was particularly brutal and horrific, made even more disturbing by CCTV footage showing Jamie with his hand being held by one of his abductors as he was walked away from a crowded shopping mall. This murder led to an overhaul of public policy regarding young people who, according to government officials, were acting with impunity because of a 'soft' and lenient criminal justice system. The government's view was that a concern with the welfare of children had created an excuse culture where children were not encouraged to assume personal responsibility for their actions (Audit Commission, 1996, 2004; Fionda, 2005).

On being elected in May 1997 New Labour signalled the potential for a more thoughtful approach to young people, especially with its assurance to tackle the exclusionary outcomes of previous government policies via joined-up and evidence-based policies which were according to the oft-quoted Blair mantra *tough on crime, tough on the causes of crime*. More specifically the Blair regime placed the onus on preventing offending by targeting young people and their families. For example, Hughes and Muncie (2002: 10) cite the government as stating in 1999 that 'if a child has begun to offend they are entitled to the earliest possible intervention to address that offending behaviour and eliminate its causes'. This pledge was welcomed by many who prioritized the welfare and human rights of young people, but a preoccupation with ASB started to permeate discourses about crime and disorder so the two become barely distinguishable from each other (Squires and Stephen, 2005). Indeed ASB featured in the Crime and Disorder Act 1998 where it is defined in terms of people 'acting in a manner that caused or was likely to cause harassment, alarm or distress to one or more persons not of the same household as (the defendant)' (Home Office, 1998). At a later date the Anti-Social Behaviour Act 2003 broadened the definition to include any behaviour that 'is capable of causing nuisance or annoyance to any person'. Consequently ASB is very much about the reaction or possible reaction to people based on subjective criteria and giving scope for the boisterous, noisy, irritating behaviour of young people to be labelled as distressing, alarming and annoying. Moreover, it can lead to the '"quasi-criminalization" of the normal behaviour of children [and youth]' (Fionda, 2005: 243).

ASB, youth and crime policy under New Labour: enforcement strategies to tackle ASB

Recent responses to ASB are embedded in the Respect Agenda, which draws on the vague definitions of ASB rehearsed above and employs civil law measures, including ASBOs; parenting contracts and orders; and dispersal orders. These measures have redefined youth and crime policy as well as the child protection system (Jamieson, 2005).

ASBOs
ASBOs are there to protect communities from ASB. They include conditions stopping a person behaving in certain ways and from entering particular geographical areas for at least two years. Early research showed the dominance of

a housing management perspective in the response to ASB (i.e. Housing Act 1996 injunctions, etc.). However, research published by Burney (2002) points out that young people and their rowdy and unruly behaviour were treated as a priority by key agencies on the ground, largely in response to calls from members of the general public. For example, the UK government published a White Paper, *Building Communities, Beating Crime* (Home Office, 2004b), which called for crime reduction partnerships to respond more effectively to anti-social behaviour (Squires and Stephen, 2005). In addition, the *National Policing Plan 2003–2006* directed chief officers and local authorities to include in their local plans a strategy to address youth nuisance and anti-social behaviour (Home Office, 2005a: 9).

As a result of the Bulger case, which abolished the presumption of *doli incapax*, the ASBO can be enforced against any person aged 10 years or more. It is a civil order, but a breach of conditions is an indictable offence meaning that a person can receive a custodial sentence of up to five years. A potential penalty for a juvenile (i.e. over 15 years of age or a persistent offender aged 12–14) breaching the conditions of an ASBO is a two-year detention and training order, a sentence including a year spent in custody with the remainder of time being a community-based punishment managed by a youth offending team. Younger children between the age of 10 and 11 can be given a community penalty. A fundamental problem at the heart of the ASBO is its nebulousness in the sense that the distinction between civil and criminal law is fuzzy. It can criminalize non-criminal behaviour and Smith (2007) shows that on 10 September 2003 over half of 66,107 recorded incidents of ASB were already defined as criminal. Furthermore, the ASBO can be used to tackle criminal activity when there is a lack of substantial evidence to demonstrate criminal responsibility. This happens because as a civil order the standard of proof ('balance of probabilities') is lower than it is for criminal cases ('beyond reasonable doubt'). Effectively, Article 6 of the Human Rights Act 1998 is not observed because the right to a fair trial is foregone. An overarching problem is that ASBOs can lead to criminal charges through the 'back door' (Burney, 2005) without any reference to the principles of 'due process' (Packer, 1968). Breaches can lead to criminalization and with specific reference to young people, in the first four months of 2005 some 200 receptions into young offender institutions were of people breaching their ASBOs (Smith, 2007).

The enforcement of ASBOs is dependent on increased levels of surveillance to ensure banned youths are not doing the things they are prohibited from doing. This is ensured by publicizing specific details – including photographs – about the reasons why an order was meted out and the restrictions imposed on the young person. This is essentially a form of 'naming and shaming', arguably out of proportion with the seriousness of the behaviour in question. The net widening of mechanisms in social control is further epitomized by the creation of 101 non-emergency call centres, set up to provide information and advice to deal with ASB and community safety matters (Home Office, 2006a and b). This surveillance is based in communities consisting of preventive and exclusionary practices. This involves conflicting concerns with care, control and enforcement, although it would appear that enforcement is prioritized above care and welfare, evidenced by the following Home Office statement:

> The ASBO legislation does not require an assessment of the needs of a child before an order is made. Where an assessment is considered appropriate, this should be carried out, but should not delay the ASBO process. ASBOs issued to young people can be reviewed annually to assess how they are working, whether the prohibition in ASBO need to be reviewed or whether there is a case for varying or discharging it. (2006a: 11)

Again, there is the targeting of actual and potential behaviour without sufficient reference to the needs of and mitigating circumstances of 'offenders'.

An outcome of this punitive atmosphere is a heightened sense of fear and anxiety, especially in those social spaces where young people gather, and there is the social construction of dangerousness and representations of a criminal 'Other' (Reiner, 2007; Young, 2007). A tool that has been implemented to prevent people from socializing in public places is the 'dispersal order', including the power to take children home, which can be used alongside fixed penalty notices, ASBOs and anti-social behaviour contracts.

Dispersal orders
The dispersal order is used by police to disperse groups of two or more people 'if they believe their presence or behaviour has resulted, or is likely to result, in a member of the public being harassed, intimidated, alarmed or distressed' (Home Office, 2007a and b). Significantly, it is only necessary for a police officer to believe that the possibility of the above exists, hence the police engage in prediction based on crude profiles assessing the risk of offending rather than guilt proven beyond reasonable doubt. The police, including Police Community Support Officers (PCSOs), have additional powers for dealing with children under 16 who are out on the streets unaccompanied by an adult after 2.00 hours and they can take a child home, using reasonable force if necessary (Home Office, 2007a and b). This intervention is justified, by appealing to welfarist principles, as a form of child protection, although we suggest that an outcome is the penalization of normal behaviour amongst children. Just 'hanging out' and 'chilling' is treated as suspicious, abnormal and ultimately anti-social. Most crucially, though, the safeguards protecting people on the street from abuses of power is limited and the authorities and members of the public more or less have a licence to determine what they regard to be troublesome. Once again, the rhetoric surrounding dispersal orders is premised on caring for young people yet

in reality there is room for exclusion and social control to the extent that the cultural rights of children and their right to associate in particular places is outlawed as part of an attempt to 'sanitise public space' (Burney, 2005) and reclaim and/or re-impose the respectable values of civil society.

The parents of anti-social children are also made more responsible for the behaviour of their protégés.

Parenting contracts
Poor parenting skills are often identified as a cause of juvenile delinquency and the Respect Agenda calls parents to account, making them responsible for reinforcing a sense of respectable morality. Government policy has argued that strong families are a prerequisite for stable and orderly communities and that dysfunctional families produce anti-social children. Parenting contracts were designed with such families in mind. These contracts are voluntary written agreements, joining together parents with schools, local education authorities and youth offending teams, to respond to the needs of children who commit truancy or are excluded from school. Parents are required to effectively supervise their child to make sure they stay away from certain places or attend school (Home Office, 2006b). Some contracts – again voluntary ones – require parents to attend parenting classes to assist them in coming to terms with ASB by offering support. For those parents who do not comply with these contracts there is a sanction, the parenting order.

Parenting orders
These are designed for those parents who do not voluntarily agree to take on board responsibility for their anti-social children. These orders are made in the civil courts if there is a problem with a young person's behaviour in relation to children on an ASBO or those young people who are convicted criminals. YOTs (Youth Offending Team) and LEAs (Local Education Authorities) may also apply for an order if a child has, or is alleged to have, engaged in ASB and if they are truanting or excluded from school. Parents are also required to develop their parenting skills and non-compliance with this objective can lead to a maximum fine of £1000 or the imposition of a curfew order.

Curfew orders can necessitate 24-hour supervision of children, which is not always achievable in the case of families where there is a history of denied welfare and pre-existing marginalization. In other words, some parents may not enjoy full citizenship rights, and parenting orders and contracts exacerbate the impact of this marginalization. There is a proclivity to treat these parents as idle and feckless without looking at the structural obstacles getting in their way. The imposition of discipline and financial penalties can worsen the situation and in some instances children will bear the brunt of this. A policy intended to reduce ASB may be counterproductive (Goldson and Jamieson, 2002).

Thus, the Respect Agenda and the ASB framework is all about changing how people behave in line with acceptable modes of conduct defined along the lines of respectability. This is undertaken by appealing to the rights of all, but in actual fact already marginalized and vulnerable groups are further victimized, including in this instance young boys. Despite government rhetoric to be *tough on crime and tough on the causes of crime* the Respect Agenda results in the crim-inalization of incivilities, and the twin objectives of caring for and controlling young people produce contradictions, not least a willingness to divorce an understanding of social problems from a material social context.

Compromising the human rights of children: victimizing boys

At the centre of the policy response to ASB is a degree of compulsion to bring about change in people's behaviour. With reference to the Human Rights Act 1998 and the Convention on the Rights of the Child 1989 the emphasis on the ASB of male youth does not give sufficient attention to their cultural rights with regard to freedom of thought, association and assembly. As Waiton (2001) shows, ASB is 'adult-centric' in the sense that the ASB of children is defined in opposi-tion to the norms of adulthood. Due respect is not always given to the interests of children who are not only discriminated against on the grounds of their age and gender, but also on the basis of the social and behavioural attributes of their parents. In particular, the anti-social behaviour order (ASBO) is a civil response, which may be used against any person aged 10 years or over who behaves anti-socially. As Hopkins Burke and Morrill (2004) show, ASBOs concern civil matters where 'behaviour need only be proved on the balance of probabilities' rather 'than beyond reasonable doubt' as it is in criminal cases. Crucially, an ASBO can be imposed against people who have not done anything criminal, but it is a criminal offence to breach an ASBO, possibly leading to a five-year prison sentence. There are four themes that need to be considered.

1. Definitions of ASB are ambiguous and many discussions of this phenomenon concern the acceptability of behaviour rather than behaviour that is criminal. Defining acceptable behaviour is a subjective exercise and actions that are acceptable for one person may not be acceptable for another person. For example, there are certain types of behaviour which are acceptable to young people (e.g. 'hanging around') but are not acceptable to older people. Acceptability not only concerns behaviour but factors such as dress codes. The clothes young people wear (i.e. hooded tops) may symbolize ASB. In the last analysis, this can infringe on the cultural rights of children and their capacity to associate freely.
2. The government's emphasis on ASB is full of contradictions. When ASB legislation was passed into law the New Labour government at that time was concerned with addressing poverty and neglect amongst young people. At the same time, ASBOs

were being used to target young people. Rather than addressing their problems, young people were at greater risk of being labelled as criminals are. Thus children experience discrimination on the grounds of their age.

3. The ASB agenda tends to concentrate mainly on the individual offender, thus ignoring wider social and economic factors (Cook, 2006). The thinking behind ASBOs is an example of being tough on crime. ASBOs can be used to coerce people to conform to wider expectations about behaviour. A consequence of paying too much attention to controlling the people who act anti-socially is that the wider, socio-economic causes of this behaviour are not addressed.

4. The civil standard of proofing effectively opens a back door to criminal conviction (Hopkins Burke and Morrill, 2004: 236) where the right to a fair trial is effectively renounced. The ASBO is a civil order, which means that the anti-social person is not necessarily arrested and read their rights. They are also not required to attend the court for a hearing. If an 'offender' does not comply with this order there is a law enforcement sanction. As such civil law can be used as a crime reduction tool.

Concluding thoughts

This chapter has outlined the complex experiences of men as victims of crime. In the first part we argued that in considering victimization it is necessary to avoid reifying gender because it is not necessarily significant in relation to all types of offending behaviour and a distinction was drawn between offences against property and offences against the person. We argued along similar lines to the chapter on women as victims that it is violent crime, especially interpersonal violence, where gender differences in victimization are most evident. As a result of the influence of second wave feminism on victimology, most attention is quite rightly directed towards women and girls as victims of violent masculinities that are not tackled head on at a structural level by the state and the law enforcement and correctional agencies within its purview. However, more recently writers have started scrutinizing the complex pattern of victimization and its impact on men. Most of this victimization, especially the alcohol- and drug-fuelled turf wars that sometimes culminate, in the most extreme cases, in murder, is carried out by men. More than that, the distinction between offenders and victims is rarely clear-cut because men and boys in certain marginalized milieu are both victims and offenders. We also showed that some men are victimized by women, which goes against the grain of some preconceptions that have been held by feminist scholars. Despite the existence of male victimization by women this is statistically negligible and men are culpable for most of the victimization that impacts on men.

We then addressed the salience of human rights discourse in coming to terms with the victimization of men. We followed up a discussion introduced in the chapter on male offenders, which called for such men to take on board personal responsibility for their actions, by suggesting that the evidence base shows that some men do tend to engage in risky behaviour that brings about their own victimization. This allusion to the notion of victim precipitation is likely to attract considerable criticism but there is conceivably a case for responsibilizing victims, especially those who also victimize, and to convince them of the need to accept a rights-based agenda. A visit to a casualty or A&E department at a weekend reveals the consequences of the brutalizing effects of the carnivalesque on all young people, but mainly men. To counter any potential victim blaming we argued that certain masculinities are criminalized as a result of over-punitive policies. This argument was fleshed out in relation to the anti-social behaviour of boys and male youths where we argued that legislation has been introduced which renders vulnerable the human rights of this group. It is argued that young men from all areas of society, especially those from poorer socio-economic groups, need their rights buttressing if they are to respect so-called civilized values.

Summary

- It goes against the grain of deeply embedded cultural attitudes that men can be victims and when men report victimization it is often said that it is an affront to their sense of what it is to be a man. However, men are frequently victimized and this chapter outlined the extent and prevalence of the types of victimization they experience. An important point is that many men and boys occupy the status of both offender and victim and that the two can from time to time become indistinguishable.
- In contrast to women, who are much more vulnerable in the private sphere, men have a higher risk of becoming a victim in public space. Most officially recognized interpersonal violence is perpetrated against men and boys by other men and it was suggested that male victims can actively avoid some risky criminogenic environments.
- While victimology has rightly highlighted the appalling treatment of female victims by criminal justice agencies, the male victim has not fared particularly well either. The factors underlying the neglect of the male victim are different, though, and are related in part to masculine identities and a lack of understanding of the needs of male victims by the police, courts and wider society.
- The causes of male victimization were reviewed and it was suggested that certain unpopular victimological concepts such as victim precipitation have perhaps been jettisoned prematurely with regard to violent crime in the night-time economy.
- There are established ways of looking at crime victims and this chapter attempted to contest some of our preconceptions about the victimization of men. It is our view that young men and boys can be victimized by the effects of state power and through a consideration of the policy response to ASB we described how this group can be perceived as victims, as well as offenders. A human rights agenda is one way of recognizing the unfair and unjust treatment of young people, as well as being a means to counter punitive policies.

STUDY QUESTIONS

- What does criminology and victimology tell us about men as victims of crime?

- Assess the adequacy of the criminal justice response to the specific needs of male victims of crime.

- Critically explore the reasons why young men are so vulnerable when it comes to becoming the victims of violent crime.

- Assess critically the claim made in this chapter that we ought to recognize the anti-social behaviour of boys as a form of victimization.

- What practical steps can be taken to reduce the victimization of men?

FURTHER READING

In addition to the general introductions to victimology authored by J. Goodey, *Victims and Victimology: Research, Policy and Practice* (2005) and Spalek's *Crime Victims: Theory, Policy and Practice* (2006). Various studies commissioned by the Home Office cited in the chapter provide important sources of knowledge on the prevalence and nature of men's victimization, especially of interpersonal violence. However there are some excellent studies looking at the fear of crime and male rape respectively, including: Goodey's 'Boys Don't Cry: Masculinity, Fear of Crime and Fearlessness' in *British Journal of Criminology* (1997) and Graham's 'Male Rape and the Careful Construction of the Male Victim' in *Social and Legal Studies* (2006). Also use the index to find the relevant pages in Walklate's *Gender, Crime and Criminal Justice* (2nd edn) (2004) and Newburn and Stanko's *Just Boys Doing Business: Men, Masculinities and Crime* (1994). Winlow and Hall's *Violent Night* (2006) focuses on the inter-relatedness of victimization in relation to men and masculinity. Overall, there are a limited number of readings dedicated to the victimization of men and it will be necessary to search carefully through the indexes of various victimological texts looking under men and masculinity.

Notes

1 Given Hood-Williams' (2001: 41) insightful observations about the 'et cetera clause' any consideration of the linkages between different structures and social divisions is fraught with difficulties and would require more attention than is feasible in a book of this size.
2 Lesbians and bisexuals were combined with gay men in this statistic.
3 It should be noted that this covered the year of the 7/7 bombings where there were three times more female victims of these explosions, which is a far from typical event that slightly distorts the overall percentage.

6

Gender and Criminal Justice Workers

Chapter Contents

OVERVIEW

Chapter 6 provides:

- A discussion of the differential employment of men and women in the criminal justice sector.
- An evaluation of the quantitative and qualitative dimensions of gendered patterns of employment.
- An analysis of gender-based discrimination in the criminal justice system.
- A critical assessment of the impact of heterosexist and hegemonic masculinities on the policing functions of police officers and private security workers.
- An initial explanation of the influence of power on the gendered dynamics of work in the criminal justice sector. It is shown that power weakens the influence of human rights-based values, thus perpetuating gendered patterns of inequality.

KEY TERMS

cult of masculinity	heterosexist ideology	power
diversity	ideology	sexism
elitism	pluralism	third way
equal opportunities	police and policing	
hegemonic masculinity	police culture	

Introduction

In the next two chapters the gendered nature of criminal justice organizations is reviewed. We depart from the symmetrical approach utilized in the chapters focusing on offenders and victims, introducing a number of themes relating to the experiences of men and women workers throughout the sector. The next chapter explores the theme of career progression to show how discriminatory ideas and practices obstruct the mobility of female professionals and how this tendency is out of kilter with the rights-based approach we have been advocating. As a precursor to this, the specific aim of this chapter is to examine the location of men and women in the criminal justice system in terms of the numbers employed by different agencies and their respective positions of power and influence in these organizations. We start from the premise that there are inequalities existing between men and women, confirmed incontrovertibly when this page was written by the final report published by the now disbanded Equal Opportunities Commission (EOC)[1] where it is observed that there are stark gender gaps and that sex discrimination is rife for women in the workplace and at home. However, the pattern of inequality is far from straightforward and it is necessary to look behind the numbers to show how organizational cultures produce and sustain sexist attitudes, beliefs, processes and practices. By the end of the chapter it is demonstrated that the effective power of hegemonic masculinities underpin the workings of the professional groups operating in an increasingly pluralized criminal justice system. This network of agencies behaves in such a way that privileges the interests of men at the expense of women and shows how this state of affairs is diametrically opposed to a human rights agenda, which values the principles of equality, opportunity, diversity, fairness, dignity and balance.

To achieve the aforementioned aims the chapter is split into three main sections beginning with an 'audit' of the criminal justice system, which counts the number of men and women working in the staple or core professions: the police; courts; probation service; and prison service. As well as these organizations we consider the Department for Constitutional Affairs, Youth Justice Board, Forensic Science Service, the Parole Board, Independent Monitoring Boards (formerly Board of Visitors) and the Serious Fraud Office. We also very briefly draw attention to an under-researched group of para-professionals, or those people brought into the criminal justice sector who lack the full expertise and powers of professionals (i.e. the police, probation and prison officers) yet who are proving influential. This group of para-professionals is largely an effect of the pluralization of criminal justice, who are playing an increasingly pivotal role in crime policy yet who remain un-researched, especially the gendered nature of their activities (Senior et al., 2007). While this part is mainly descriptive there are discernible patterns requiring some elucidation. The limitations of relying on statistical data are acknowledged and the properties of the relationship between numerical and other hidden inequalities are identified.

The second section provides a more qualitative take on gendered inequalities throughout the crime control industry, although there is a bias towards policing, which reflects in part our own research interests, but also the type of research that has been undertaken by a range of criminologists. We use the word *policing* deliberately because our analysis extends beyond the *police service* or force to investigate other providers of security and surveillance, especially the private sector. We show in some detail how masculinist and heterosexist ideologies permeate all of these organizations, most evident within the organizational cultures of policing agencies, which bolster male dominance in terms of the power and influence of men, especially though not exclusively, over women. A key point of this section is that the sexism of the police service can be censured and subjected to sanctions and regulation whereas the masculinities of nightclub bouncers are less easily monitored and managed.

In the third part we account for the apparent failure of equal opportunities policies, despite the production of various statements of good intent and seemingly positive anti-sexist initiatives. To do this we apply the concept of power to convey how attitudinal and institutionalized forms of sexism preserve male interests within and between professional groups. It is argued that despite damning criticisms of male dominance it has not been fundamentally challenged in some areas of crime and public policy and that its local workings lead to more subtle and insidious forms of discrimination and injustice. Over the last three decades or so, but especially from 2000 onwards, there is clearly a higher degree of compliance with a rights-based discourse, but full commitment to it is less easy to evidence. We argue that deeper structural and attitudinal changes are needed to address gendered inequalities in the criminal justice professions, a point followed up in the next chapter.

A gender audit – men and women working in criminal justice

The activities of criminal justice agencies are gendered in myriad ways and their external orientation towards gender issues, which has been traced thus far in this volume, is intimately related to their internal orientation. In other words, the differential and inequitable treatment of men and women as gendered subjects is in some ways mirrored by what goes on inside the police, the courts and correctional agencies. There is a numerical dimension to this as well as a qualitative angle.

The police service

As gatekeepers to the criminal justice system it has already been noted that police work is gendered in terms of the differential treatment of male and female offenders and victims. In the case of sexual and domestic violence police attitudes are ambiguous and the devaluation of women can be routinized and despite reforms sexist assumptions still remain in some areas of police work. This externally gendered orientation is, at least hypothetically, intimately related to the number of practitioners who are women though that is clearly only part of the story. Historically the number of women joining and staying in the police service have been low and the numbers did not grow appreciably until the 1970s (Heidensohn, 2003). Overall, there are more male than female police officers, an over-representation most glaringly obvious at the senior levels of the force hierarchy. On 31 March 2005 there were 142,795 full-time police officers in the

43 forces of England and Wales, including the National Criminal Intelligence Service and the National Crime Squad).[2] Of this number 30,162 were female, which is the equivalent of 21 per cent. In the previous year 20 per cent of officers were women (Bibi et al., 2005: 5). By March 2006 the female population in the police service was 22 per cent (31,273 of 143,271) (Fawcett Society, 2007: 29) suggesting some enhanced, albeit still negligible, representation.

In the police service there is a clearly demarcated hierarchical rank structure and the service is organized in a quasi-military style (Walklate, 2004). At the top are the chief police officer ranks, with the chief constable being the highest rank-ing officer (the equivalent for the Metropolitan Police Service is Commissioner) followed in descending order by superintendents, inspectors, sergeants and the police constable. Table 6.1 shows that only 10 per cent of senior posts or those at the rank of chief inspector and above are held by female police officers, whereas 24 per cent of constables are women. In other words, there are relatively more women serving in the least senior ranks of this occupation.

Table 6.1

Rank	% of male officers	% of female officers
ACPO ranks	90	10
Chief Superintendent	93	7
Superintendent	90	10
Chief Inspector	90	10
Inspector	89	11
Sergeant	87	13
Police Constable	76	24
Total ranks	**79**	**21**

Source: Adapted from Bibi et al., 2005: 5

However, it should be noted that compared to the previous year the 10 per cent figure for the ACPO ranks in Table 6.1 is an improvement on 8 per cent in 2004. According to an Equal Opportunities Commission report (EOC, 2006, cited in Fawcett Society, 2007) it is estimated that 101 out of 269 senior officers (i.e. the ACPO ranks) should be female if there is to be a higher degree of equity.

In addition to police officers there are police staff, a body consisting of fewer male employees and on 31 March 2005 there were 49,856 female police staff (Bibi et al., 2005: 19). As a percentage in 2006, 36 per cent of police staff employ-ees were men. If we consider ethnicity as a factor 2886 BME staff were female out of a total of 4181 (Bibi et al., 2005: 19). Thirty-two per cent of special con-stables were female (Bibi et al., 2005: 10). Amongst Police Community Support Officers (PCSOs) there is a higher proportion of females: out of a 6268 total, 3685 are men and 2583 are women showing that there is a higher proportion of women working in this role in contrast to fully sworn-in police officers. The equivalent number for BME PCSOs is 654 males and 237 females (Bibi et al., 2005). Expressed as a percentage, in 2006 58 per cent of PCSOs were men (Fawcett Society, 2007: 30).

Thus women are concentrated in the less senior and influential positions in the world of policing, which indicates that there is potentially a problem with their progression, an issue followed up in the next chapter. When looking at the numbers of police officers the key issues are recruitment and retention. In 2005–6 33 per cent of recruits were female, which is a positive development in the sense that this number is higher than the percentage of existing officers. Despite this there is a relatively low turnover of police officers and police careers tend to be long so the impact of this, if it continues, is not likely to be conspicuous for some time. ACPO has said 'it will take between 17 and 23 years to achieve the Home Office target for 2009 of 35 per cent for women police officers' (ACPO cited in Fawcett Society, 2007: 29). Significantly, this is only likely to be achieved if a course of 'affirmative action' is driven forward by the government.

Beyond the numbers and the under-representation of women amongst police officers there are cultural problems, which need to be addressed (see below).

The Crown Prosecution Service (CPS)

It is only in relatively recent times that the police have not been responsible for prosecuting individuals. Since 1986 the Crown Prosecution Service, or the CPS as it is known now, decides whether or not a case should be taken to court so people can be prosecuted. Nowadays the police are only responsible for the investigation of an alleged offence and preparing a case for the CPS, which at least speculatively reduces the impact of the police culture and its 'cult of masculinity' (this is elaborated below; also see Waddington, 1999). On 1 January 2006 there were 8357 persons employed by the CPS with more female representation (66 per cent) compared to males (34 per cent), although there is a higher proportion of men employed in positions of relative seniority (Home Office, 2006d)

The prison service and probation service together belong to the National Offender Management Service (NOMS), introduced by the Carter Review (2003) with the aim of creating an integrated corrections agency joining together community-based and custodial penalties.

The prison service

We already know from the chapters on offending behaviour that most prisoners are men although the proportion of women in this population started to increase from the late 1990s (Gelsthorpe, 2006). This is mirrored by the gendered pattern of employment where male officers outnumber females significantly. The prison service is structured like a militaristic organization and its working practices are heavily imbued with aggressive masculinities where security and control are of tantamount importance. Out of a total of 48,809 employees 66 per cent are men and as with various other agencies it is clear that there are relatively more male officers (79 per cent) and operational managers (80 per cent). There are relatively fewer men employed in other grades (51 per cent). If we look at the Governor grades, in 2004 there were 1044 (81 per cent) men in this position but only 248 (19 per cent) of women (Home Office, 2004a). Hence just like the police service, men occupy the more senior positions in the prison service.

The probation service

According to one survey, the National Probation Service (2005) employs a total of 22,873 staff of which almost two-thirds were women. Altogether, women outnumber men by an approximate ratio of 2:1. In other words, in contrast to the police service, there is in statistical terms an under-representation of men: 64 per cent of Probation Officers (POs) and 74 per cent of Trainee Probation Officers (TPOs) are women. There is a smaller proportion of female Senior Probation Officers (53 per cent), but they are still numerically better represented. Of the 42 chief officers of probation, half are women. At an even more senior level five out of 10 Regional Offender Managers are women, including the Chief Executive (Fawcett Society, 2007: 30). If we look at this information in more detail women have a greater representation in the operational job category and other roles and there is a reduced representation of men in Probation Service Officer and Senior Practitioner roles. This is consistent with the higher representation of women as POs and TPOs noted above, and it is reasonable to assume that people in these posts will progress through the seniority structure. Women do not dominate all areas of probation, though, and there has been an increase in the number of men employed in the Psychologist job group.

Taking the staff population, 76.44 per cent of staff are female, although this figure is skewed by the fact that there are 90.45 per cent women staff working in the Support Staff Administration job group. Turning to more senior staff support roles there is a higher proportion of men averaging out at 56 per cent (National Probation Service, 2005: 5). These disparities could be explained with reference to the higher proportion of older men employed in this category, although women in this category tend to have a greater length of average service, another criteria widely used by employers to determine promotion prospects. In the National Probation Directorate (NPD), the civil service arm of the NPS, 57.39 per cent of staff are men (National Probation Service, 2005).

Probation officers are placed under tremendous pressure and staff sickness is a significant problem, but most importantly probation has been unable to resist radical reforms to its organizational structure and functions. A recent development is the introduction of the principle of contestability in the National Offender Management Service. As Senior et al. (2007) demonstrate, this is an idea that has its origins in economics and was taken up by Martin Narey, in his former capacity as Head of Correctional Services. Narey described contestability as a mechanism that may be used to raise the standard and quality of services by opening up major areas of work for competition. Functions and roles typically carried out by state agencies could also be delivered by the private and voluntary and community sectors. It signalled the end of state monopoly of crime and public policy. The issue here is that the gendered nature and ethos of organizations in the private and voluntary sectors could be very different to the probation service and the commitment of the NPS to 'advise, assist and befriend' offenders could be further abandoned by organizations motivated more by a need to demonstrate economic rather than ethical viability.

Other criminal justice agencies

The Department for Constitutional Affairs (DCA)
This department emerged in 2003 and is responsible for the day-to-day running of the Court Service, in particular the Magistrates' Courts, the Crown Court and the Appeals Court. It appoints magistrates and judges although the Fawcett Society (2007) has said that the Judicial Appointments Commission (JAC) appointed in April 2006 must act independently of the DCA. It also oversees the Legal Services Commission. As stated in its Equality and Diversity Plan published in May 2000 in the aftermath of the Macpherson inquiry (1999) the DCA has striven to achieve a target of at least 50 per cent female employees, which was achieved for most positions in 2005 (see Table 6.2). Overall 67 per cent of workers in the CPS are women.

Table 6.2

Women pay band	2002	2005
1, 2, 3, A & B	67.9%	67.9%
4, 5 & C	63.5%	63.8%
6, 7, D & E	54.9%	54.9%
8, 9, F & G	41.6%	43.9%

Source: www.dca.gov.uk/deptobj/sda/manage.htm (accessed 1 May 2007)

It is clear that while women are over-represented in most pay bands they lag behind in positions of seniority and only 13 of the 42 Chief Prosecutors are female (Fawcett Society, 2007: 28). The CPS is committed to gender equality and it has issued an Equality and Diversity Expectations Statement to ensure that members of the Bar working with or seeking work with the CPS will have equal opportunities policies in place. It is also committed to creating more gender friendly and flexible working arrangements (Fawcett Society, 2007: 28).

The judiciary
Information about judicial officers shows a clear bias with women being under-represented in all positions (see Table 6.3).

Table 6.3

Position	Total	Men	Women
Lord of Appeal in Ordinary	12	11	1
Head of Division (excluding the Lord Chancellor)[3]	4	3	1
Lord Justice of Appeal	37	35	2
High Court Judge	108	98	10
Circuit Judge	643	576	67
Recorder	1358	1172	186
Recorder in Training	17	13	4
District Judge (including Family Division)	433	349	84
Deputy District Judge (including Family Division)	823	620	203
District Judge (Magistrates' Courts)	128	101	27
Deputy District Judge (Magistrates' Courts)	168	130	38
Total	**3731**	**3108**	**623**
% of total	**100**	**83.3**	**16.7**

Source: adapted from www.dca.gov.uk/deptreport2005/pdf/dca2005a.pdf (accessed 30 April 2007)

As noted above, the Judicial Appointments Commission was launched as part of an attempt to redress this stark gender imbalance but as the Fawcett Society rightly observes:

> ... even if the JAC is successful in increasing the number of women who successfully apply to become judges, this will take a long time to have a significant impact on the gender balance of the judiciary. Similarly, the number of female Queen's Counsels is very low and even if the new application procedure is successful in increasing diversity, it will take a long time for it to have a substantial effect. These reforms to introduce fairer selection procedures are important and will have positive effects in the long term, but the pace of change is slow. (2007: 4)

The legal profession more generally is a male-dominated profession especially at higher levels and this is elaborated in Chapter 7.

In addition to the core criminal justice agencies there are other players where details about the gender of employees are collated.

The Youth Justice Board (YJB)

The YJB was created to oversee the youth justice system, including Youth Offending Teams (YOTs), which are multi-agency teams set up by the Crime and Disorder Act 1998 to deal with youth justice matters. In April 2006 (Home Office, 2006d) 184 people were employed by the board, comprising 78 (42 per cent) of women and 106 (58 per cent) men. As with many other agencies there are no women in the three most senior grades (G3, G5, G6) and men are dominant in all grades with the exception of the bottom two grades.

The Parole Board

This takes decisions about when and if to release prisoners. The Board employs relatively few staff and of 241 employees 59 per cent are male (Home Office, 2006d: 21).

The Independent Monitoring Boards (formerly Board of Visitors)

Of 1785 staff 51.71 per cent of staff are men (Home Office, 2006d: 21).

Forensic Science Service

This organization employed 2595 staff in March 2006 with 42.5 per cent male employees, although the issue of seniority is relevant because there are slightly more men (50.7 per cent) in managerial posts (Home Office, 2006d: 21).

Victim Support

This charitable organization exists to offer help and assistance for crime victims, possibly following a referral by the police. In 2004–5 it employed 6162 staff, of which 1593 were male. Volunteers working for Victim Support cannot be forced into reporting their gender and for this reason there is missing data in some 5000 cases (Home Office, 2006d: 22).

Criminal Injuries Compensation Scheme

This is in place to compensate some victims of violent crime and in 2004–5 it employed 123 people: 58.5 per cent women and 41.5 per cent men (Home Office, 2006d: 22).

Serious Fraud Office

This employs 290 staff, which when broken down by gender shows that 57 per cent of employees are male, with 68 per cent of managerial posts being occupied by men (Home Office, 2006d: 23).

NACRO

This organization has charitable status and is dedicated to reducing crime and making society a safer place. It aims to reduce crime in order to give actual offenders and those at risk of becoming offenders a stake in society. It is committed to reducing various forms of disadvantage and social exclusion. In terms of its staff profile 38.5 per cent of its workers are men with 61.5 per cent being women (NACRO, 2005).

A group of employees who are becoming increasingly influential in criminal justice policy are what Senior et al. (2007) call para-professionals, which is part of a trend toward the pluralization of providers of criminal justice services. From the 1990s onwards there were new opportunities for a range of players and stakeholders, not least the expansion of the VCS and private sectors in the so-called crime reduction industry. To give an example, a raft of posts have been created in the anti-social behaviour industry. In addition, the core players in criminal justice are also being transformed by the de-professionalization of their status. There has effectively been 'downward hierarchical theft' where the roles and responsibilities of criminal justice professionals are being handed down to those whom professional groups perceive to be relatively under-qualified or unqualified and inexperienced people, such as unqualified justice workers and posts in the legal profession. The point is that the gendered nature of these rising organizations is yet to materialize, although it could transform gender relations and the machinations of the criminal justice professions.

The limitations of statistical information

The figures compiled for this section provide, if not a contradictory then a rather confusing picture. At a simplistic level it may be argued that the criminal justice system is sexist and that it systematically disadvantages the women it employs. If we take the police and prison services then this argument would have some veracity but other agencies, such as probation and the CPS, employ more women. Thus if the outcomes of the various activities of different agencies are assessed according to the number of men and women employed then the probation service does not appear to be discriminatory. However, despite the appointment in June 2007 of the first ever female Home Secretary, we know that men occupy many senior positions and that hegemonic masculinity can be evidenced in a number of areas. The form hegemonic masculinity assumes varies from agency to agency although we have a fuller picture of how masculinities are manifest in relation to policing. The gendered dynamics of working in the probation, prison and court services are less well-documented and for that reason the next section draws on the voluminous literature on policing and its gendered organizational cultures.

Gendered inequalities and organizational cultures

The concept of policing; and – after detailing our rationale for this – the existence of masculinities in the context of police work; (and very briefly the night-time economy) are outlined.

Policing: the gendered nature of the police and private security

Jones and Newburn argue that policing consists of:

> those organised forms of order maintenance, peacekeeping, rule of law enforcement, crime investigation and prevention ... which may involve a conscious exercise of coercive power – undertaken by individuals or organisations, where such activities are viewed by them and/or others as a central or key defining part of their purpose. (1998: 18–19)

Take another example from Bowling and Foster:

> 'Police' refers to a particular kind of social institution, while 'policing' implies a set of processes with specific social functions. 'Police' are not found in every society, and police organisations and personnel can have a variety of shifting forms. 'Policing', however is arguably a necessity in any social order, which may be carried out by a number of different processes and institutional arrangements. A state-organised specialist 'police' organisation of the modern kind is only one example of policing. (2002: 980)

The idea of policing is therefore not restricted to what the police do and is concerned with a set of processes and practices rather than an institution. The police, in other words, perform a policing function but policing can be undertaken by non-police agencies as well. Indeed the police are, in historical terms, a relatively new phenomenon with a more specific role: 'the police are nothing else than a mechanism for the distribution of situationally justifiable force in society' (Bittner, 1974: 39).

As the quotations taken from Jones and Newburn (1998) and Bowling and Foster (2002) cited above both show, there are a range of individuals and organizations drawn from the public and private sectors that are involved in policing. At this stage it is still not any clearer what policing *is*, however. In essence policing is a form of social control and security, related to the surveillance of particular geographical areas but above all specific populations or groups of people. Examples of surveillance include the CCTV cameras installed more or less everywhere; private security staff at shopping centres; and night-club bouncers (Hobbs et al., 2003). The list is endless and it soon becomes clear that the police are just one provider of control, security and surveillance. The underlying aim of these activities is to make sure society is disciplined and orderly and that any unruliness and disorder are kept to a minimum. It is in this context that various masculinities are played out, which have a ruinous effect on the working lives of many women and, in actual fact, men too. An argument that is developed is that the heterosexist orientations of both the public police and private security are inhibitors of a fully-fledged human rights remit for employees. However, the publicly-funded police are potentially more amenable to regulation and censure, whereas the violent masculinities of the private sector are less easily channelled in such a direction.

The police culture

This is a concept that most students of criminology are familiar with. It is an idea that accounts for the disjunction existing between police policy as it is written and what actually happens in practice. The idea was first developed in the United States and was adopted by several British criminologists to describe the actions of rank and file officers and how they do not correspond with the formal written statements of senior police officers (Holdaway, 1983; Reiner, 2000). There is a debate about the different factors that constitute this occupational culture although most scholars accept this phenomenon is not homogeneous but heterogeneous. However, there are some overarching characteristics, in particular the 'cult of masculinity' (Reiner, 2000; Foster, 2003). The observation of Van der Lippe et al. is our starting point:

> Understanding police culture as a social construct is necessary for gaining insight into how notions of masculinity and femininity influence the organisation, and for gender policies to be made effective. (2004: 394)

The masculinity of police officers has been linked with other elements of the police culture, such as the quest for action and excitement. This is also associated with violence, a capacity conventionally associated with men. As stressed earlier the police service is organized along similar lines to the military and the ability to use force, quite legitimately, is central to its mandate. Male police officers, like male offenders, have been shown to celebrate physical hardness and toughness. They also engage in leisure activities that are gendered, such as heavy drinking and pursuing women (Waddington, 1999: 99). Given the emphasis placed on these attributes female police officers are often made to feel uneasy, especially as feminine qualities are denigrated. The masculine culture of police officers is also heterosexist and homophobic in its outlook. Research published in the 1980s shows, interestingly, how police officers conflate homosexuality with a deviant underclass, which is illuminating especially because there are homosexual police officers (Smith and Gray, 1983: 111). Police work is also presented as 'heroic' (Waddington, 1999: 117), which chimes with some of the accounts of men as victims and offenders (see Chapters 3 and 5; see also Whitehead, 2006; Winlow and Hall, 2006). It would be helpful if some of the ways in which this 'cult of masculinity' is manifest are sketched.

A relatively recent study was conducted by Foster et al. (2005), a disturbing piece of research, which documents widespread sexism in the British police. It delineates the calamitous consequences of this sexism for the future of policing a diverse society. The research was primarily interested in the impact of the Macpherson (1999) inquiry on race and policing although this was situated in the context of wider forms of discrimination such as those experienced by women and LGBT groups. The Foster et al. (2005) study discovered that toleration of racism, especially prejudicial banter in the 'canteen', had declined post-Macpherson (1999), whereas sexist and homophobic attitudes and beliefs were more likely to go unchallenged. Changes in these areas were superficial and while officers were anxious about potential disciplinary action being taken against their racism, this did not apply so readily to heterosexist talk. It was found that derogatory attitudes and beliefs about women and gays were not confined to the rank and file and only some senior police officers. For example:

> ... one officer was told by her inspector to 'run along little girl and do you job'; when she complained about his comment she was asked 'is it your time of the month?' Another officer said she was paired with a male officer during a nightshift, and other men on the team repeatedly phoned her to ask 'are your legs still closed'? Other women reported being called by derogatory terms, such as 'dizzy blonde', 'Coco the clown' or 'dolly'. Women, in all sites, were routinely referred to as 'girls'. In one site a female civilian officer described 'sexual banter ... you know, rude, sexually crude. (Foster et al. 2005: 40)

This heterosexism also underpinned offensive remarks relating to homosexual officers and one scenario recounted in the study shows one officer teasing another because the former perceived the latter to be 'vain' and 'gay'. Such attitudes make many women and gay and lesbian police officers feel isolated, excluded and undervalued. Some respondents felt that gay men were more vulnerable to discrimination than lesbian women who were seen as less threatening to the masculine identify of male police officers. There is also a perception that women and gay people have to work harder than their colleagues to achieve recognition for their efforts. A particularly worrying finding in this study is that police managers and supervisors either seemed unwilling to challenge, or were unaware of the existence of, this problem (Foster et al., 2005).

The consequences of this rampant heterosexism are potentially damaging for the police service because it may lead to problems with recruiting female and gay officers in the future or lead those in the organization to consider an exit from the job. The aspiration to have a police service that is representative of the diverse communities it serves would therefore falter. These problems are identical to those experienced by BME officers, even if the source of discrimination is very different (Rowe, 2004). Another issue is that the internal problems experienced by an organization are likely to be projected outwards, a point already demonstrated by the over-policing of marginalized masculinities (see Chapter 3).

Westmaarland (2001) echoes the above findings, although there are some novel twists and turns in her ethnographic work, based on unprecedented access to frontline operational policework. Her methodology enabled her to analyse police work and its cultures in a variety of settings. It is a compelling study, which revisits the police culture literature in light of traditional concepts of male and female. The unbridled sexism previously discovered was again uncovered although how this is experienced by female officers deviates from some earlier work. For example, some male officers who expressed sexist attitudes and beliefs while at work were dismissed as 'sick' and 'pathetic' by their female counterparts (Westmaarland, 2001: 175). More than reproducing plentiful evidence reinforcing what is already known about the behaviour of men at work, Westmaarland scrutinized other aspects of police work such as ideals about professionalism and competence where there is evidence showing that policing is still perceived to be an essentially male activity.

The gendered inequalities in police work persist but they are not equally applicable in all areas of police work. Westmaarland (2001) argues that it is not just family protection and domestic violence units to which women are attached and that they are involved in certain areas of patrol role, which until recent times were inaccessible to them. As well as entering these areas women also proved in some instances to be relatively more successful than their male counterparts. Interestingly, it also became apparent that the women officers in this study chose these roles rather than them being imposed as a matter of course. Although policing has undergone something of a transformation in relation to some activities, other masculine roles remain sacrosanct and the 'masculinity' or 'masculinities' of specialisms such as firearms remain under the control of male officers. In other words, there is more gender equality but this is confined to certain functions, specifically not 'driving, shooting and fighting' (Westmaarland, 2001: 175).

Because the core functions of police work, especially the symbolic and actual physical use of force require 'male' attributes, such as force and strength, there are issues relating to embodiment (Collier, 1998). Westmaarland avoids lapsing into a simplistic analysis that would assert that men are physically bigger and stronger. Instead she makes the point that high-octane jobs are not just based on the use of brute physical force but that men and women use their bodies in different ways and there is something inherently different about how men enact masculinities in contrast to women.

It is not just the public police where masculinity is an issue. There is an emergent literature examining door supervisors, which is part of a trend described as the pluralization of policing. This is most evident in the area of commercial security, an expanding sector that provides policing for areas of 'mass private property' (Shearing and Stenning, 1981), such as shopping centres, sports stadia and gated communities. Private security firms who employ 'bouncers' also effectively police the night-time economy – the pubs and clubs in town and city centres (Hobbs et al., 2003). It is here that we can observe the work of predominantly men who are in control of mainly intoxicated people in a hedonistic and chaotic environment, exemplified by the subtle, rich and thick ethnographic description found in the works of Winlow (2001) and Monaghan (2004). Although the subject matter was similar these two writers adopted a different critical stance in their respective analyses with the former referring to political economic change and deindustrialization and the latter looking at embodiment.

This not the place to review in detail their methodologies but this work does reveal some illuminating information for our understanding of the gendering of criminal justice professions. Door supervisors perform an increasingly important function in maintaining order in an unruly night-time economy and their work complements the work done by the police as well as that work which the police do not do. It is an overwhelmingly male occupation and most men working in this role conform to notions of 'hegemonic masculinity', they are heterosexual and their sense of embodiment is central to their work. The research shows that the banter of bouncers is remarkably similar to police officers and both groups of workers celebrate a cult of masculinity where there is talk about women, drinking and violence. At one level of analysis the nature of their work is very much alike although the bouncer lacks the legal status that is enjoyed by the police officer. As an individual who needs be able to look after himself, or at least give of that impression, the bouncer is rather vulnerable, especially because his actions are sometimes illegitimate: how much violence can be acceptably used to maintain order in a pub or club is the question they face routinely. More importantly for the purpose of our analysis, the bouncer occupies two statuses: (1) as a potential perpetrator of unlawful violence and (2) as a victim of violence from a reveller who is a customer. As far as a human rights agenda goes, this is of limited relevance to employees in this area of the economy, yet the work they do infringes very much on the rights of the people they encounter.

Interim summary

The preceding pages in this section have explored how masculinities have been enacted in various organizational settings. The usage of public and private forms of policing as exemplars shows that heterosexism pervades these occupations, although they are not occupationally specific and similar attitudes will be found amongst corporate and political elites. What is especially interesting is that the police service is subject to various government- and state-led initiatives that are in place to ensure compliance and to outlaw and stamp out sexism.

The pervasiveness of the police culture continues to be registered by administrative and critical criminologists alike and gendered discrimination is therefore an obdurate feature of contemporary policing. There are many explanations for this, although the concept of power is illuminating for our purposes (Lukes, 1986).

Addressing human rights: the gendered working of power

Thus the concept of power is potentially very useful for coming to terms with conflicts and contradictions arising when we study gendered organizations and the ascendancy of particular value frameworks, such as hegemonic masculinity. An understanding of the power of governments at a macro level is essential for grasping the dynamics of organizational cultures at a micro level and the mediating influence of players at a meso level. More specifically, it is contended that some conceptions of power are useful because they offer a preliminary explanation of some of the reasons why men and women remain in unequal positions in criminal justice. At a superficial level things should be equal, or at least more equal, now. Equal opportunities legislation and a range of anti-discriminatory initiatives have been introduced, most recently the Equalities Act 2006 and the CEHR, yet despite calls for affirmative action to reduce sexist discrimination in the workplace inequalities still exist. An appreciation of the concept of power and its workings in organizational settings can go some way towards appreciating this contradictory state of affairs. While legislators and campaigning reformers have counselled that legislation and policy are the most appropriate mechanisms for instigating meaningful change, the predominance of a cult of masculinity at all levels of institutions, and a preponderance of men in influential and powerful positions, is still an obstacle to equality. It is argued that the political agency exercised by governmental elites preserves the existing status quo in the criminal justice sector. Economic goals such as the financial probity of agencies and their ability to meet over-simplified and inappropriate performance targets (i.e. 'what gets measured, gets done') are prioritized above progressive politics, such as the human rights agenda. Since the late 1990s the government has pledged that it will modernize the public sector although this has occurred without any fundamental changes to the social structure, in particular gendered inequality. How does the concept of power help us to understand this?

There are several conceptions of power, or more accurately, 'effective power'. Power may be channelled through many outlets and can be exercised diffusely (pluralists) or centrally (elites) (Mills, 1956; Dahl, 1958). In addition to these perspectives, which put social agents at the centre of their analytical frameworks there is also a structural dimension (Lukes, 1974, 1986). It is not feasible to do justice in the literature on power, and only a few issues are selected here for our purposes (see Clegg, 1989 for a detailed overview). Power is distributed inequitably amongst various social, economic, political and cultural groups, not least men and women. Numerous commentaries imply that power is simply imposed from above, but one must also account for the fact that in the policy-making process, if anything is to happen at all, some kind of consent and consensus is required from below, however tacit that may be. This is fully in accord with the Gramscian (Gramsci, 1971) position that the dominance of one group needs to be accepted by subordinate groups.

How is this consensus and consent constructed? Bachrach and Baratz's (1970: 16) 'two dimensional view of power' (Lukes, 1974, 1986) elaborates on Dahl's (1958) pluralist 'one dimensional' view of power. The pluralist conception of power held by the latter focuses on the conduct of decision takers, which entail observable conflicts between the different groups (e.g. men and women police officers) who are each aiming to further their interests. The actual route or course of action that they take reflects the interests of each of these groups. In other words, 'where the interests [of groups] are seen as equivalent to revealed preferences' (Lukes, 1986: 9). In their critique of Dahl's (1958) pluralist model, Bachrach and Baratz introduce the second face of power. As they put it:

> … in conceiving of elite domination exclusively in the form of a conscious cabal exercising the power of decision making and vetoing, he overlooks a more subtle form of domination; one in which those who actually domi-nate are not conscious of themselves simply because their position of dominance has never seriously been challenged. (Bachrach and Baratz, 1970: 16)

The 'overlooked' form of domination in decision-making they refer to is:

> … non-decision making, that is the practice of limiting the scope of actual decision making to 'safe' issues by manipulating the dominant community value, myths and political institutions and procedures. To pass over this is to neglect one whole face of power. (Bachrach and Baratz, 1970: 18)

This second face of power describes covert conflicts between actors over actual as well as potential issues. Thus, non-decisions, whereby particular issues like the proliferation of heterosexist occupational cultures are kept off the agenda, are as significant as actual decisions. It reveals the ability of the players involved to determine what is on the agenda so that any of the decisions taken do not threaten the position of the dominant political groups.

Lukes (1974) describes a third face of power, which shows that even if a group is unaware of a conflict of interests, this does not deny the existence of a conflict.

This disputes the hypothesis that power is only exercised where conflict is observable. This does not dispense with overt and covert conflicts, but illustrates how power may operate to shape and adjust aspirations and beliefs in order that they do not reflect people's interests. This third dimension of power, known as 'latent conflict' is used to question the view that if consensus exists, power is not being exercised. In Lukes' own words there are:

> ... many ways in which potential issues are kept out of politics, whether through the operation of social forces and institutional practices or through individual's decisions. This, moreover, can occur in the absence of actual, observable conflict, which may have been successfully averted – though there remains an implicit reference to potential conflict. What one may have here is a latent conflict, which consists of a contradiction between the interests of those exercising power and the real interests of those they exclude. (Lukes, 1974: 24–5)

The key issue here is ideology and it would appear that in light of the continued inequality experienced by female employees working in criminal justice occupations heterosexist and masculinist ideologies downplay this fact. The existence of legislation and initiatives is misrecognized as an equivalent of equality in practice.

Ideology is enmeshed in the policy process, both at a macro level and micro level. The former includes the dominant political and economic values of the day, such as social democracy and neo-liberalism, elements of which both underpin government policy in the early twenty-first century. According to the mission statements and founding goals of recent governments, there is an emphasis on human rights and words such as equality, opportunity, diversity and fairness are in circulation, though in practice these principles do not necessarily materialize.

Hewitt (1992: 44–5) referred to the elasticity of ideologies, which helpfully illustrates how different as well as similar values, or 'contrasting but complimentary principles', are arranged in such a way that a 'coherent logic' is developed to justify a particular course of social action or inertia. At a micro level there are operational ideologies which are sometimes in conflict with those at macro, meso and micro levels. For example, competing ideological perspectives can be mobilized, between and within these levels of analysis. The ideas which acquire, in the words of Gramsci, the 'solidity of popular beliefs' in organizational cultures and practices are explicitly different from the government's rhetoric or political ideology. Furthermore, the occupational cultures of street level bureaucrats (such as police officers, security staff) forms part of an all-encompassing agency culture which includes other levels, ranging from middle to senior managers. The diverse range of ideas underscoring representations of gender, including masculinity and femininity, belong to street level bureaucrats, as well as senior, albeit more *streetwise* bureaucrats who network with influential civil servants and powerful government officials. It is at such points that the ambiguities in sexist and heterosexist banter come into play.

At a macro level policies and initiatives are created step-by-step, reacting to changing societal, economic, political and ideological conditions. Firstly, we look at the impact of structural factors mentioned above, and secondly, the ways in which these impinge on actors at a micro level. If individual Home Secretaries are taken as an example there is little to unify them in terms of the diversity of their individual intellectual standpoints, foibles and idiosyncrasies. Individuals are undoubtedly relevant but there are other important factors such as the influence of political ideology, of which a recent example is the 'Third Way', an idea developed through the influential writings of the social theorist Anthony Giddens (1999, 2007). The Third Way signalled an attempt to move beyond the distinction drawn between the political left and right, and refers to a raft of social democratic reforms and programmes intended to update or modernize government and public sector activities. Martin provides a nice précis of the situation in the UK:

> A fundamental component of New Labour's Third Way is the emphasis on modernising government. This is sold as a package of reforms and programmes, which can be used to update government and public services, and which works as a means to move beyond the assault on public services that occurred under the Conservatives. (2003: 165)

The Third Way is a project that has not been fully realized but it does have ome distinctive features that are closely related to the restructuring of state forms, in particular Jessop's (2000) account of the ongoing and incomplete transition from a Keynesian Welfare National State (or KWNS) to the Schumpeterian Workfare Post-National Regime (or SWPR) (Hay, 1999; Jessop, 2003). This partial transformation has been achieved through a response to the neo-liberal and New Right-led reforms of the state and government. For example, the Third Way is partly a continuation of managerialism or the New Public Management (NPM), including the '3Es' (economy, effectiveness and efficiency), privatization, quasi-markets, organizational restructuring, downsizing and contracting (Newman, 2000; Martin, 2003; Clarke and Newman, 2004). The modernizing imperatives underlying the Third Way are not simply about adopting these earlier reforms but also the introduction of other value frameworks to compensate for the worst excesses of the free market ethos held by neo-liberal conservatives. Politicians belonging to the social democratic left subscribe to social values such as equality of opportunity and social solidarity evidenced in the areas of childcare, schooling and education; social security; and income maintenance. In terms of practice, the Third Way also includes an attempt to rethink the process of management and governance itself, demonstrated by initiatives such as 'Best Value' (BV) in the UK: this placed emphasis on public consultation, democratization and joined-up partnership working.

Above all the Third Way and its modernizing impulse involves the following:

- the devolution of responsibility downward from central to local government, although budgets continue to be set by the former;
- services have to be delivered more economically, effectively and efficiently;
- there is increased targeting of resources.

The resources made available to different agencies in different policy areas vary substantially and the social problems identified as priorities may be counterproductive, largely because economic interests override social interests. Due to the obsession with 'what gets measured, gets done' criminal justice agencies will dedicate time and energy to activities that are prioritized by the government, and the human rights of employees is not necessarily one of them. Even if there is a rhetorical commitment this does not necessarily become a guiding principle of policy and practice. Also, as an upshot of neo-led reforms of the public sector, the welfare state no longer has available the resources and government support needed to deal with the needs of a diversifying and fragmented society. The subordination of social policy to the requirements of economic policy can result in the neglect of some social issues and even in some cases politicians can evade responsibility for particular policies that their government had devised. Moreover, they can blame policy failure on other levels by invoking the ideologically determined distinction between policy and operations as a way of abnegating responsibility. There is also the matter of 'delegated discretion', described by Hill as 'sinister' in the sense that:

> ... hierarchies may leave discretionary decision making to fall into a specifically biased pattern – for example, involving racism. They leave the responsibility for action they accept, but will not publicly condone, in the hands of subordinates. (1993: 11)

We substitute racism with sexism.

Further down the organizational hierarchy the codified statements issued by policy-makers and legislators are not necessarily translated into practice, highlighting the difference between policy as it is written and policy in action.

The ideological perspectives which characterize the relationship existing between the Home Office and powerful criminal justice policy-making bodies such as ACPO, NAPO and APO also impact on relations between other levels of the criminal justice policy-making machinery. Due to its 'elasticity', ideology can accommodate conflict, inconsistencies and contradictions, and yet still be bound by a coherent logic (Hewitt, 1992: 44–5). The divergent forces at work at macro, meso and micro levels may therefore meet. The government's ideology and rhetoric interact with the attitudes and popular beliefs which exist in other social organizations and amongst other social groups. If individual views and the perspectives of cultural collectivities alone are considered to be important, then there is little in the way of continuity. If they are interpreted as the outcome of individuals and groups giving their 'spontaneous consent ... to ... the general direction imposed on social life by the dominant fundamental groups (Gramsci, 1971: 12) that is an entirely different narrative.

In a society in which all things are equal the likelihood of explicitly sexist statements in the mission statement of either the Home Office or any agency is, if not unthinkable, certainly very unlikely. The Human Rights Act and Gender Equality Duty, for example, codify a commitment to equality and opportunity where diversity is celebrated. However, the impact of such seemingly unambiguous statements on the criminal justice system and wider society is less obvious. The criminal justice system is diffuse and macro ideologies interact with operational ideologies, which is the point where an organizational culture comes into prominence. There is no single and unified outlook, say in the police culture, but at this level street level bureaucrats do attempt to simplify a complex environment. Representations of particular hegemonic masculinity are a useful tool to help practitioners minimize occupational and environmental uncertainty. It is under these conditions that gender stereotypes sustain sexist beliefs, thoughts and occasionally deeds. This occurs at various levels where ambiguous 'popular convictions' become institutionalized in such a way that even though policy statements may purportedly cancel out such bias in effect they become an *unwitting* feature of policy and practice. The observations Macpherson (1999) made about institutional racism, we feel, are potentially germane to enrich our understanding of gendered inequalities affecting criminal justice workers. To quote Macpherson, institutional racism:

> ... is the collective failure of an organisation to provide an appropriate and professional service to people because of their colour, culture or ethnic origin. It can be seen or detected in processes, attitudes and behaviour which amount to discrimination through unwitting prejudice, ignorance, thoughtlessness, and racist stereotyping which disadvantage minority ethnic people. (1999: para. 6.34)

There is insufficient space here to review the strengths and weaknesses of Macpherson's findings and recommendations and the key point we extract from him is the often *unwitting* nature of prejudice, which indicates that discrimination may be unintentional because it is so deeply ingrained either in the minds of practitioners or in their mundane activities. In some instances it can almost lead to people denying personal responsibility for their attitudes and actions, which are seen as an effect of belonging to a specific organisation. This kind of reasoning is almost evident when we consider the heterosexist culture of the police, which in the view of one respondent in Foster et al.'s (2005: 44) study is almost 'inevitable' because of the 'macho external culture in the region'.

Restating the importance of power

The above analysis has contemplated some of the reasons why men occupy more powerful positions as workers in criminal justice than their female counterparts. It has been shown that effective power maintains inequality between the sexes through the use of ideology. Although legislation has been introduced to improve the status of women this has largely been ineffective because the government is unwilling to dedicate scarce economic resources towards a gender equality and human rights agenda. Because there is not the political will to drive forward human rights the rhetoric survives but its material impact is tragically limited as women continue to be paid less and experience various forms of sexualized harassment. Although this analysis is rather negative in tone the next chapter offers some room for optimism because although women may not experience career advancement that parallels that of men, changes have occurred and there is room for further transformation.

Concluding thoughts

In this chapter we have quantified the differences existing between men and women in terms of their representation amongst different professional groups employed across the criminal justice sector. The pattern is not clear cut: while men do tend to be numerically predominant, principally in policing, the prison services and the judiciary; they do not outnumber women in all agencies. Despite this, the agencies where there are more men than women are those that exert the most influence on the general tenor of criminal justice policy. The latter point is especially salient with regard to the positions of seniority occupied by men and the fact that it took until 2007 for the first female Home Secretary to be appointed is just the 'tip of the iceberg' when it comes to gendered inequality. There is far more to gender differences than hard numbers and we concentrated on how gender is played out on a daily basis, claiming that hegemonic masculinity subordinates women through attitudinal and systemic practices. The organizational culture of the police service was used to show how sexist and eterosexist ideologies perpetuate structured inequalities that shape the experience of practitioners, both those employed by the state and increasingly the private sector too. It was shown that a cult of masculinity is central to social control where the physical qualities of masculinity are seen to be fundamental prerequisites for a craft that is heavily dependent on the ability to actually deploy, or symbolically demonstrate a capacity for the use of, physical violence. Attempts to reform the functions of employment in criminal justice have not altered this underlying commitment. We then attempted to explain the obdurate features of a sexist orthodoxy with reference to the concept of power. The literature is replete with examples of sexist and heterosexist banter but these attitudes in themselves do not constitute a sufficient explanation of why women are systematically disadvantaged throughout the criminal justice system, hence our allusion to the sociological literature on power. This shows that power operates in hidden ways that are not easy to change, although in line with what we have said about the male offender and male victim there is a pedagogical issue: men must become fully responsibilized and recognize their autonomy as social agents. More than that, governments must not deny their political agency for driving forward agendas for change and with this thought in mind the disbanding of the Equal Opportunities Commission is not a particularly inspired or desirable piece of policy-making. The following chapter follows up this analysis of gendered forms of inequality with an examination of career progression, which is frequently used as an indicator of sexist discrimination. While acknowledging women's potential for transformational change to bring about positive opportunities for career advancement, in the context of the criminal justice professions, their career aspirations are repeatedly blocked and thwarted.

Summary

- Employment patterns in the criminal justice system for the most part mirror those found throughout the labour force. While there may be more male than female police officers and more female than male probation officers, these quantitative measures tell only part of the story. A more significant factor is the status of male and female professionals and in more or less all instances men are relatively more powerful and exert a greater influence.
- In addition to describing male dominance across the criminal justice sector the factors underlying this gendered discrimination were investigated. By referring to the police culture thesis we illustrated the pervasive influence of a cult of masculinity on the experiences of both male and female police officers. Evidence suggests that heterosexist and hegemonic masculinities influence the behaviour of both the police service and private security outfits.
- The concept of power was employed to show how hegemonic masculinity is sustained in criminal justice organizations and how it operates against a human rights-based agenda. Power functions at various levels and enables state actors to say one thing but do another. Consequently, legislation and policy statements belonging to the HRA and the CEHR are effectively ignored or subverted. A key point is that gendered inequality is central to the workings of criminal justice agencies and that well-intentioned reforms are seldom as progressive as they seem.

STUDY QUESTIONS

- Outline the main trends in terms of the distribution of jobs by gender in the criminal justice system.

- Critically explore the main reasons why the proportion of men and women working in the criminal justice system is important for the study of gender and crime.

- Assess the relevance of the police culture for understanding the gendered nature of police work.

- What, if anything, can be done to address gendered forms of discrimination in criminal justice?

- Evaluate the usefulness of the concept of power for explaining the patterns of gendered discrimination in the criminal justice system.

- What can a human rights perspective tell us about the experiences of men and women working in the 'crime control industry'?

FURTHER READING

There are not many books which focus exclusively on masculinities in relation to the criminal justice professions. A helpful starting point, written from a feminist perspective, is the work of the Fawcett Commission, which highlights the main issues relating to female – and indirectly male – employees (see in particular: Fawcett Society *Women and Justice: Third Annual Review of the Commission on Women and the Criminal Justice System* (2007)). However, see the relevant chapter in Walklate's *Gender, Crime and Criminal Justice* (2nd edn) (2004). Waddington's *Policing Citizens* (1999) refers to the 'cult of masculinity' in relation to police culture and Winlow's *Badfellas* (2001) is an excellent ethnographic study of bouncers and masculinities in the night-time economy. Also see Messerschmidt's *Masculinities and Crime: Critique and Reconceptualization of Theory* (1993) for some comments on gender and the criminal justice professions.

Notes

1 As mentioned, the EOC was replaced in 2007 by the Commission for Equality and Human Rights, an all-purpose organization set up to deal with all aspects of inequality and discrimination on the grounds of sex, race, disability, sexual orientation, etc.

2 On 1 April 2006 NCIS and NCS were replaced by the Serious Organised Crime Agency (SOCA).

3 On 1 April 2007 there were five Heads of Division, none of which were women (see: www.judiciary.gov.uk/keyfacts/statistics/women.htm)

7

The Criminal Justice System: A Gendered Site

para ①

Chapter Contents

OVERVIEW

Chapter 7 provides:

- An overview of the broad movement towards developing diversity in society.
- An introduction of the laws that govern and tackle discrimination.
- An overview of the benefits of achieving diversity within organizations: the case of social justice; the business case; the asking of new questions and concerns; and alternative ways of working – and a discussion of how these might be played out in the police service and the legal profession.
- An insight into the gendered nature of organizations through an analysis of Acker's (1990) gendered organization theory.
- An analysis of the gendered nature of the police service through a focus on the temporal dimension and the development of flexible and part-time working.

KEY TERMS

commission for equality and human rights	flexible working	judge
criminal justice system	gender equality duty	judicial diversity
discrimination	gendered organisation theory	policewomen
diversity	gendered substructure	secret soundings

Much of the work within the field of gender and crime and indeed within this book has been concerned with exploring women's and men's experiences as offenders and victims. Our analysis would be incomplete without giving attention to those professionals working within the criminal justice system. The poor retention rates for women working in criminal justice remain a key cause for concern. The previous chapter has already outlined the location of women and men in the criminal justice system as professionals, demonstrating the stark imbalance of men to women in positions of power. It also demonstrated some of the ruinous effects of organizational culture on women and some men. This chapter outlines the concept of gendered organizations and focuses more specifically on the issue of career progression as a key measure of gender discrimination in the criminal justice system. It builds on the previous chapter by offering some explanation of women's continued lack of progress within criminal justice organizations.

The chapter is divided into two main parts. The first part contextualizes the debate by providing an account of the broader call for developing diversity within organizations generally and criminal justice organizations more specifically. In Britain, the increasing requirement to demonstrate equality, fairness and diversity has now been firmly cemented into public policy with the arrival of the Equalities Act 2006 and the 'gender equality duty' in 2007. It is in this context that we situate the debate within a rights-based framework. Unlawful discrimination and the harassment of workers is an important human rights issue and the canon of human rights law now provides a comprehensive framework for challenging the various forces that have created and sustained discrimination based upon sex. The extent to which criminal justice organizations have drawn upon this framework to improve the position of women will become clear as we explore some of the initiatives currently taking place within criminal justice organizations to encourage a more representative workforce. We also consider the potential benefits of a more gender-balanced and gender-aware criminal justice system for those professionals working in criminal justice and for those who come into contact with criminal justice agents, be they offenders and/or victims.

The discrimination that women working in criminal justice organizations now face is far more insidious than that faced by their historical counterparts. With discriminatory behaviour less blatant and visible, its identification requires us to adopt a much more complex approach. The second part of this chapter draws on the theory of gendered organizations (Acker, 1990) and uses the police service and the legal profession as case studies. We outline the way in which criminal justice agencies and the career trajectories within them are deeply gendered at structural, cultural, and individual levels. In our analysis of the police career we focus on the way in which the police service conceives of and organizes 'time'. In doing so we develop a more structural account and consider the way in which the police career structure itself acts as an inhibitor to women's progression. In our examination of women working in the legal profession, we focus on the judicial appointments process. Here we outline the selection process and consider the way in which arrangements have resulted in a lack of judicial diversity, with the virtual exclusion of women from the judiciary and the self-perpetuation of men (Griffith, 1997).

The call for diversity

The need to develop a fairer and more equitable workplace has been the concern of reformers for some time now. Indeed employment equality legislation has expanded considerably since the 1970s to include more groups and to cover more aspects of employment. More than 30 years since the Sex Discrimination Act 1975 came into force in Britain, women have made significant inroads in the workplace. Women are now visible in public life and in areas that were previously closed to them. Despite women's achievements in criminal justice work the previous chapter noted that their representation in leadership positions remains disappointing. In its annual survey *Sex and Power: Who Runs Britain? 2007*, The Equal Opportunities Commission points out that the pace of change at the top in many areas remains painfully slow, and in some cases has even gone into reverse. The appointment of Britain's first female Home Secretary, Jacqui Smith, in June 2007 demonstrates this point well. While Smith's arrival marks a much-needed and welcome milestone for women in criminal justice work, her appointment also saw the overall number of women in the cabinet almost halved from eight to five.

The general commitment to tackling discrimination can be found in human rights law in Article 14 on the Prohibition of discrimination. It asserts that:

> The enjoyment of the rights and freedoms set forth in this convention shall be secured without discrimination on any ground such as sex, race, colour, language, religion, political or other opinion, national or social origin, association with a national minority, property, birth or other status.

Some other grounds for discrimination are now clearly accepted as coming within the scope of Article 14, for example discrimination on the basis of someone's sexual orientation. It is important to state here that Article 14 is not free-standing. For there to be a breach of Article 14 the area in which a person is discriminated against has to come within the scope of one of the other Convention articles. This means that the way in which you are discriminated against has to be connected with one of the other articles. A more direct approach to tackling the discrimination against women can be found in the Convention on the Elimination of All Forms of Discrimination Against Women [CEDAW] where it is explicitly acknowledged that 'extensive discrimination against women continues to exist', and emphasizes that such discrimination 'violates the principles of equality of rights and respect for human dignity'. The Convention gives positive affirmation to the principle of equality in Article 2, which requires that the state take:

> [a]ll appropriate measures, including legislation, to ensure the full development and advancement of women, for the purpose of guaranteeing them the exercise and enjoyment of human rights and fundamental freedoms on basis of equality with men.

For the purpose of this chapter, Article 11 of CEDAW more specifically targets the elimination of discrimination of women in employment. Article 11 (1 b–d) asserts that:

> States Parties shall take all appropriate measures to eliminate discrimina-
> tion against women in the field of employment in order to ensure, on
> a basis of equality of men and women, the same rights, in particular: ... (b)
> The right to the same employment opportunities, including the application
> of the same criteria for selection in matters of employment; (c) The right to
> free choice of profession and employment, the right to promotion, job
> security and all benefits and conditions of service; (d) The right to equal
> remuneration, including benefits, and to equal treatment in respect of work
> of equal value, as well as equality of treatment in the evaluation of the
> quality of work.

We consider this commitment more closely in our discussions about women's
experience of progression and promotion in policing and in the legal profession.

The benefits of gender balance

Before exploring the mechanisms underpinning women's lack of representation
within the higher echelons of the criminal justice system, we map out the rationale for greater gender balance in working life and outline the benefits of a
gender-aware criminal justice system. The literature points to a whole host of
reasons for campaigning for a better gender balance in organizations. We group
these broadly under four main themes: social justice; the business case; asking
new questions and concerns; and alternative ways of working and apply them
to the case of criminal justice work.

Social justice

In line with the ethos of this book, gender equality is related to fundamental
notions about the quality of social justice, human rights and the nature of
democracy. Internationally, gender balance is considered as a fundamental basis
for democracy and is often constitutionally protected. Perhaps the strongest
international statement of the fundamental need for gender balance in decision-
making thus far has been the 1995 Beijing Platform for Action. Its commitment
to the empowerment of women is based on the conviction that:

> Women's empowerment and their full participation on the basis of equality in
> all spheres of society, including participation in the decision-making process
> and access to power, are fundamental for the achievement of equality, devel-
> opment and peace. (United Nations: The Beijing Declaration 1995)

The Platform for Action explicitly aims for a 50:50 gender balance in all areas of
society placing full participation in decision-making at the forefront. At the level
of the nation state, the government in the United Kingdom, for example, directly

advocates complete parity at the top levels of public decision-making with its 'Target 50:50' programme. Introduced in April 2007, the Gender Equality Duty now places a proactive duty of legal responsibility on the public sector to promote equality and eliminate discrimination between women and men both as an employer and as a public service provider. In the criminal justice context, the gender equality duty will require public bodies to have due regard to the need to eliminate unlawful sex discrimination and to promote equality of opportunity between women and men. Achieving a gender balance in a democracy is seen as an important way to improve the quality of society with the viewpoints of different groups taken into account. We have already demonstrated that the majority of those working in criminal justice agencies are male and white. Given that the business of criminal justice professionals is the administration and delivery of justice and fairness, it follows that if those working in the criminal justice system were more representative of society as a whole, the criminal justice system would have a greater chance of securing greater fairness for all – offenders, victims and practitioners alike. The Lord Chancellor, Lord Falconer, encapsulates the idea that diversity increases a sense of justice, when he states that:

> Diversity also increases justice. Justice cannot be done unless it carries broad support: the aggregated assent of the people in wanting justice to be done. That assent rests on a number of issues – probably most centrally, that the justice being done is the justice people want done. But that confidence in justice rests too on confidence in those dispensing justice. (Falconer, 2005)

Research has shown, for example, that the lack of diversity in the judiciary has had an impact on confidence in the system among the wider community and that this is especially true in the case of women users of the court system (Hoyle and Zedner, 2007). In New Zealand, women who had been to court have been recorded as registering a much lower sense of confidence that they had been treated fairly than men (Morris, 1997, cited in Davis and Willams, 2003). In the UK, women who had never been to court evinced less confidence than men that if they went to court with a problem they would receive a fair hearing (Genn, 1999) and in the Australian context, the three volumes of findings of the Australian Law Reform Commission's 1994 inquiry into gender equality in the law, outlined numerous areas in which women felt that they were treated unfairly by the legal system (cited in Davis and Williams, 2003).

The business case

If the arguments of moral and social justice are not substantive or persuasive enough then the business case for greater gender balance is often more convincing.

Inherent in this is the idea that having a more diverse workforce produces better results. Having a workforce that is unbalanced, consisting primarily of men, is one that is not realizing its full potential. Chair of the Equal Opportunities Commission, Jenny Watson, states that:

> We all pay the price when Britain's boardrooms and elected chambers are unrepresentative. Our democracy and local communities will be stronger if women from different backgrounds are able to enjoy an equal voice. In business, no one can afford to fish in half the talent pool in today's intensely competitive world. (2007)

From this perspective there is some specific interest in proving the economic value of gender diversity. It should come as no surprise then that the 'business case' has taken ascendancy over the moral case. In recent decades, women have become better qualified and motivated to take up public roles. With young women entering the labour market better educated than their male counterparts (Eurostat, 2005) a workforce consisting primarily of men is clearly one which is not realizing its full potential. Using this argument, unequal opportunities are not only a matter of injustice but also primarily a matter of wasted talent. The retention rates for women working in criminal justice remain a key cause for concern. The Commission for Women and Criminal Justice (2004) for example, reports an exodus of women in their 30s from the legal profession. The impact of women's departure from the profession is profound. Not only does it result in a loss of talent to the profession, it also results in fewer women at a senior level from which to draw the judiciary.

Asking new questions and concerns

It has also been argued that better gender awareness and balance in decision-making improves policy and democracy because it leads to the introduction of new questions and concerns. More specifically, greater gender balance in organizations offers the opportunity to ask the 'woman question' (Bartlett, 1990). Through asking the 'woman question' the gender implications of a social practice or rule can be exposed. As a result we may be better positioned to see how existing legal standards and concepts might disadvantage women. Indeed those involved in asking the 'woman question' have denounced the idea of law as a universal and neutral system of adjudication (Smart, 1989). Rather, it has been argued that legal concepts of 'impartiality' and 'objectivity' are just viewpoints of dominant groups, and therefore hide a male bias (Graycar and Morgan, 2002). Chapter 4 on women as victims has already highlighted the impact of feminist activism on the reform of various laws, including sexual offences, rape and domestic violence. In doing so, feminist writers have worked hard to expose the gendered nature of law, legal rules and legal practice. Asking the 'woman question' in rape cases, for example, has resulted in a much more open discussion about why the defence of consent focuses on the perspective of the defendant and what he 'reasonably' thought the woman wanted, rather than the perspective of the woman and the intentions she 'reasonably' thought she conveyed to the defendant. Without asking, differences associated with women are taken for granted and may serve as a justification for laws that disadvantage women.

With regard to policing, Heidensohn (1992: 247) speculates that an equality agenda has the potential to encourage innovation and change into policy with an increased focus on crimes such as rape, domestic violence, and child sex abuse. Hanmer and Saunders (1991) argue that the employment of women is an issue, both in relation to requests by women and agencies in the community for women officers and the transformation of a masculine police culture in order to provide a more satisfactory service for women. The idea of reorienting service delivery to 'policing by women, with women and for women' (Walklate, 1993b) is not new and can be traced to the work of early women in policing. Heidensohn (2000: 60) argues that it is possible to draw out the parallels between early pioneer women involved in social control in the last century and their modern day counterparts in this century. A key feature of the pioneers' case was 'their universalizing of the problems for which they saw policewomen as the solution: essentially these were "vice", trafficking in women and abuse of children'. She goes on to stress that contemporary organizations still stress a common, universal agenda, this time however, it is 'domestic violence, trafficking and child abuse' (Heidensohn, 2000). Homant and Kennedy (1985) conclude that women officers are significantly more involved and concerned in domestic disputes than male officers.

Alternative ways of working

It is the idea that women have alternative ways of working to men, however, that has perhaps received the most attention in recent years and has caused the greatest controversy. Before we outline these arguments, a brief note on our position here. We are mindful of the problematic implications of such an idea. In essence, established works rest on the notion that there are basic differences between the sexes. As a result, they essentially define a dichotomous model of behaviour in which 'feminine' behaviour is posited against 'masculine'. The problem here is that it is all too easy to fall into the trap of essentializing the 'feminine' and 'masculine' into single categories thus failing to acknowledge the diversity that exists between and amongst women and men. Such studies run the risk of perpetuating many of the myths that have dominated discourses about women and work, further entrenching and sustaining the often simplistic and sexist justifications for excluding women's participation in organizations, particularly in leadership roles. Nichols (1993: 12) warns against recreating a 'new maternal metaphor of management' in which elaborate extensions of prevailing sexual stereotypes and our traditional beliefs about the way women and men should behave are translated into an organizational context. Mindful of this, we review the growing caucus of work on women in policing and law that supports the idea of difference between women and men.

Over the past three decades a number of studies have emerged that suggest that increasing the number of policewomen has the potential to alter the ways in which the police carry out their role. Studies by Bloch and Anderson (1973); Sherman (1975); Linden (1983); Grennan (1987); Lunnenborg (1989); Belknap and Shelley (1990); and Spillar (1999) all conclude that women officers are less aggressive, and more likely to reduce the potential for a violent situation to develop by relying on verbal skills and a communicative rather than an authoritative policing style. The idea that women police are more likely to be perceived as 'friendly and service oriented' by members of their communities can be seen in Miller's (1999) work on gender and community policing in which she argues that women's perceived skills are finally finding a legitimate place in police work and law enforcement.

The link between the presence of women and an alternative style of law enforcement can be seen across the globe. Following the beating of Rodney King, the Christopher Commission (1991) deplored the 'hard-nose' posturing of Los Angeles policemen, declaring that male officers' aggressive style 'produces results at the risk of creating a siege mentality that alienates the officer from the community' (cited in Appier, 1998: 168). The Commission urged the Los Angeles Police Department (LAPD) to develop a new style of policing based on communication rather than confrontation, noting that policewomen are less likely than policemen to 'abuse the public'. More specifically, it pointed out that despite the fact that women composed 13 per cent of LAPD's sworn personnel during the period 1986–1990, none of the LAPD's worst offenders in cases of using excessive force was a woman. In sum, the Commission concluded that hiring women police officers holds the key to substantially decreasing the incidence of police violence (Report by the Women's Advisory Council to the Los Angeles Policy Commission, 1993).

This picture is also replicated in Australia. The potential to bring about change through an increased presence of women in policing lies at the heart of the Fitzgerald Report (1989). The report identified several factors that contributed to the corruption, misconduct and mismanagement exposed in the Queensland police force. They included: a rigid, over-centralized hierarchical structure; inequitable recruitment, training and performance appraisal and promotion practices; and an insular organizational culture, in which criticism of other police was seen as 'impermissible' (Fitzgerald Report, 1989: 202). In response to such criticisms, women police were awarded the status of 'change agents', particularly charged with the task of reducing the level of corruption within policing. Women were identified as important players in the movement to erode a 'police code' that protects officers guilty of misconduct or corruption. The Wood Commission Report into the New South Wales Police made similar recommendations regarding the potential of women to achieve a greater diversity through the dismantling of 'inappropriate associations' (Wood, 1997).

An interesting reading of women's contribution to policing can be found in the work of the National Centre of Women Police (NCWP) in the USA in which an economic rationale for employing policewomen over men has been emphasized. Their work suggests that 'the average male officer on a big city police agency cost taxpayers somewhere between two and a half and five and half times more than the average woman officer in excessive force liability lawsuit payouts' (NCWP, 2002 cited in Heidensohn, 2003: 29). As a result, they suggest that women may be better suited to policing than their male counterparts. For 'women not only can do the job of policing equally as well as men, but in fact hold the key for substantially decreasing police violence and its costs to the taxpayer, while improving the ability of the police to respond to violence against women' (Spillar, 1999: 5). In this instance, the full integration of women into policing has been transformed into an opportunity for a constructive solution to the costly problems of police violence. Such a cost benefit analysis of employing more women in policing is particularly welcome. It may provide the necessary evidence and rationale for encouraging more women into policing and for shifting the conceptualization of police work as men's work. It will also no doubt appeal to those involved in promoting quality of service and value for money in policing.

Brown's (1997) vision of gender balance in police leadership further predicts the development of new methods of management and leadership. The female police leader has been singled out for her potential to bring about positive organizational change. In her study of senior policewomen, Silvestri (2003) argues that senior policewomen are engaged in a qualitatively different way of working from that traditionally associated with police leadership. Senior policewomen demonstrated the use of interactive styles by encouraging colleagues to share power and information to reinforce open communication and create loyalty. Such styles share much in common with Rosener's (1990) description of transformational approaches in which values of mutuality, interdependence, inclusion, co-operation, nurturing, support, participation, self-determination, empowerment and personal and collective transformation are prized (Ferguson, 1984; Martin, 1993). Such values are perceived to be in direct opposition to the practices that prevail in most corporations. Male forms of management, consistent with hegemonic forms of masculinity, attach emphasis to the core values of transactional leadership characterized by values of separativeness, competition, and individual success (Jackall, 1988; England, 1989; Leidner, 1991; Martin, 1993). Underpinned by the principles of participation, consultation and inclusion, the benefits of transformational style in policing are clear.

This idea of difference can also be seen clearly in studies that focus on women working in the legal profession. Commentators have argued that women offer alternative and positive improvements to the quality of justice dispensed (Goldman, 1979; Menkel-Meadow, 1986; Grant and Smith, 1991; McGlynn, 1998). The basis of such a claim is that women bring a 'new dimension of justice' (Goldman, 1979: 494) to the bench, namely that women 'enhance the likelihood that a certain perspective (the symbolically female one) is brought to bear' (Grant and Smith, 1991: 73). The origins of the difference-based justice arguments can be found in the work of Carol Gilligan (1982) whose work centres on the idea that women are more likely than men to bring with them an 'ethic of care' in their interactions with others. When applied to women working in law, this line of argument suggests that women might practise law differently than their male counterparts. Ultimately, confrontational adversarial processes might give way to more mediational forms of dispute resolution (Rifkin, 1984; Menkel-Meadow, 1985, 1987, 1988). Bartlett (1990: 863) supports this idea by noting that women approach the reasoning process differently to men, resisting universal principles and generalizations, approaching 'problems not as dichotomised conflicts, but as dilemmas with multiple perspectives, contradictions and inconsistencies'.

In an excellent and critical review of material that has attempted to justify gender equality on the bench Malleson (2003: 1) warns of the perils of such difference-based approaches noting that they are 'theoretically weak, empirically questionable and strategically dangerous'. She challenges the idea that women bring with them a 'feminine voice' and suggests that this has more to do with the nature of work that women judges tend to be given and their career profiles in general than with an expression of their biology. Women judges are, for example, more likely than men to have worked in areas such as family law and employment law where issues of discrimination are more familiar and which tend for the most part to use less aggressive and adversarial techniques. As a result she argues that:

> It has become commonplace for commentators on women in the legal profession to argue that the greater presence of women will bring out a reorientation of the legal system away from formalism, objectivity, universalism and adversarial methods of conflict solving towards the subjective needs to individuals and a greater use of alternative dispute resolution as such as mediation. (Malleson 2003: 3)

Sceptical and critical of the assumption that more women will lead to an improved delivery of justice Malleson (2003: 8) reviews a number of international studies on the relationship between sentencing decisions and gender. Overall she concludes that there is no clear or consistent difference between men and women on the bench but rather that the research is 'contradictory and inconclusive'. Indeed she notes some instances where women were more likely to impose a custodial sentence on women than their male counterparts (Steffensmeier and Herbert, 1999 and Gruhl et al., 1981 cited in Malleson, 2003: 6). The dangers of presenting women's approaches as 'different' to men on the bench are further emphasized by Baroness Brenda Hale, a keen advocate of gender equality in law. She notes that:

> Women do not want to claim that they look at things differently from men, partly because this would be manifestly inaccurate in many cases and partly because it would make them less qualified to be judges. (Hale, 2001: 13)

Here, Hale is referring to the fundamental concept of judicial impartiality. The judicial oath requires that judges do justice to all manner of people without 'fear or favour, affection or ill-will'. If a judge were seen to be taking a more favourable or empathetic view of women's perspectives, values and interests, this would raise serious questions about their capacity for upholding the principle of impartiality. While this argument should not hold much weight, given that judicial partiality is commonplace today among male judges (Malleson, 2003), it is a powerful argument and one that will easily jeopardize women's attempts to join the judicial élite.

To sum up briefly, the cumulative and resounding message of many of the studies cited above is that women may be engaged in the project of delivering criminal justice in a distinctly different way to their male counterparts. They also lend further support to the idea that increasing the number of women in policing and the legal profession may do much to transform and improve the workings of the criminal justice system. In making our plea for better gender balance, we are not suggesting that an increase in the number of women in criminal justice work (indeed in any organization) will result in organizational change, but rather, by 'being there' women may bring new and different perspectives on employment issues and so may become catalysts for change within their organization (Colgan and Ledwith, 1996). More women working as criminal justice professionals will not automatically lead to instances of asking the 'woman question' but a better gender balance may present more opportunities to ask.

In short, we push for a better gender balance within criminal justice organizations. We believe that such a balance will have a powerful effect on both the lives of workers and on those who come into contact with criminal justice agents. More specifically we support the idea of more women in criminal justice work as a matter of social justice. The rationale for the equal participation of women and men in the criminal justice system should not be based on women's potential contributions as women, but rather that their presence be viewed as an intrinsic and essential feature of a democracy. It is inherently unfair that men enjoy a near monopoly of power in criminal justice work. As Hale writes:

> In a democratic society, in which we are all equal citizens, it is wrong in principle for that authority to be wielded by such a very unrepresentative section of the population. (2001: 18)

With the rationale for greater gender balance now firmly established, we turn our attention to exploring why, despite numerous attempts to introduce equality, gender balance continues to be an unattainable goal for criminal justice organizations. To recap briefly, we have already argued that whilst integration has occurred theoretically within criminal justice organizations, women (and indeed some men) are not fully accepted by their male colleagues and continue to be subject to sexual harassment, discrimination and differential deployment (Holdaway, 1983; Heidensohn, 1992; Burke, 1993; Fielding, 1994; Martin and Jurik, 1996; Brown and Heidensohn, 2000; Adams, 2001). Many of these studies offer excellent accounts and interpretations of the ruinous effects of organizational culture on achieving gender balance. Though we do not want to dilute the contributions of such works we hope to offer an alternative, albeit complimentary, insight into why, despite some impressive attempts, gender balance continues to be such a stumbling block for organizations. In this final part of the chapter we draw on the work of Acker (1990) to demonstrate the way in which criminal justice work is gendered at individual, cultural and structural levels.

The gendered organization

While the criminal justice system has a number of distinguishing characteristics, its gendered nature continues to be a powerful and defining feature. The previous chapter demonstrated the fact that the criminal justice system remains quintessentially male in composition. While providing us with a good starting point and insight into the gender make-up of criminal justice organizations, such information tells us little about the way in which an organization defines its work and its workers. In order to understand the gendered nature of criminal justice work and workers, we branch out into the field of organization studies. Out of a growing dialogue between feminist theory and organization theory a concern with the way in which organizations are themselves gendered has emerged (Ferguson, 1984; Cohn, 1985; Baron and Davis-Blake, 1986; Beilby and Baron, 1986; Reskin and Hartman, 1986; Hearn and Parkin, 1987; Cockburn,

1988; Hearn et al., 1989; Acker, 1990, 1992; Reskin and Roos, 1990; Boyd et al., 1991; Mills and Tancred-Sheriff, 1992). Through this work, we can see systematic attempts to theorize the processes through which organizations and occupations are gendered at both institutional and individual levels. In her influential paper 'Hierarchies, Jobs, Bodies: A Theory of Gendered Organisations', Acker (1990) argues that organizations are arenas in which both gender and sexuality have been obscured through gender-neutral, asexual discourses, concealing the embodied elements of work. As a result, job positions and management hierarchies assume a universal, disembodied worker. One of the key features of this approach is that it provides an understanding of the ways in which gender divisions are actively created and sustained in the processes of organizational life. Her approach emphasizes that men and women encounter gender meanings, relationships and identities which are embedded in the social setting itself, as part and parcel of the roles and scripts deemed appropriate for that setting. Hence gender is defined here as a contextually situated process and is conceived of as an emergent property of social situations rather than as an individual characteristic. Instead of a characteristic that people have, gender is something that individuals *do* with their behaviour and organizations *do* through the gendering processes and structures. Such gendering processes mean that

> [a]dvantage and disadvantage, exploitation and control, action and emotion, meaning and identity, are patterned through and in terms of a distinction between male and female, feminine and masculine. (Acker, 1990: 146)

Through the creation of symbols and images that explain and justify gender divisions, organizations further perpetuate and sustain the gendered order. Here interactions between individuals are crucial as they enact dominance and subordination and create alliances and exclusions; images here are constructed and confirmed. In so doing, individuals consciously construct their own understandings of the organization's gendered structures of work and hence provide the appropriate gender response, in terms of behaviours and attitudes (Acker, 1992: 252–3). This may, for example, include the creation of the correct gendered persona with roles and scripts deemed appropriate for that setting (Hall, 1993). Consisting of both a cognitive element (inferences that permit understanding and comprehension) and a behavioural element (activated performances) in a particular social setting, the concept of scripts describes a 'predetermined, stereotyped sequence of actions that defines a well known situation' (Schank and Abelson, 1977, cited in Hall, 1993: 457). It is through being organizational members that workers inhabit a world of shared meanings, of shared rituals, symbols, languages, practices, rationales and values. In turn, these shared meanings easily translate into scripts that workers draw on in their day-to-day work and interactions characteristic.

For Acker, the bureaucratic organization has a 'gendered substructure', that is, the social practices that are generally understood to constitute an 'organization' rest on certain gendered processes and assumptions. In defining this substructure, she notes:

> The gendered substructure lies in the spatial and temporal arrangements of work, in the rules prescribing workplace behaviour and in the relations linking work places to living places. These practices and relations, encoded in arrangements and rules, are supported by assumptions that work is separate from the rest of life and that it has the first claim on the worker. (Acker, 1992: 255)

It is within this gendered substructure that the 'ideal worker' is routinely constructed and reproduced. Here, Acker is arguing that organizational designs and established norms are far closer to men's lives and assumptions about men than to women's lives and the assumptions made about women. It is men's bodies, men's sexuality and men's relationships to procreation and production that are subsumed in the image of the disembodied worker. We draw on Acker's ideas below to explore some of the organizational arrangements that govern a career in policing and law. In doing so the embedded ideas about femininity and masculinity and the 'gendered substructure' can be exposed.

Women in policing

The police organization is a powerful site where symbols, images, and forms of consciousness that explicate and justify gender divisions are created and sustained. To suggest that the nature and substance of police work and identity are characterized by a 'cult of masculinity' (Reiner, 1992; Fielding, 1994) remains uncontested within the police literature. The police organization in Britain is a good example of a strict linear organizational career, operating a single entry system of recruitment with all officers without exception beginning their careers as constables. From here, career advancement is achieved through climbing a highly structured career ladder through a series of ranks. At first glance the police service appears to offer its members a gender-neutral career ladder within which to advance, with all officers, male and female, beginning their careers at the bottom of the organization. On closer inspection, however, it becomes clear that the ideology of internal recruitment together with a rank-governed progression system has particularly damning consequences for women wanting to progress. With the majority of police officers congregating at the bottom of the police structure, it should come as no surprise that the chances of promotion in such an organization become severely limited (Bayley, 1994). While female and male officers both experience the effects of such a system, by its very nature, there is a high degree of predictability about male promotion prospects built into a linear organizational career structure (Halford et al., 1997).

If we examine 'time' in its most literal form, we can see that the route travelled by police officers in their quest for higher rank is a long one with the upper limit of a police officers' length of service normally being 30 years (Bland et al., 1999). At the outset, the potential length of a career in policing suggests ample time for new recruits to plan and develop a strategy for reaching the top. Greater scrutiny, however, reveals that this long career path may not work in favour of all officers, holding particular significance for women who have interrupted career profiles to meet family commitments (Silvestri, 2003). In his study of chief constables, Reiner (1991) notes that after the initial hurdle of promotion (from constable to sergeant), those who realistically want to have a chance of becoming chief constable must move fairly rapidly through the middle management ranks. He notes that this follows 'from the simple arithmetic fact that most prospective chiefs reach sergeant rank in their late twenties so they have just over 20 years to achieve seven further promotions before they reach their early 50s, after which age few chief constables are appointed' (Reiner, 1991: 78). The police career is premised on an 'ideal' type of worker in which the possession of a 'full-time, long and uninterrupted career profile' reigns (Silvestri, 2003, 2006).

Our focus on the temporal dimension has particular relevance for wider contemporary debates about women, work and rights. The issue of how best to achieve an improved work–life balance is a key part of the human rights agenda for improving the position of women in employment. Article 11 (2c) of CEDAW states that:

> In order to prevent discrimination against women on the grounds of marriage or maternity and to ensure their effective right to work, States Parties shall take appropriate measures to: ... (c) encourage the provision of the necessary supporting social services to enable parents to combine family obligations with work responsibilities and participation in public life, in particular through promoting the establishment and development of a network of childcare facilities.

Developing a better work–life balance has also been at the forefront of broader governmental thinking and policy development. It has been the subject of a Department of Trade and Industry's (DTI) initiative, 'The Work–Life Balance Campaign'; a Green Paper on 'Work and Parents Competitiveness and Choice' in 2000; a Work and Parents Taskforce in 2002; and the 2003 Treasury strategy document *Balancing Work and Family Life*; as well as various government research initiatives (Hogarth et al., 2001). Launching its campaign 'It's About Time' in September 2003, the Trades Union Congress (TUC) argued that 'Long hours, greater pressure of work, flexibility that only suits the employer and stress are the biggest problems in today's workplace'. The Equal Opportunities Commission (EOC) reinforces this by emphasizing that:

> Britain's long-hours culture is bad for men, women and families... [it] prevents many men who wish to play a fuller part in their children's lives from doing so. It also blocks the progress of many women towards senior positions at work, because these sorts of hours are incompatible with responsibility for a family. (Equal Opportunities Commission, 2004: 4)

The inclusion and movement towards more flexible working practices incorporating an improved work–life balance is being hailed as indicative of organizations that are serious about developing and managing diversity successfully within their organizations. The positive effects of alternative working practices are wide and far-reaching and raise important questions for the career progression of women in criminal justice occupations.

The police service has taken an active role in trying to improve the recruitment and retention of women police officers. In line with other organizations, it has been working towards developing flexible working practices for its employees. The current push towards developing alternative working patterns in the police organization emerged over nearly two decades ago. In 1990, the Police Advisory Board agreed to the establishment of an experimental scheme to introduce part-time working and job-sharing for police officers across six forces. The issue was revisited in 1999 when ACPO created a working group to develop guidelines for the service on flexible working practices. Studies have speculated about the potential benefits that such changes could bring, and these have included improvements in: sickness records; retention; productivity; morale; commitment; together with an improved ability to attract potential new recruits. With respect to policewomen, evidence from Tuffin and Baladi (2001) demonstrates that such developments have in many cases retained the contribution of women officers who would have left the service if they had not been able to reduce their hours in order to meet childcare commitments. They note that each officer retained with more than five years' service saves the force a minimum of £23,000 (to replace the costs of recruitment, probationer and ongoing training for an operational officer). The sum becomes conceptually far greater when we begin to take into account the loss of experience that has been invested in officers. The response to initiatives so far has been disappointing. An HMIC Report on *Developing Diversity in the Police Service* in 1995 found a poor take up of these schemes and pointed to the resistance of middle management in terms of understanding the benefits of flexible working practices. Six years later, Tuffin and Baladi's (2001) work confirms HMIC findings by indicating an increase of one per cent for those officially classified as involved in flexible working practices (rising from one per cent in 1995 to just over two per cent in 2000). Following the launch of the Gender Agenda[1] in 2001, however, we can see a renewed interest in the development of greater flexibility in the working practices of police officers. Armed with the task of making gender central to the police agenda, Brown (2003) notes that this women's network offers perhaps the most likely initiative capable of shifting the paradigm of policing. Through asking the 'woman's question', she argues that:

> [T]he Gender Agenda raises consciousness about the long hours culture, including breakfast and twilight meetings. It challenges stereotypical thinking and offers alternative practices. Its vision is that of a 'moral' and 'ethical' approach which ensures that all staff, regardless of their membership of any identifiable category, are neither advantaged nor disadvantaged in pursuing their duty or their career. (Brown, 2003: 185)

Though somewhat premature to assess the impact of the Gender Agenda, indications from the British Association of Women Police's (BAWP, 2003) *Gender Agenda Force Survey* suggest that a more coherent and forceful approach to developing the role of women in policing is taking place. Important discussions have been ongoing regarding officers' eligibility to undertake alternative working practices. And, while part-time working is now open to police officers at all ranks, this was not always the case. There were some important exclusions to the operation of working practices, in particular the restrictions in police regulation for the provision of part-time work for those in higher ranks. The opportunity to take up part-time working was only available for probationers to inspector ranks. It was at more senior levels that the opportunity for flexible working practices all but disappeared. For more senior ranks, the requirements for 'on call' decision-making, under the Police and Criminal Evidence Act 1984 serve as a continuing barrier and justification against the development of flexibility. Research conducted by the Superintendent's Association has, however, questioned the need for 'on call' decisions to be taken by superintendents and suggested that many chief inspectors felt that such requirements were archaic and did not fit with the strategic role of superintendents in modern policing (Davies, 1998). The current position is that no member of staff has an absolute right to work part-time but they do have a right to have their applications considered (Police Regulations, 2003).

The ability to work long hours, to 'give time', has become one of the most desired management attributes in an increasingly competitive environment. Rutherford (2001) reminds us that time is an important resource to be drawn on in order to progress in an organization. The intensification of a management culture characterized by the ability 'to get things done' has become a key feature of organizational life in recent years. Visibly working long hours has come to be an indicator of commitment and stamina. 'Time-serving' is a core constituent of the police career and is a fundamental resource for building the necessary identity of the police leader (Silvestri, 2003). While part-time work and other flexible practices offer women in principle the chance to engage in the work of policing more meaningfully, to suggest that this would have a dramatic impact on the number of women in policing and police leadership is short-sighted. Julie Spence, President of the British Association of Policewomen sums up these fears well when she states that 'part-time work continues to be charac-terised by a mentality that constructs those who assume flexible forms of work-ing as part-able and part-committed' (cited in Jenkins, 2000: 23). Utilizing alternative working patterns does not count towards the profile of earning or demonstrating either credibility or commitment. On the contrary, the police career is one that tends to define the career as at odds with domestic responsi-bilities. If women in policing choose to limit their working hours or opt to under-take them in an alternative configuration, they do so in the knowledge that they may also be limiting their career opportunities (Stone et al., 1994; Adams, 2001; Silvestri, 2003). The reality for many women is that unless they can combine work and caring roles successfully they are unlikely to reach the top in great numbers.

The police organization's commitment to developing flexible working prac-tices is a reality and should be encouraged. It offers an important strategy for ensuring the retention of trained staff, and at the same time it offers workers the opportunity to balance the demands of work and home life. More significantly, developing alternative working practices offers an important starting point for challenging an organization whose identity is substantially shaped by such fixed 'male' working patterns. It also shows a willingness to adhere to Article 11 (2c) of CEDAW, outlined earlier, on the provision of support for combining the oblig-ations of family and work. The development of policy alone, however, will not achieve the open and flexible working environment that officers need if they are to take up such working options. If part-time work is not considered to be 'real' policing, then flexible working policies will have limited real effect for those who wish to take advantage of them (both men and women). Particular atten-tion needs to be paid by senior management – their role as communicators of messages – to job worth. Those in senior management need to actively demon-strate a commitment to different forms of working by taking action to ensure that awareness of information and the potential to undertake alternative ways of working are more fully supported, both by the officers they manage and among their managerial peers. There also needs to be the development of a more cre-ative dialogue on the possibilities of working more flexibly at all ranks; only then can women in senior management sustain their roles more ably. Above all, engaging in flexible ways of working should be recast as evidence of officers' ability and not inability to perform the job of policing.

Women in the legal profession

The feminist critique of law, both as an entity (body of knowledge) and as a profession, has been powerful and multi-faceted. The overarching criticisms have focused on three major themes: the specific practices of law; the content of legislation; and the exclusion of women from its profession. Though inextricably linked in exposing the gendered nature of law, the status of women working in the legal profession is the focus of this section. Although on the face of it, women working in law have made real progress and some perceived glass ceilings are being shattered, there are a number of areas which give cause for concern. In particular, as the previous chapter showed, women tend to remain clustered at the lower levels of the legal profession. Britain is not alone here. In their overview of 19 countries,[2] Malleson and Russell (2006) demonstrate that achieving diversity within the judiciary has become a key concern of legal systems across the world.

Women working as solicitors and barristers continue to experience deeply entrenched cultural and practical barriers to career progression with large numbers of them leaving the profession (Fawcett Society, 2006). Examining the selection procedure of an organization tells us much about the gendered patterning of jobs, tasks and hierarchies. In this section we focus on the considerable criticism that has been directed at the way in which judges are appointed. Until recently, there were no advertisements for judicial office. Applications were subject to being invited to the post. Selection processes lacked any clearly defined selection criteria. Rather, the selection process for judges in the High Court involved the Department for Constitutional Affairs gathering information about potential candidates over a period of time by making informal inquiries, seeking personal opinions (known as 'secret soundings') from leading barristers and judges. It is the role of these 'secret soundings' that has proved consistently controversial among legal commentators for their discriminatory impact on women and other under-represented groups wishing to join the ranks of the judiciary (Malleson, 1999, 2002; Malleson and Banda, 2000; Rackley, 2007). Essentially, the process of secret consultations has meant that being 'well qualified' is not necessarily enough to secure selection for senior rank. Rather, the candidate needs to be 'well known' among the group of judges and senior members of the profession whose personal opinions are sought. Those lawyers outside the so-called 'magic circle' of élite chambers are disadvantaged by the process as are many lawyers from minority backgrounds, and many women lawyers (particularly those with family responsibilities), given their under-representation at the senior bar (Malleson and Banda, 2000). In this way the secretive and discriminatory nature of the selection process ensures that women are unlikely to have equal access to the promotions process. The continuing need to be 'known' in order to be appointed, and the role of social networking in the consultation process were cited as key factors in deterring women lawyers from applying for Silk or Judicial Office (Malleson and Banda, 2000). Malleson sums this up succinctly when she states that:

> Outsiders are inevitably at a disadvantage in a system which relies on the opinions of insiders. (1999: 93)

Changes to this system are afoot. Indeed since the 1980s various Lord Chancellors have worked hard to actively support the goal of increasing judicial diversity – see Rackley (2007) for a good account of the various initiatives. The call to secure a more diverse judiciary only really became a possibility with the appointment of Lord Irvine as Lord Chancellor after the Labour election victory in 1997. During his time as Chancellor a number of research projects and initiatives exploring the concept of judicial diversity were commissioned.[3] One of the most notable developments during his time as Chancellor was the creation of the Commission for Judicial Appointments in 2001 to audit the Queen's Counsel and judicial appointments process. It is under the former Lord Chancellor, Lord Falconer, however, that some of the greatest strides towards achieving judicial diversity were introduced.

A number of important changes have been proposed under his leadership, including opportunities of job-sharing, career breaks and a mentoring scheme (Falconer, 2005). In 2005 he introduced the judicial diversity programme expanding these developments by encouraging applications and raising awareness; removing barriers to appointments; and meeting the needs of a more diverse judiciary. More recently, the Constitutional Reform Act 2005, established a new and independent body to oversee judicial appointments: the Judicial Appointments Commission (JAC). Set up in April 2006 the JAC has taken over the selection of judges from the Lord Chancellor. The motivation here was to remedy some of the serious and chronic problems in the old system outlined above by ensuring that judicial appointments are fair, transparent and made on merit (Rackley, 2007). Some of the main changes which the JAC has brought in are: a new, simplified definition of merit with five core qualities and abilities required to make a good judge; a fairer system for filling High Court vacancies in which all candidates must now apply for vacancies and short-listed candidates will participate in face-to-face discussions to explore their qualities and abilities, and references will be sought fairly and openly; a more streamlined and objective application process in which the length of the application form has been reduced from more than 20 pages to 9; and an improved marketing of vacancies in which advertising will be better targeted to encourage more people to apply (Rackley, 2007). Describing the new system, JAC Chairman Baroness Usha Prashar notes:

> The days of 'secret soundings' and 'taps on the shoulder' are long gone. Today's judicial applicants will be assessed on who they are, not who they know. (www.judicialappointments.gov.uk)

While such changes provide a much-needed source of optimism for the future of the judiciary – indeed, application figures for Queen's Counsel show that 16 per cent of the first group of applicants are women, compared with 10 per cent of applicants being female in the last round of the previous system (www.qcapplications.org.uk) – we should remain attentive to Acker's (1992) work on the way in which organizations are gendered. For Acker (1992), gendered processes operate on many levels from the explicit and institutional to the more subtle, cultural forms that are submerged in organizational decisions. They include the way men's influence is embedded in rules and procedures, formal job definition, functional roles and the accumulation of competence, skill and merit. Ideas about femininity and masculinity are embedded in organizational arrangements and the opportunities to accumulate 'merit' are structured along gender lines (Burton, 1992). With 'merit' at the forefront of changes to the judiciary, there is growing concern and cynicism among commentators about the extent to which such changes will benefit women. The extent to which 'merit' is a neutral standard by which to judge applicants to the profession is highlighted by Davis and Williams when they note that:

> [W]hile merit should incontrovertibly be the starting point when making judicial appointments, it is of minimal help as the sole criterion for appointment and may in fact mask (conscious or unconscious) bias in decision making. (2003: 11)

In this way 'merit' is seen to have what Thornton (1996) terms an 'essential subjectivity' to it. Here, decision-makers have the power to construct what they deem to be meritorious using their own frameworks of understanding. The argument then follows that, given that decision-makers are by and large men, the criteria of merit tends to reflect the attributes and concerns stereotypically seen as 'male'. As Thornton notes:

> [T]he 'best person' to occupy a position of authority has tended to be unproblematically defined in masculinist terms that reflect the values of the public sphere. (1996: 33)

Herein lies the contradiction of using 'merit' as a way of achieving a fairer system of recruitment. For a candidate appointed on 'merit' alone will be appointed without regard to their gender or ethnic origin. The aim of increasing diversity then becomes a much more difficult task and may serve to exclude 'outsider judges' even further. We concur with Rackley's (2006: 86) assessment when she asserts that Lord Falconer's belief that there is 'no conflict between merit and diversity, is at best, somewhat optimistic, and, at worse, deliberately naïve'. Without an acknowledgment of the gendered nature of 'merit', it is all too easy to join in with the mantra that assumes that 'all things are equal now'. This approach continues to foster the myth that if women work hard(er) to accumulate 'merit' they will succeed and be rewarded (Silvestri, 2003).

Concluding thoughts

We have demonstrated the powerful ways in which the police service and the legal profession systematically discriminate against and achieve social closure for women. Bringing about change in any organization is a difficult and often protracted process (Chan, 1997) and despite a wide range of attempts to increase gender balance throughout the criminal justice system progress towards integration and gender equity has been 'glacially slow' (Brown, 1998).

The police service and the legal profession have shown a strong resistance towards any potential modification of their career structures. In this sense, pushing for alternative ways of working may appear a fruitless exercise. On the contrary, challenging existing arrangements presents a radical challenge to criminal justice organizations and its agents. Any strategy that offers the potential to fracture and break down the hierarchical nature and loosen the stranglehold that men hold in positions of social control is a project worth pursuing. Unlawful discrimination and harassment within the workplace holds serious implications, not only for those in power, but also for those at the receiving end. To restate our position, unlawful discrimination is an important human rights issue. The values of equality, opportunity, diversity, fairness and balance are at the very heart of delivering good and effective justice. The aim then should be to turn these values into tangible differences to the lives of women and men working in criminal justice professions.

Whether the criminal justice system will be changed by the presence of more women remains to be seen – we are a long way from achieving diversity. We do not believe that change will come about simply with the recruitment of more women in criminal justice. To achieve meaningful change within organizations we need to think beyond the numerical. Such an approach will not impact upon the deep-rooted gendered assumptions that characterize the criminal justice system. By concentrating efforts on how best to improve the number of women in criminal justice work, strategies have been directed at helping women to cope with discriminatory policy and structures. Little if any effort has been directed at critiquing or dismantling those structures that constrain women's progression. Ideas about criminal justice work continue to operate within existing parameters and remain characterized as 'men's work'. With regard to the legal profession, initiatives have not fully confronted the extent to which familiar yet particular images of the judge and judging continue to infuse and distort current discourses on adjudication (Rackley, 2007). As a result, the woman judge is characterized as a:

[S]uspicious interloper or dangerous outsider. Her inescapable deviance from the judicial norm disrupts the homogeneity of the bench, revealing the unavoidable, yet largely unacknowledged, gender dimension to traditional understandings of adjudication. (Rackley, 2007: 76)

The same can be said of the female police leader. Perceived as an 'outsider' to the project of policing, she remains the 'ultimate oxymoron' (Brown and Heidensohn, 2000). Heidensohn sums up men's resistance to women in criminal justice work as:

> ... emanating from a struggle over the ownership of social control ... it may also reflect a deeper concern about who has a right to manage law and order. (1992: 215)

The increased presence of more women (and indeed greater representation from other groups whose background differs from that of the majority) has the potential to bring about change in both the substantive law and the interpretation and the application of law and may work to secure a radical overhaul of criminal justice professions more generally. Achieving a greater diversity across the broad spectrum of criminal justice workers will increase the level of public confidence and legitimacy in those who administrate the delivery of social control and justice (Malleson, 2003; Rackley, 2007). It will also move a step closer to assuring compliance with the spirit of non-discrimination at work in human rights law.

Summary

- The situation described in Chapter 6 was one where men are in a dominant position and the purpose of this chapter is to consider some attempts to address this. The policy response to gendered discriminination is part of a more general movement that recognizes diversity in society.
- We have examined in some detail the introduction and effectiveness of legislation to reduce the degree of inequality experienced by women. It was argued that the cultivation of more diverse and representative organizations can produce several important benefits. The first is that a strong case for social justice can be advanced. Secondly, it makes sound business sense to have a more diverse workforce. Thirdly, recognition of gender difference has fostered new ways of thinking about the world of work and what can be done to improve the work–life balance of employees. These three potential improvements all necessarily involve raising gender specific questions.
- Acker's gendered organization theory was applied to explain how criminal justice professions, in particular the police and legal system, have responded to various 'gender agendas'. In the context of policing we discussed the significance of temporal dimensions to working practices, as well as the creation of opportunities of flexible employment, like part-time working.

STUDY QUESTIONS

- Discuss the idea that the police service is deeply gendered at structural, cultural and individual levels.
- Why are there so few senior policewomen?
- Critically discuss the barriers to progression that women working in the legal profession experience.
- Outline the problems with adopting the principle of 'merit' in the selection of judges.
- What are the benefits of achieving diversity in criminal justice organizations?
- Think critically about what the possible impact might be of having social control reside in the hands and minds of men.
- Are there any rational reasons why the ratio between women and men working in the criminal justice system should not be 50:50?

FURTHER READING

The journal *Gender, Work and Organisations* provides a good source of related articles on the general nature of gender and organizations. Acker's 'Hierarchies, Jobs, Bodies: A Theory of Gendered Organisations' in *Gender and Society* (1990) provides a good starting place for those interested in understanding the gendered nature of organizations. Martin and Jurik's *Doing Justice, Doing Gender* (1996) provides an overview of the general gendered nature of criminal justice professions. For those particularly interested in policing see Brown and Heidensohn's *Gender and Policing* (2000); *Women in Control: The Role of Women in Law Enforcement; Sexual Politics and Social Control* (2000); Silvestri's *Women in Charge: Policing, Gender and Leadership* (2003). For those interested in women working in the legal profession see numerous articles by K. Malleson including 'Justifying Gender Equality on the Bench: Why Difference Won't Do' in *Feminist Legal Studies* (2003) and Malleson and Russell's *Appointing Judges man Age of Judicial Power: Critical Perspectives From Around the World* (2006). See also McGlynn's *The Woman Lawyer: Making the Difference* (1998).

Notes

1 Launched in 2001, the Gender Agenda has been developed by an executive group representing the British Association of Women Police, Action E, the Senior Women Officers' Conference, the Police Federation, the ACPO Women's Group, the Metropolitan Association of Senior Women Officers, and the European Network of Policewomen.

2 Editors Kate Malleson and Peter Russell provide a comprehensive overview of judicial appointment systems in established, western democratic systems (Scotland, England and Wales, Canada, the United States, New Zealand, Australia, the Netherlands, Italy, France and Germany); international courts; and emerging democracies; as well as transitional states (Israel, Egypt, South Africa, Namibia, Zimbabwe, Japan and Southeast Asia, Russia and China).

3 During his time as Commissioner, Lord Irvine was involved in commissioning reports and funding research; publishing information booklets and Annual Reports on the application process (including statistics about the proportions of appointments from under-represented groups); holding information sessions to promote awareness of the process; and the development of innovative measures, such as 'work shadowing' of judges by interested applicants.

8

Conclusions

Chapter Contents

This book has covered a lot of ground in a relatively short space, drawing attention to the continued, if not growing, significance of gender in relation to our understanding of crime and disorder. The book shows the differential experiences and inequitable treatment of men and women as offenders, victims and criminal justice workers. This discrimination may not be as obvious as it was in the 1970s, for example, but it is still there in increasingly insiduous forms. Criminologists have made major empirical and conceptual advances since the 1960s when feminist scholars first exposed the institutionalized sexism of academic and administrative criminology. All students of the discipline will nowadays be familiar with, or at least aware of, the contrasting experiences of men and women in the criminal justice system, however superficial that knowledge may be. Also, and quite perversely, gender differences exist in a society that is committed to a human rights agenda, which currently presents politicians and policy-makers with a largely unrealized opportunity to treat all citizens equitably, especially in the sense that their freedom and dignity is respected. It is also a chance to create a more equal and just society, where fundamental human rights co-exist with wider economic, social and cultural rights. In reality none of these are actually enjoyed by everyone in the criminal justice system or crucially in the wider socio-economic context in which it is embedded.

In this, our final chapter, the complex pattern of inequality existing amongst men and women as offenders, victims and professionals is reviewed. Following that it is argued that there are several drivers in global crime, which create a number of paradoxes in criminal justice policy. For example, it is suggested that the principles of the new public management (NPM) and modernization; emphases on victim-centred justice; the penal populism and public protection; decline of the rehabilitative ideal; the prioritization of the assessment and management of risk; and the commercialization of crime control all have a bearing on the gender and crime debate (Senior et al., 2007). The links are not always obvious and need to be teased out but it is argued that these factors contribute towards the shaping of gendered relations in criminal justice and ultimately wider society. These broad-brush developments may perpetuate existing inequalities between men and women, in addition to creating new opportunities for change. It is not our intention to bemoan the current situation without there being some recognition of the scope for making progress towards a more humane society in which there is mutual respect and tolerance, and where gender relations are not based solely on conflict and discrimination. Most crucially, we make our final statement about the relevance of the human rights agenda as an antidote to gendered inequality with reference to a political economy of crime (Reiner, 2007a, 2007b). At the time of writing, the British Prime Minister, Gordon Brown, indicated that there will be a British Bill of Rights embedded in the constitution. Again, whatever the outcome of these deliberations a rights-based agenda provides opportunities and, paradoxically, obstacles for the offenders, victims and employees all caught up in the criminal justice web.

An overview of key debates

This book was organized in a way that has hopefully lent some coherence to a complex set of issues and debates about gender and crime taking place in criminology and criminal justice. The main themes covered included offending behaviour, victimization and criminal justice policy and practice, the latter focusing in particular on employees in the criminal justice sector. Throughout this text we have endeavoured to tap into the tension existing between, on the one hand, the clear divisions that exist between men and women in each of these areas; and on the other hand, attempts to introduce a framework that recognizes the potential unifying features of difference, which is underpinned by a commitment towards repairing the damage done by divisive ideas and practices. This is where the human rights agenda comes into play. As noted earlier on in this book our ambition is to take us further than the 'black letter law' approach to human rights, opening up the debate to the wider theoretical and empirical concerns of students of criminology. In line with the relevant conventions and protocols first mentioned in Chapter 1 human rights is all about respecting the freedom, equality and dignity of everyone based on an appreciation of justice. Each and every human being possesses an equal moral status on the grounds that they share in common their humanity. Having said that, as well as these universals, there is also social diversity, for example gender, class, race and ethnicity, which can place pressure on the universal. There is a tension between unifying human qualities while recognizing multiple forms of division and differentiation.

Let us review our attempts to achieve the above aims before moving on to consider the intellectual and practical difficulties confronting scholars in the future.

The female offender

Chapter 2 scrutinized the experiences of women as offenders, tracing from a historical perspective the status of this actor in criminological inquiry. Historically the study of crime has been male-centred and a range of sexist assumptions have tainted criminological theorizing and the workings of the criminal justice system. When the female offender is not being ignored she is being pathologized and treated as abnormal and aberrant. Feminist scholars rendered the gendered visible, the nature of the discipline calling for a more nuanced account of crime and disorder where the differential experiences of male and female offenders are made explicit. The key point is that women do not offend as much as men and that their offending behaviour is of a less serious nature. There have periodically been moral panics about female crime, embodied in the form of the 'mean girl', but all reliable sources of information about offending behaviour show clearly that female offending is relatively minor. Despite this the woman offender finds herself in an increasingly punitive environment, demonstrated tellingly by the dramatic increase in the number of women being given custodial sentences. The chapter illustrated in painstaking detail the gender specific problems experienced by female inmates in an environment designed with men in mind, drawing attention to the dehumanizing practices in contemporary penal policy. The deleterious effects of prison life on women's psychological and physical health; their unsettled as opposed to resettled futures on release from custody; and the indirect harm caused to children deprived of the guardianship of their mothers contribute towards a denial of their human rights. We argued that while the National Offender Management Service more or less complies with the Human Rights Act 1998, there are limitations to the black letter law approach inasmuch as human rights defined more widely are not enjoyed by all people in society and that the indignities faced by women in prison are inconsistent with human rights principles more generally.

The male offender

Chapter 3 went on to explore the male offender. Consistent with certain aspects of the feminist critique of criminology we acknowledge the greater degree of involvement of men in crime. Official statistics and other forms of criminological research show unequivocally that crime, especially violent crime, is more likely to be committed by men and boys than women and girls. The activities of the police, courts, probation and prison services all attest to this simple fact. An attempt was also made to consider the contribution of some male criminologists who foreground gender in their respective analyses of criminal behaviour through various adaptations of the concept of masculinity/masculinities, including structural and psychosocial versions. This body of work provides a range of complementary although not always compatible explanations of criminality at various levels of analysis, ranging from the individual psyche to global processes. We argued that structural approaches in particular, which draw attention toward marginal working- and under-class masculinities, show how male offenders experience discriminatory forms of policing resulting in a denial of their citizenship and human rights. Notably, this approach is consistent with certain variants of critical criminology and there is the danger that male offenders are treated as victims of an unjust criminal justice system, which is far from our actual intention. While we recommend that the human rights of unpopular and sometimes undeserving individuals are protected there is also a need for male offenders – and some critical criminologists – to recognize that offenders, but especially violent men, inhibit the human rights of others, especially their individual victims and the fearful communities in which they live. Psychosocial approaches which focus on the potential for change in the male subject offer some limited scope for optimism with this aim in mind, although in the last analysis structural and psychic factors restrict the nature of change that can be instigated by individual men.

Criminology has traditionally been concerned with understanding and responding to offending behaviour and in doing this the victim has been neglected. Nowadays the victim is at the centre of academic and policy debate and in the next part of the book our attention turned towards the victim of crime. Although crime victims were in the past under-studied by criminologists, following two important interventions it is not possible to think about crime without full consideration of this important component of the so-called square of crime formulated by left realist criminologists (Lea, 2002). Firstly, there emerged a new field of inquiry, namely victimology, although this perpetuated many of the sexist mythologies associated with criminology resulting in victim blaming. Secondly, the work of pioneering feminist criminologists highlighted the plight of the female victim, especially women who were victimized by the violence of some men.

The female victim

State-funded and independent research shows that victimization is not distributed evenly amongst men and women and that women are particularly vulnerable to the worst excesses of male violence mainly in the private sphere. Evidence reviewed in Chapter 4 also showed that while chivalrous attitudes do exist in the criminal justice system, female victims consistently say that they experience secondary victimization in the form of relatively poor treatment by the police when they report that they are the victims of domestic and sexually motivated violence. The dreadful situation first highlighted by feminist researchers from the 1970s onwards has brought about some changes to police policy and practice although there is still a long way to go to ensure that there is adequate protection of and care for victims of male violence. In this chapter, it was argued that the victims of domestic violence share much in common with victims of torture, not least because of the repeat or multiple victimization that takes place. Indeed the main characteristics of the latter are all evident and we suggest that the human rights-based remedies developed to tackle torture are also appropriate for domestic and sexual violence. Above all, both violent men and an unsympathetic or non-responsive criminal justice system need to be called to account for their routine disregard of the fundamental human rights of some of their victims. Thus male offenders are responsible for most victimization and many of the more serious harms experienced by women are perpetrated by men, but this does not mean that men are not victims too.

The male victim

While criminologists quite rightly tend to focus on the violence experienced by women, Chapter 5 stated that men are also victims of violent acts. As the journalist Madeline Bunting (2007) put it, 'Being male carries real penalties, and these are deeply written into understandings of masculinity'. This observation is especially pertinent in relation to victimization. This chapter showed that men are frequently victimized by other men, especially in the context of the night-time economy, although this is often under-reported. The reasons for this are complex although a significant factor is that, when looking at this category of men, their status as victims and offenders is fluid and interchangeable. Men are also victims of domestic violence carried out by female partners and this chapter accounted for the relative dearth of knowledge about this aspect of victimization. Building on the argument posited in Chapter 3 it is necessary for men who victimize, in particular those that are both *victimized* and *victimizers*, to become responsibilized by taking stock of the fact that their behaviour inhibits human rights. In this chapter we also suggested, quite controversially, that young males whose behaviour is labelled as anti-social are actually victims of a process of criminalization. Under successive New Labour governments boys and juveniles involved in anti-social – invariably sub-criminal – behaviour, have been demonized. We argue that while their actions may create fear and distrust they are in actual fact victims of neglect and stereotyping, especially as a result of a lack of economic, but especially emotional, investment in their uncertain futures. We suggest that often vulnerable young people need to be treated in a way that is respectful of their social and human rights and that the imposition of the British state-led Respect agenda and school exclusions is not necessarily the most appropriate solution.

In all of the above chapters a key actor is the criminal justice professional and we have seen how their activities create and/or sustain gender specific outcomes in their dealings with the wider public either as suspects and offenders or victims and witnesses.

The criminal justice practitioner: a gendered perspective

Chapter 6 moved on to outline the gendered dimension of the police, courts, probation and prison services to show how gender is also salient for the people working in the system. The number of practitioners who are men and women in each of these sectors is pertinent: the numerical dominance of men in the police and prison services is of interest, but in itself it does not tell us much about how these organizations operate. For that reason we examined the cultures of masculinity that pervade these organizations to show how women and some men and their masculinities are subordinated. We also introduced some of the work that shows how the commercialization of social control means that private sector agencies, such as 'bouncers', are integral elements required for the maintenance of a gender imbalance in crime reduction. The overarching aim of this chapter is to show that power is important for understanding the division of labour across the criminal justice sector and that this not only compromises the human rights of offenders and victims but also employees. Masculine power, for example, facilitates overt forms of sexual discrimination and less visible discrimination that discredits freedom of expression and respect for private and family life.

Chapter 7 examined in depth the criminal justice system as a gendered site, showing how the respective careers of men and women are played out in the police service and legal profession. Changes in organizational policy and in law have made significant and positive changes to the way in which women and men are recruited and achieve career progression. Women and men working in the police service and the legal profession do so within what appear to be gender-neutral systems. Outwardly, there are no visible and apparent restrictions to the progression of men and women within organizations. Yet research has shown us that despite a number of reform initiatives, women continue to be under-represented in criminal justice work, especially at senior level. Women continue to experience discrimination, albeit in a less blatant and visible form. The 'gendered substructure' in which gendered assumptions about criminal justice work and workers can be found remains a fundamental and defining feature of criminal justice agencies. If we look behind the guise of gender neutrality we see a criminal justice system subscribing to and working within the parameters of an 'ideal worker' – this ideal worker continues to be male. While women have equal opportunity to participate in and compete for positions of authority they do so within existing 'male' systems. The chapter demonstrated the considerable gap that exists between policy and practice. At a cultural level, women remain 'outsiders' in the project of social control and the delivery of justice. The increased presence of women (and indeed greater representation from other groups whose background differs from that of the majority) has the potential to bring about change in both the substantive law; the interpretation and the application of law; and may work to secure a radical overhaul of criminal justice professions more generally. Above all, achieving greater diversity is a matter of equity and social justice (Diamond, 2007).

The bulk of this book has addressed the central issues covered in the gender and crime debate and we have added our own, hopefully original, albeit exploratory take on the topic. Finally, we now tease out some broad currents in crime policy occurring in late modern societies across the globe, with a specific focus on the British context. It is to these drivers in global crime that we now turn.

Gender, crime and human rights: towards a contextual framework

The introduction to this chapter referred to the following six global drivers of crime and we draw extensively on the work of Senior et al. (2007) to consider these developments.

- New public management (NPM) and modernization;
- Victim-centred justice;
- Penal populism and public protection;
- Decline of the rehabilitative ideal;
- Risk assessment and management;
- Commercialization of crime control.

As the main features of the above are sketched we explore their resonance in debates about gender and crime, also comprising an assessment of the applicability of human rights discourse. Most attention is dedicated to the NPM, as this political rationality is especially influential. Our organizing argument is that while we have placed gender at the centre of our reflections on criminology and criminal justice there is still much work to be done because on a day-to-day basis gender is often implicit and taken for granted. The issues identified throughout this book are not in the minds of everyone and absence of this knowledge means the human rights of men and women in criminal justice are experientially marginal. Furthermore, there is the influence of authoritarian austerity, which underpins the drivers discussed below. The main features of this authoritarian austerity are the strong and strict influence of the government (the authoritarianism), which limits what can be said and done in criminal justice. Moreover, a rather narrow range of economic and technocratic considerations, often resulting in severe and harsh policy outcomes against individuals and communities (its austerity) restricts its determination of the direction of criminal justice policy and practice. There may be talk, as well as legislation, driving forward human rights and a respect for gender equality, but other politically determined choices and courses of action frequently overshadow this. It is to these that we now turn. The trends described are global in their significance although the focus is on the British context to aid explanation.

New public management and modernization

The principles of NPM, especially that of performance management, have impacted unevenly across the public sector in general and the criminal justice system in particular. We take stock of its influence on policing, youth justice, the courts and correctional agencies. NPM is a set of principles and practices which have influenced the general direction of criminal justice policy since they were set in train in British society by successive Conservative governments from the 1980s onwards and later adapted by New Labour. According to Rhodes (1997, see also Newburn, 2002; Raine, 2002; 6, 2006) the main features include: a shift to disaggregating of units, including the creation of Next Steps agencies and the growth of regulatory bodies; de-professionalization and de-privileging staff groups seeking to reduce the control over policy and practice by 'experts'; hands-on professional management, often creating responsibility without authority; explicit standards, procedures and measures of performance management; greater emphasis on output controls and managing by results; shift to greater competition; and stress on private sector styles of management practice (Travers, 2007). This set of politically motivated tactics is principally concerned with the maximization of economic competitiveness and social considerations such as human rights – equality, dignity, justice, etc. – are marginalized. Performance management is an exemplar of NPM principles (Diamond, 2007).

Performance management
Performance management has been utilized as a mechanism for assessing and auditing the performance of public sector agencies, including the criminal justice system. In real terms this has resulted in the setting of targets, attempts to control outputs and the development of minimum standards. The measurement of performance is oriented towards activities that can be quantified and more abstract beliefs and values such as gendered equality and human rights are neglected. It is seen as a politically neutral exercise although this is disingenuous because the choices made reflect a narrow range of interests.

To take a concrete example, in the 2000s the Police Performance Assessment Framework (PPAF) was introduced. This was an assessment conducted jointly by Her Majesty's Inspectorate of Constabulary (HMIC) and the Home Office Police and Crime Standards Directorate (HOPCSD), including advice from the Association of Police Authorities (APA) and the Association of Chief Police Officers (ACPO). Throughout the 43 constabularies of England and Wales over thirty performance indicators were assessed, which were aggregated into seven areas of performance: (1) reducing crime; (2) investigating crime; (3) promoting safety; (4) providing assistance; (5) citizen focus; (6) resource allocation and (7) local policing (www://police.homeoffice.gov.uk cited in Senior et al., 2007). These areas are what most people would reasonably expect, but there are few calls for the police to respect the freedoms of citizens and there is a missed opportunity to measure gendered discrimination and any possible human rights deficit that may exist.

Youth justice and performance management

Target-setting has governed the development of youth justice at all levels since 1997 and is seen by government as a method of performance management in youth justice. In this sector the rights of young people – principally boys – have been neglected as a result of agencies pursuing economic goals. New Labour's White Paper *No More Excuses* (Home Office, 1997) homed in on delays in processing offenders through the courts. While the word justice and a concern about reducing offending appear in this document the overarching aim is to achieve efficiency gains. Over time it would appear that national targets have not always been achieved and that there have necessarily been shifts of emphasis within an evolving system. Nonetheless target setting is central to the operations of the Youth Justice Board (YJB) and the situation is very much as Brown describes it:

> Performance is increasingly described in terms of deliverables: deliverables not being overarching successes such as real reductions in harmful behaviour but rather measurable, target-output achievement. (2005: 97)

More than this it is evident that performance targets and subsequently the processes used to manage them are centrally determined. For instance, the YJB exerts close control over the content of plans for youth justice at a local level. These plans observe national priorities such as parental responsibility, the speedy administration of justice, restorative justice philosophy (i.e. bring offenders and victims together) and the principles of effective practice (Smith, 2003). Following Smith's reasoning the key issue here is the extent to which these plans do not include recognition of factors that some practitioners may consider to be good practice. There is nothing here about:

> promoting anti-discriminatory practice or protecting the rights of young people in any other way; there is nothing about addressing welfare needs ... [or]... promoting opportunities for young people through education .... (Smith, 2003: 84)

To these illustrative examples we add the differential treatment of boys and girls and the vulnerability of their human rights. Boys, for example, are far more likely to 'fail' at school, especially if they are white and working class (Cassen and Kingdon, 2007).

The delivery and assessment of performance by the YJBs is based on key elements of effective practice and its structure for assessment, planning, interventions and supervision, which is based on a problem-solving approach. This draws on the reliability and validity of criminological research and comprises assessment, an evaluation of issues, the application of guidance and an evaluation of outcomes. The production of evidence-based policy of this type can be seen in the 15 KEEP booklets, which outline all there is to know about youth justice, thus limiting the requirement for fully trained and knowledgeable professionals (Senior et al., 2007). Another outcome of this approach is that young people are lumped together into groups sharing particular characteristics, paying scant attention to individual needs and experiences. This is an issue Pitts (2003: 6) has addressed when he draws attention to the government and its *pragmatic* use of criminological knowledge. Evidence-based knowledge is gathered through the application of the methods belonging to an emergent crime science, but not necessarily for 'intellectual illumination', rather the 'political legitimation' of policy goals (Pitts, 2003: 6). The aforementioned goals, which are inspired by an authoritarian austerity are sacrosanct and recognition of the human rights of young people and their susceptibility to gender-based forms of discrimination remains peripheral.

Performance management in the courts
The measurement of performance in this part of the criminal justice system is evident in various ways, although the treatment of victims and witnesses has attracted considerable attention. Anyone who has visited the courts will understand that they are unwelcoming places with few facilities available for victims and witnesses. In particular, the standard of services available to meet the needs of often anxious and sometimes traumatized victims and witnesses is inadequate. It is not unknown for victims of violent crime to be seated in the same areas as the perpetrator of their victimization, a situation that is now widely recognized as unsatisfactory. In line with the Victims' Charters (see Chapters 6 and 7) performance management is now equated with enhancing the experiences of consumers of courts services. Accordingly, the courts now provide a more customer oriented service. This is especially clear in response to the complex needs of female victims of crime where a rights-based discourse has informed provision. The courts may commit to investing in new and better facilities but these are vulnerable to rapidly changing budgetary-based decisions. Overall, economic considerations are prioritized and budgets are managed very closely to the extent that any aspirations to cater for the needs, and rights, of victims are cancelled out (Senior et al., 2007). Working in an environment where balancing the books is a major preoccupation it is also increasingly difficult for the courts to work with other agencies, such as the police and CPS, as well as the voluntary sector. The consequences of this can be seen if we consider the plight of rape victims where attrition rates are high, maintaining highly gendered patterns of victimization.

In the context of the courts service, information technology (IT) systems are essential for enhancing management systems and the process of auditing. Targets are centrally formulated and enshrined in a unified HM Courts Service Business Plan, which is published on an annual basis and includes plans tailored for individual areas. A recent HM Courts Service Business Plan (2006–7) refers to a range of strategic targets, which on the surface would seem to drive forward a human rights-based agenda in which gender is recognized. For example, the needs of different citizens must be acknowledged if access to justice is to be made meaningful for all. The plan refers to, amongst many groups, victims of crime and defendants in criminal cases. The promotion of access to justice is laudable, especially when it is backed up with addressing declining public confidence in the courts and the lack of respect for the values of criminal justice. Unfortunately, the plan juxtaposes these aims alongside the speed of the process and the necessity to keep costs to a minimum. Fitzpatrick et al. (2001) show how appropriate performance indicators are set with the effective and efficient delivery of services very much in mind, rather than fairness, equality and rights. We do not wish to say outright that improved access and greater confidence are incompatible with reduced costs, and delays are inevitably incompatible in principle, but in practice they tend to be so (Senior et al., 2007).

In sum, there is much in what we have said above to make us optimistic and the rhetoric here chimes with human rights. We can also discern the cognizance of gender issues. However, the focus remains too fixated on the quantifiable measures of the court process and not on its central mission. Raine (2001: 114) captures this well in a description of the emphasis on the quantifiable – 'throughput rates, waiting times and length of sentences' – at the expense of qualitative dimensions of service delivery. The latter would include the future effects of how a case is handled on those involved, whether the victim or offender is taken into consideration. Under New Labour (1997–2007) there was undoubtedly a commitment to human rights and it did more than previous governments to take seriously gender inequality but these diverse needs of offenders and other court users were not fleshed out. Again, government interests may rhetorically promote the rights of court users, whereas in reality, economic considerations such as efficiency and cost effectiveness are preferred to indoctrinate the tone and direction of policy.

Performance management and the prison and probation services
The prison service is a highly regimented organization and there is a clear hierarchical structure of command and control. The performance culture affecting the services described above has been adopted and adapted more straightforwardly by the prison service. The service has accepted that its survival is in part dependent on demonstrating the effectiveness of its performance, and while from time to time operational staff may question the wisdom of certain indicators there is general compliance, not least because the allocation of resources is closely linked to the achievement of targets. The probation service, with its very different professional orientation, took longer to welcome the ethos of performance management.

Senior et al. (2007) contend that performance measurement is politically determined and that this can lead to contradictions within an organization. The existence of different timescales, where targets have been set for a particular time period can soon be outdated if politicians push policy in another direction during that period, is an example. This can be counterproductive because areas of good practice can be disregarded because they are out of kilter with a new initiative. The danger is that good practice (e.g. something that 'works') is not necessarily the equivalent of good performance. Regarding the probation service, which has proven its capacity to meet targets, there have been surprising developments, not least the introduction of other service providers from the voluntary and private sectors. The situation outlined above shows that the policy-making process is volatile and that short-termism is the name of the game. Under these circumstances a commitment to gender equality and human rights is likely to be subordinated.

Interim summary
The principles of the NPM developed throughout the 1980s and 1990s were adopted and reshaped by New Labour modernizers in the 2000s although the underlying logic of the 3Es is still germane. There is scant evidence to suggest that there will be any diminution of its significance and authoritarian austerity is central to modes of governance across the world. All agencies nowadays are expected to achieve what they did in the past – and possibly more – by using existing funding regimes more prudently. It is likely that more will have to be done with less through working 'smarter' in an increasingly competitive environment. All criminal justice agencies are likely to be subjected to this disciplinary mechanism although it is feasible that this will become second nature as policy-makers and practitioners comply with and commit themselves to these goals. Other goals such as gender equality and human rights are there, and there is compliance, even commitment, to these values, but they are way down a list of increasingly economic and technocratic priorities.

Victim-centred justice

During the last two decades of the twentieth century the criminal justice system in England and Wales experienced an increased workload due to a focus on victims and witnesses, culminating in victim-centred justice (Goodey, 2005; Spalek, 2006). As noted in the main body of Chapters 4 and 5, since the early 1990s successive British governments have introduced so-called Victims' Charters in 1990 and 1996 (Home Office, 2001), followed by the Victims' Code of Practice, coming into effect in 2004 with the passing into law of the Domestic Violence, Crime and Victims Act 2004 (Spalek, 2006). Although the Conservatives did launch the first Victims' Charter (Home Office, 1990), it was New Labour that invested much more resource into this area (Williams, 2003). We now look at the status of the gendered victim in the context of certain criminal justice agencies.

The police service and victims

This organization became much more attuned to the needs and rights of victims and the introduction of the second Victims' Charter in 1996 led to 'one-stop shops', which made the police responsible for keeping victims informed about progress with their case (Senior et al., 2007). In reply to the activism of feminists, victim statement schemes were created to encourage victims to articulate their personal experiences of victimization (Hoyle and Young, 2003). In the aftermath of the Macpherson inquiry (1999) deficient services experienced by victims, particularly amongst minority ethnic groups, were exposed. Moreover, there are provisions in the Crime and Disorder Act 1998, which allow for victim consultation in those cases where a young offender receives action plan and reparation orders. A year later, the Youth Justice and Criminal Evidence Act 1999 called for victims to receive an invitation to go to youth panel meetings. However it is restorative justice that perhaps signals most explicitly the arrival of a victim-centred justice. All of the above developments impacted on the police service, although some elements of the police culture (see Chapter 6), especially an ideology of penal punitiveness (see 'Public protection and penal populism' below) have been shown to be in contradistinction to this principle. However, it is perhaps the extremely high attrition rate in rape cases that suggests that the police still have much work to do to respond to the rights and needs of victims.

The courts and victims

In an earlier section of this chapter there was a discussion about the growing influence of consumerism on the courts and the services they offer. This customer focus has led to numerous actions, not least a government response to the Victims' Charters and the pledge to rebalance the criminal justice system so victims and their needs are respected and guarded. There are nowadays more services for victims and witnesses in the courts although many still do not feel safe and adequately protected. The existence of a statutory code attests to this and the courts are now obliged to consistently provide good quality support and advice, as well as information, to protect all victims equally. We welcome this, especially because of the differential experiences of men and women are acknowledged as part of this, but there are still problems (Senior et al., 2007). In our chapters on victims we made the point that there is regretablly a tension in crime and public policy between the respective needs of offenders and victims. In the mid-2000s New Labour showed more even-handedness in its rebalancing act, but as Williams and Canton (2005) rightly point out the rights of victims are often portrayed as if they are irreconcilable with those of offenders. Thus an apparently benevolent and politically neutral move to look after victims of crime can deepen forms of exclusion experienced by defendants and offenders. In the words of Williams and Canton:

> One is bound to suspect that this politicisation is part of a deliberate strategy to flush out opposition to victim-focused changes, so that opponents can be accused of woolly-minded, sentimental support for the civil liberties of criminals. The attempt to justify harsher sentencing of offenders and curtailment of civil liberties in the name of victims is not new. (2005: 2)

Interim summary

Thus in a relatively short time period victim-centred justice may not have come to dominate crime policy but it has a much higher profile and this seems set to continue. Broad swathes of public, political and practitioner opinion are embedded in assumptions about the irredeemable nature of some offenders and the need to discipline them more forcibly are perceptions that are based on an appreciation of the victim. Western European criminal justice systems still have safeguards to protect suspects and offenders and they enjoy formal human rights not enjoyed by victims; however the victim has a new status. It seems impossible that at any time a government will give up on victims. The continued functioning of criminal justice partly depends on the effective valorization and inclusion of victims as a justification of its other more punitive and exclusionary policies. There is, of course, restorative justice, although its future is likely to be limited because of growing public intolerance with nuisance offenders (i.e. the current criminalization of anti-social behaviour) and because it is of little use in the case of mainly male serious and violent offenders. Also, it is necessary to reiterate an observation aired earlier on in the book where we ventured the view that it is not always possible to see victims and offenders as occupying different camps because some young men are victims and offenders at the same time.

Public protection and penal populism

Public protection has been a fundamentally important consideration as society becomes ever more fearful of various hazards and potential harms. Significantly it is men who cause most concern in this regard. Our homes, workplaces, and public space all feel less safe, as people become more knowledgeable about the everyday significance of crime and anti-social behaviour. Sex offending once confined to families is now a virtual as well as an actual phenomenon and the rowdy behaviour of young people is increasingly criminalized as anti-social behaviour. High profile cases of seriously dangerous predatory violent criminals haunt not only the public but probation, parole and prison personnel too who sometimes make flawed life-and-death decisions about the releasability of these offenders. Anthony Rice, a man with a history of violent offending behaviour, was released from prison prematurely on the grounds that his human rights were being violated. Tragically, on being released he went on to kill again because there were not adequate provisions in place to manage the risks he posed. Human rights discourse is increasingly making the citizenry aware that governments should assume responsibility for looking after their safety and security. If this book were written ten years ago it is unlikely that few scholars would have anticipated the long-term consequences of 9/11 in the US and 7/7 in the UK. While this is not explicitly a crime issue it has placed a burden on the criminal justice system, augmenting the work of the police, courts and security services. What these events effectively did was to transform the human rights agenda in two ways. Firstly, human rights abuses have been resituated at an international level, lessening the focus on domestic problems. An example of this is a Law Lords ruling that the activities of British troops abroad are regulated by the Human Rights Act 1998, in particular the prohibition of torture (*Guardian*, 14 June 2007). Secondly, recent events of terrorism have further strengthened a more punitive approach. The increased use of stop and search/stop and question by the police and the ongoing debate about extending the time for which terror suspects can be held, all indicate a less sympathetic climate for civil liberties and human rights. It is arguable too that the discourse of 'ordinary' crime has changed as a direct consequence of a focus on terrorism. In describing anti-social behaviour for instance some commentators make a subliminal connection to this global agenda in the way in which the terms of the debate are being conducted. References appear in the papers which conflate the nuisance behaviour of 11-year-olds as exerting terror on local communities (Senior, 2005).

Government policies designed to protect the public are closely allied with penal populism and evidence that the public hold punitive attitudes towards criminals. The perilously overcrowded prison estate in Britain makes it one of the most punitive societies in Western Europe (Liebling and Maruna, 2005; Padfield and Maruna, 2006; Pratt, 2007). Prison overcrowding has produced further paradoxes in the sense that in the summer of 2007 over 1000 prisoners (out of a total of almost 10,000) who were serving indeterminate sentences for public protection (IPP)[1] were not being released on time. This population includes some lifers, but mainly individuals who are at risk of harming themselves or others. They are mainly men. This group of inmates were nearing the end of their sentences but could not be considered for release by the parole board because they had not attended compulsory programmes that are a condition of their release. Some prisoners in this position claim that they are being detained arbitrarily, which is a breach of the Human Rights Act 1998 (*Guardian*, 4 June 2007). Ironically, given the government's orientation towards economy and efficiency it was estimated that the IPP could lead to a £10 million 'jail backlog' (*Guardian*, 23 June 2007).

Although crime went down by 30 per cent between 1997 and the mid-2000s, alongside lower risks of victimization, the prison population continues to expand (Garside, 2006). John Reid, the New Labour Home Secretary until the spring of 2007 stated that more prisons would be built to respond to public demand and the decisions of sentencers. It is worth noting that the rate of increase started to slow in the summer of 2007, although it is too early to tell if this is a blip in the context of a much broader punitive trend. It is notable that the Chancellor of the Exchequer until June 2007, Gordon Brown, remarked that there were no resources to honour this pledge, a clear illustration of the influence of NPM. Overall, it would appear that *penal punitiveness* is becoming more and more irrational and contradictory by the day.

When John Reid was Home Secretary large sections of the public expressed their fears about dangerous male offenders in the community who posed risks that had not been assessed or managed appropriately. The actual risk of becoming a victim of one of these offenders or being a witness of their crimes is negligible although public fears do need to be addressed. Anxiety about the adequacy of public protection – including the vulnerable as well as the respectable majority – mirror not only government priorities but also the deep-seated concerns of both 'middle England' and socially excluded communities (Respect Task Force, 2006; Hughes, 2007). Popular punitiveness is most clearly demonstrated by the intolerance of 'loutish' and anti-social behaviour, especially that of boys, which is resulting in the criminalization of non-criminal activities (France, 2007).

It was Rod Morgan, on his resignation as head of the YJB in 2007, who questioned such an openly punitive approach to young people. In the current climate there is not much evidence to show a curbing of this desire to punish not just serious and organized crime, such as human trafficking, but also relatively petty incivilities. The targeting of suspected terrorists can conceivably be vindicated although there needs to be a balance to make sure legally innocent citizens are not subjected to unwarranted attention. Crucially, human rights may not be routinely violated and are rarely mentioned although civil liberties advocates voice their worries. In their clamour to satisfy public demands to punish, the gender specific issues faced by those bearing the brunt of this punitiveness is rarely mentioned outside of academia and the conference circuit attended by researchers and those campaigning for the human rights of prisoners. The deleterious impact of this climate on women in particular and the blighted futures of male prisoners are not high on the government's agenda.

The courts
The courts frequently experience attempts by the executive government to interfere with its workings, particularly when government attempts to produce legislation that is sufficiently punitive. This is often legitimated by appealing to public opinion, although research into sentencing decisions and public opinion shows a fair degree of consensus between the two, thus questioning the interference of government (Roberts and Hough, 2002). This research finding does not stop the tabloids representing the use of voluntary drug treatments for paedophiles, as 'chemical castration' (*Guardian*, 14 June 2007). Nevertheless, the Carter Review (Carter, 2003) noted sentence lengths reflecting more severe sentencing practice, and tariffs for the most serious violent offenders have been increasing since the mid-1980s (Carter, 2003). As a result of this punitive climate the experiences of prisoners have changed and they spend, on average, more time inside prison with increased delays in their consideration for a release date. It would also appear that ideas about rehabilitation are less influential than ever before when assessing the releasability of a prisoner. The need to carry out a risk assessment where public protection is paramount is the order of the day. In sum, then, there is a situation where the executive arm of the law is more and more interventionist, often leaving the judiciary relatively impotent. If there is a successful defence of the law against abuse this is usually countered by a change in the law to overcome that obstruction (Senior et al., 2007).

Decline of the rehabilitative ideal

The decline of the rehabilitative ideal belongs to the past and Martinson's (1974) 'nothing works' pessimism was effectively challenged in the 1990s by the 'what works' agenda and the burgeoning of 'evidence-based' research, suggesting on the contrary that future offending behaviour may be reduced (Wiles, 1999; Davies et al., 2000; Hough, 2004). This is underpinned by a belief in progressive change based on scientific evidence. It is all about making sure interventions are targeted at the right people, at the right time, and in the right place (Tilley, 2005). Initiatives designed to reduce crime need to be refashioned to meet individual requirements. This emphasis has influenced probation policy and practice in the past although offender management and corrections now dominate. Other agencies in criminal justice are also sceptical about rehabilitation. In contrast to probation officers, police opinion is more likely to refer to retribution and incapacitation of offenders, offering some support to a view that the rehabilitative ideal is perceived to be in crisis because of the ascendancy of penal populism (see above) and, as shown in the next section, techniques of risk assessment and management.

Declining faith in the efficacy of rehabilitation is a trend that has resulted in the justification for a policy of mass imprisonment where criminals are warehoused or contained. There is a lack of trust in community-based punishments leading, for example, to an increase in the female prison population. This logic is applied to all criminals and has resulted in the imprisonment of individuals who have committed relatively minor offences. Many prisoners serving short sentences do not benefit from interventions intended to tackle offending behaviour and they re-enter society more damaged (in terms of mental and physical health) than when they entered the prison estate. A failure to reintegrate rehabilitated offenders leaves prisoners, especially women, in a vulnerable position with regard to human rights.

Risk assessment and management

Ideas about risk are right at the heart of the criminal justice system and are there to predict and classify offenders on the grounds of their dangerousness. Risk can be assessed in various ways, including the use of clinical assessments designed for individual offenders to work out dynamic and static risk factors. Some models of risk examine psychological variables whereas others look at sociological factors. An important aspect of risk is that it is regarded as a scientific crime reduction tool. For our purposes its deployment of predictive profiling means its commitment to human rights principles is weak and its imprecision means it overstates the protection it can provide to victims of serious violent, often sexually motivated, crimes. The section below suggests that risk assessment and management in relation to probation, youth justice, the courts and the police is heavily influenced by penal populism and a waning belief in the capacity of offenders to commit themselves to change.

Correctional agencies and the management of risk
The probation service has relied on risk management for its work with violent men and prolific male offenders, and there is the expectation that its measurements will be accurate (Kemshall, 2003). While risk assessment is a permanent feature of probation work there are more novel features in current practice, especially the usage of actual accounting, which is supposedly based on scientific procedures. This helps to predict both the risk of reoffending and the more complex and potentially sensitive risk of harm to self or others (Senior et al., 2007). Actuarial justice can, in Feeley and Simon's (2004) view, be contrasted with liberal ideas about justice that were created to determine the culpability and guilt of individual suspects and offenders as part of an overarching reformist and reintegrative strategy. These assumptions were characterized as untenable in the late twentieth century, especially the focus on individualized justice. Actuarial justice more or less abandons any pretensions that rehabilitation or punishment are

effective and that instead policy-makers must devise, 'techniques for identifying, classifying and managing groups assorted by levels of dangerousness' (Feeley and Simon, 1994: 173). Accordingly, justice is no longer individualized but is oriented towards assessing and managing the dangers presented by 'groups' and 'aggregates' such as 'permanent-marginal' underclass-type populations. Thus actuarial justice can maintain the marginalized masculinities described in Chapter 3, though more often than not this logic is applied more routinely to individual violent men.

The careful assessments associated with high-risk male offenders such as those represented in the improved MAPPA arrangements demonstrate progress towards public protection, agency co-ordination, and targeted interventions. However whether that satisfies the public appetite for risk surveillance of whole populations, particularly an overwhelming male group of sex offenders, is less easy to assess. Sex offenders have been subjected to increased levels of scrutiny demonstrated by the use of registers and panels (Senior et al., 2007). Still, senior policy-makers in government seem reluctant to face the fact that their expectations about the degree of risk protection that can be provided are essentially unrealistic and unobtainable in practice. Moreover, the human rights of those subject to this type of risk assessment may be denied. Increasing public protection is feasible and there are interventions that can yield positive results yet for these strategies to be successful it would be necessary to use intrusive surveillance technologies that are out of touch with the values of a civilized society. Furthermore, such strategies do not guarantee the prevention of reoffending. It is by its very nature impossible to prevent new offenders offending because they have not formally been measured and therefore do not exist. Despite this there are occasional demands for so-called 'pre-delinquents' to be identified and tagged as a precaution against future unspecified offending. Again, this process is gendered with boys most commonly being identified as dangerous. Indeed, anti-social behaviour orders converts *nuisance* youngsters into *criminals* simply through a breach process.

The issue of unrealistic expectations is a factor that the probation service has faced when dealing with the fallout of the Monckton Enquiry in 2006. In this case, probation staff committed several errors, and the enquiry shows the contradictions impacting on probation policy and practice. It examined the issue of whether or not procedures followed and the decisions taken in this case were correct. The problem is that practitioners are urged to give their full attention to agency protocols although in doing this they are prompted to gloss over those issues usually dealt with as a matter of professional judgement (Senior et al., 2007). This proclivity to devote more time and attention to protocols also ignores a finding taken from the desistance literature, namely that change in individual offenders is often highly individual (Maruna, 2001; Farrall, 2002). As Bottoms has pointed out, an outcome of this is that risk assessment procedures will result in the calculation of false negatives and false positives (Bottoms, 1977). Subsequently, it is possible that a potential risk of offending is therefore not detected, which means that a victim is not adequately protected. Conversely, in contradistinction to Articles 5, 6 and 7 of the HRA it is possible that certain categories of male offenders are going to be wrongly assumed to be guilty.

It has been shown that from time to time risk and penal populism co-exist and any effective method of offender management, especially of serious offenders, will include an element of public protection. Risk management is therefore an essential part of the system. It must be noted, though, that defining a situation or a person as a risk and in need of a policy response is a political decision. Research evidence shows that it is violent men who are most likely to be labelled as a risk and in need of higher levels of surveillance and incapacitation.

Given that over a 10-year period, commencing in the mid-1990s, crime rates have fallen it could be argued that risk of crime victimization in general has reduced. Yet the tone of debate both in the popular press and in government circles is one of increasing concern about the risks to individuals and this is fed by occasional high profile cases which genuinely do challenge our protective capacities, for example the Soham murders[2]. Another feature of this process is the primacy of the private sector in delivering protective services – electronic surveillance, prison escorting, satellite tracking, lie detectors, etc. Their desire to develop their business and in a market in which contestability seems somewhat absent, can lead to an unregulated desire to extend control. As will be shown a little later on, the private sector is under no particular pressure to monitor the gender impact of its activities (i.e. there is no section 95 requirement) nor are human rights considerations pre-eminent. It has been argued elsewhere that unless there is a balance between the aims of protection, rehabilitation and restoration (Raikes, 2002) then the system ceases to be fit for purpose. The danger with risk is that it becomes a form of both proactive and retrospective profiling, potentially leading to a diminution of the human rights of some male offenders and suspects.

Risk and the courts
What is the role and influence of risk assessment and management in the courts? It is a responsibility of the judiciary to sit on parole hearings, including those instances where considerations about 'risk to the community' have a material impact on release date (Senior et al., 2007). Hudson (2003) has observed that practitioners are risk averse and the control of this phenomenon is based on conservative definitions of what it is to be dangerous, especially with reference to the optimum time for release and assumptions about certain categories of more or less exclusively male offenders who should never be released.

Currently, it seems that every time a person who is released commits another serious offence the outcome is an ever more cautionary atmosphere, restricting the discretion used in assessing early release applications. As Senior et al. (2007)

comment there is a paradox because on the whole the parole and lifer system works well and its judgements are sound. Despite this there are occasional outbreaks of moral panic accompanying the release of certain groups of potential releasees. Thus the courts may perpetuate stereotypes about some male offenders, overstating the threats they pose to the public (e.g. false positives).

Risk and youth justice
If our attention switches now to young people where, again, we are talking about boys, risk assessment and management is highly punitive and it can cancel out a needs-based focus. Risk assessment procedures for young people increasingly resemble those used in the adult correctional services. There is, as Brown argues, a youth justice system based on penal populist principles where:

> The so-called 'actuarial new penology' retains most of the aspects of the punitive 'old' penology within a framework of governance that is increasingly managerialized and interventionist in its 'centralized decentralization'. Inherently net-widening in both criminalizing incivilities and allocating punitive powers to non-justice based agencies and individuals, and is increasingly distanced from any notion of rights or social justice for young people in its aggressive promotion of a somewhat barbaric populism. (Brown, 2005: 99)

In the above quotation, Brown (2005) describes a situation in which actuarial risk management is a way of explaining youth crime and its causes, as well as the nature of the policy response to it. The main goals of this system are information sharing between agencies and the continual monitoring of the progress of cases. If we revisit the problem of ASB (see Chapter 5) this approach can be seen where the number of orders issued is deemed to be a success rather than attempts to come to terms with the underlying causes of ASB. In making risk as a guide to action the pre-eminent concern about the extent and prevalence of offending behaviour is residualized. In the 1970s crime prevention strategies were perceived to be problematic because they increased rates of youth custody but, as Hudson (2003) argues, in more recent times this is seen as an aspiration of a system that supports an early intervention even if there is no evidence of an incipient criminal career. Senior et al. (2007) show how a proliferation of programmes target 'at risk' children and young people and risk accelerating a criminal career. Again, these tendencies are gender specific with boys bearing the brunt of often discriminatory attention, although socio-economic factors and ethnicity may interact with masculinity.

Under these conditions there is the potential blurring of boundaries between criminal and non-criminal behaviour and media-led moral panic about 'hoodies', for example, lends support and credibility to policies based on ideas about risk reduction instead of confronting the causes of this behaviour (Jewkes, 2004).

The processes used in response to this are couched in managerial terms but the outcome is one in which a significant number of young people are being brought into the criminal justice system even though more appropriate interventions are available elsewhere. This is an effect of what Hudson (2003) calls risk controls where penal populism and risk management merge. Fortunately, this approach to reacting to the risks presented by young people is not automatic and during the writing of this book there have been changes, albeit small. The draconian impetus behind these developments actually led to the resignation of the Chair of the YJB, Rod Morgan, in January 2007. Quite surprisingly, a little later on in that year Cabinet ministers were expressing remarkably similar sentiments. In July 2007 Ed Balls signalled a departure – at least at a discursive level – from the tough talking Tony Blair when he opined that 'every ASBO is a failure' and that the children's department needed to address ASB in a different way by integrating health and education rather than over-punitive criminal justice measures (*Guardian*, 28 July 2007).

Risk assessment and management of risk are also central to crime analysis and offender profiling, which are increasingly important tools for the police service (Ainsworth, 2001). Gender is not an explicit component of risk assessment tools used by the police, yet men are targeted most and it is their human rights that are most susceptible to infringement. This focus on risk cannot be separated from the wider belief that we live in a 'risk society' where social agencies cannot resolve social problems but rather limit the most negative effects they cause (Beck, 1992). Ericson and Haggerty (1997) have drawn on this reasoning in their analysis of 'policing the risk society', an environment in which the police play an increased role in the production and dissemination of crime-related knowledge to a range of agencies beyond the police.

Thus, to sum up this section, risk assessment and management are explicitly underpinned by the logic of actuarial justice. Rather than individualized justice, offenders are assorted into groups whose members share characteristics in common. Such an approach to risk assessment and management provides a useful profiling tool, sometimes to predict who is going to offend. Such reasoning is evidenced by attempts to bring into the criminal justice system individuals who are potentially dangerous before they have committed an offence. This pressure has been resisted thus far, though we anticipate further calls to be made for predicting patterns of offending behaviour. Professionals will continue to call for rehabilitation but the punitiveness referred to in an earlier section could lead to calls for the segregation and exclusion of offenders rather than their rehabilitation.

Commercialization of crime control

The private sector is nowadays a major provider of crime reduction and security services, ranging from the regulation of the night-time economy (Winlow, 2001;

Hadfield, 2006) to private policing (Johnston, 2000) and private prisons (Matthews, 2000). Each of the above activities focuses mainly on men and/or masculine behaviour.

In more concrete terms we can see the commercialization of crime control in a number of areas, especially the installation and monitoring of security equipment such as CCTV (Goold, 2004; Fussey, 2005). In 2001 the Private Security Industry Act 2001 passed into law a new regulatory framework, including the creation of the licensing body known as the British Security Industry Authority (BSIA). This new framework has made it possible for the private security sector to give off an impression that it is professional and accountable in its operations. Data published in 2001 by the BSIA estimated that there were 8000 security companies and 350,000 employees in this sector in the UK (BSIA, 2001). This unprecedented expansion of private security must be situated in the context of structural changes in post-industrial societies, most crucially the privatization of what was at one time exclusively public space (Shearing and Stenning, 1981). The police service in England and Wales is not in a position to actively resist such changes and there are potential benefits. However, such developments reinforce earlier patterns of policing inasmuch as interpersonal relationships between men and women, however violent they may be, are not a preoccupation of private, for-profit enterprises.

The future looks like being a lucrative place for the private sector, as the commercialization of crime control seems set to continue (Senior et al., 2007). The correctional services have already been exposed to privatization in various jurisdictions and policing functions are increasingly being performed by private security agencies. In the United States, for example, gated communities exist in many urban areas, existing as a testament to the limitations of federal- and state-funded law enforcement. Surveillance systems such as CCTV and electronic tagging were once the stuff of science fiction novels and new technological innovations are materializing all the time. Similar developments are occurring throughout western European cities but not on the scale found across the Atlantic. A hazard with this approach is that socio-economic priorities are of paramount importance. The protection of private property is the priority unless that rare population of predatory strangers is acknowledged. Caution must be exercised because technological fixes such as CCTV are not able to address the underlying causes of crime and disorder. We do not anticipate any reversal of this trend and suggest that it may expand at an unprecedented rate. This is controversial, though, as it is likely to lead to a reawakening of debates about accountability and further undermine any of the remaining significance attached to the principle of both criminal and social justice. More than that, the commercialization of crime control will see mechanisms of control reflecting the interests of those paying for it without any wider reference to democratic values, gender equality and human rights.

Concluding thoughts

If anything the reader of this book will have been introduced to a range of disputes taking place in criminology about the relative significance of gender for understanding the multidimensional nature of crime, including its causes and control. For those of you who are new to criminology we hope to have awakened you to the injustices experienced by people on the grounds of their sex and gender, showing you how women are systematically disadvantaged in comparison to men. We should state here that we are indebted to the work of second wave feminists who ensured that gender now appears on the radar of criminologists and policy-makers, as well as those writers on men and masculinity who have taken seriously this critical intervention. It is also hoped that we have sketched the bare bones of another way of looking at this debate, by incorporating human rights discourse. There is much work yet to be done for those who are persuaded, even partially so, by our argument we believe it is a potentially fruitful way forward and a useful tool kit for assessing the flawed argument that things between men and women are all equal now.

Criminological theory and crime and public policy must now pay more than lip service to gender issues and this is undoubtedly a good thing. However, in late modern societies characterized by diversity and difference social divisions have not dissipated, rather the links between gender and crime are more complex and muddy. Despite legislation and a plethora of policy initiatives across the criminal justice sector gender-based differences are still profound. We have strived in this slim volume to expose continued as well as novel forms of inequality, some of which have arisen in part out of attempts to create equality. Ironically, our usage of human rights discourse, where the emphasis is on the universal, shows that universal principles must interact with the particular. Men and women have different social experiences as offenders, victims and workers and while all should be treated equally on the basis of universal values, there are powerful contradictions producing many paradoxes. While the dignity of all human beings must be respected this right must be based on an awareness of the fact that historically male power in the criminal justice arena subordinates female interests and sustains male power and influence at structural and individual levels.

Notes

1 This sentence was introduced by the Criminal Justice Act 2003.
2 This case refers to the murder of two young girls by the predatory paedophile, Ian Huntley. Although Huntley's criminal past was known to the authorities this information was not effectively communicated and consequently he was employed as a school caretaker, which gave him access to young children.

Glossary

Anti-social behaviour (ASB) – Behaviour that is not necessarily criminal but disorderly and causing people to be fearful.

Arrest – This is when a suspect is lawfully detained, usually by a police officer.

Attrition – The process resulting in criminal cases being dropped at various stages of the criminal justice system because of one of the following factors: (a) a case is **no-crimed**; (b) a case is not referred by the police to the **Crown Prosecution Service** (CPS); (c) the CPS decide that they will not proceed with a case; (d) if a defendant is found not guilty in a court of law.

Barrister – A professional lawyer acting as an advocate in the courts.

British Crime Survey – A survey set up by the Home Office to measure crime and victimization throughout England and Wales. This survey complements the recorded crime statistics gathered by the police (i.e. **notifiable offences**).

Circuit judge – The individuals in this role are full-time judges who are appointed by the Lord Chancellor. In most instances they are barristers and solicitors who belong to what is called the circuit bench.

Class (social class) – A person's class is normally assessed with reference to their occupation. Significantly there is a strong link between a person's job and their personal wealth and income.

Classical view of the offender – According to this view, the offender is a rational person who makes a conscious decision to commit crime. The threat of punishment exists to try and deter a person from committing a crime.

Code for Crown Prosecutors – These are the policies and procedures in place to guide the activities of the **Crown Prosecution Service (CPS)**.

Commission for Equality and Human Rights (CEHR) – Set up in 2007, the CEHR drives forward human rights and equality agendas and replaced the Equal Opportunity Commission (EOC), Commission for Racial Equality (CRE) and the Disability Rights Commission. It has a legal role to enforce equalities legislation in relation to sex and gender, as well as race/ethnicity, age, sexuality, disability, etc.

Community safety – This concept refers to the general well-being of a community and focuses on a range of hazards and threats beyond just crime.

Compensation – This penalty requires a offender to reimburse the victim for their losses.

Conviction – This refers to when a person is found guilty in a criminal court.

Crime – There are many definitions of crime, but one commonly used is the breaking of the law or the violation of a legal code.

Crime control model – In this approach a priority is arresting, charging, prosecuting and sentencing offenders effectively and efficiently. Advocates of this approach assume a suspect is guilty and that this is not something that must be proven beyond reasonable doubt.

Crime prevention – In general terms, this is all about methods of stopping crime from occurring.

Crime reduction – Put simply this is any method that aims to cut the number of crimes committed.

Criminal justice agencies – The police, crown prosecution, court, probation and prison services (the latter two belong to the National Offender Service (NOMS).

Criminal justice system – **Criminal justice agencies** are seen to work together in an integrated fashion in the wider context of the **state** and society.

Criminalization – This is the process which leads to particular groups being labelled as crime prone, which means they experience differential treatment by the police, courts and correctional agencies. A person is criminalized when their criminal status is dominant.

Criminology – This is the study of crime, including a focus on its causes and ways of reducing it.

Critical criminology – Society in general and the criminal justice system in particular is oppressive and discriminates against minority groups, such as women.

Crown Court – In this court trials on indictment (i.e. more serious sentences) are heard in front of a judge and jury.

Crown Prosecution Service (CPS) – The main function of this service is to prosecute most criminal cases.

Cult of masculinity – Masculine values are celebrated and seen as more worthy than other values. This cult tends to be associated with heterosexuality, physical power and risk-taking behaviour, and is strongly associated with what men do.

Curfew – An offender that is placed on curfew is required to be found in a particular place at a particular time.

Custody – To be in custody a person is either given a prison sentence or is detained by the police.

Custody minus – This sentence is intended to punish an offender in the community, but if they do not observe the conditions attached to this sentence they face a custodial or prison sentence.

Custody plus – For this sentence an offender spends a short time in prison followed by a longer period of supervision in the community.

Dark figure – This refers to the number of offences that are either not reported to the police or not recorded by the police when they are reported.

Defendant – This is someone who is put on trial because they are accused of committing a crime.

Determinism – An explanation of criminal behaviour that assumes offending is strongly influenced by social (structural), biological or psychological factors that are beyond the control of the individual.

Discharge – Those occasions when sentencers in the courts take no further action against a suspect.

Discretion – The selective application of legislation or policy.

Discrimination – This refers to the ways in which people are treated differently on the grounds of their sex, race/ethnicity, sexuality, age, etc. This differential treatment is typically negative and results in inequality.

District judge – Trained legal professionals (i.e. solicitors or barristers with a minimum of seven years's experience) who usually serve in larger courts in urban areas, and who are salaried. Unlike most magistrates they sit alone and tend to take on more lengthy and difficult cases.

Diversity – This refers to social differences, such as sex and gender, race/ethnicity and recognizes the different needs and wants of various groups or categories of people. Difference is celebrated rather than being seen as a problem.

Domestic violence – This is violence between current or ex-partners in the context of a personal relationship. The violence used may be physical as well as including psychological and emotional forms of abuse.

Due process – In contrast to the **crime control model** the criminal justice system must prove beyond reasonable doubt that the accused is guilty. Criminal justice agencies must observe all the rules and procedures to safeguard suspects.

Electronic tagging – The use of technological devices, such as an electronic tag, to monitor the movement of offenders.

Elitism – A concept of power which suggests power and influence is concentrated in the hands of a small group of influential actors and agencies. It is often contrasted with **pluralism**.

Equal opportunities – This idea assumes that all people should be given equal opportunities in all walks of life and that their gender, race, sexual orientation, etc. should not result in them experiencing any **discrimination** or be prevented from doing things that most people do.

Ethnicity – The culture, attitudes and beliefs of a particular social group. This is sometimes used interchangeably with **race**.

Ethnomethodology – A sociological approach that focuses on the individual social actor and their attempts to produce meaningful social interaction with other social actors.

Extra legal factors – The criminal justice system is there to enforce the law in a way that is just and fair, but the administration of justice is sometimes influenced by factors other than law, such as **discretion**. Relying on such factors often involves the use of prejudicial beliefs and attitudes about particular groups.

Family life – Article 8 of the Human Rights Act 1998 states that each person has a right to a private and family life. Evidence shows that this is not always observed and in this book this can be seen by looking at prisoners.

Fear of crime – While crime impacts on many people it is also clear that people worry about becoming a victim of crime. Such fears are now taken as seriously as actual victimization because it can cause significant harm and distress.

Female offender – More than describing females who offend, this idea draws attention to changing representations of this phenomenon, such as 'girl gangs', and the association of female crime with masculine forms of behaviour. The female offender is contrasted with stereotypical idea about female passivity.

Female sex offender – In relation to the female offender this notion concerns attempts to **search for equivalence** between male and female offenders, showing that females are capable of committing the most heinous crimes committed by men.

Feminist criminology – Approaches which highlight the differential and inequitable treatment of women in society.

Fine – A sentence of court involving a financial penalty.

Flexible working – Instead of rigid working patterns, such as the 9–5 routine and long, unsociable hours, this approach recognizes a need for different ways of working. Part-time working and 'flexi-time' are examples, but most significantly there is an appreciation that work needs to be balanced with other life commitments (e.g. parenting and other caring relationships).

Gender – The socially constructed categories of male and female.

Gender equality duty – This makes public authorities legally responsible for promoting gender equality and for tackling unlawful sex discrimination. Agencies need to be proactive rather than relying on members of the public making a complaint.

Gender relations – This idea was developed by Connell (2002). Rather than looking at gender in terms of static categories, such as men and women, he draws attention to the interaction between men and women, which produces more dynamic relationships between the two sexes.

Gendered organization theory – It is widely assumed that organizations such as the police service are gender neutral organizations where men and women experience organizational activities in the same ways. By contrast, this perspective shows that men and women have markedly different experiences at individual, cultural and structural levels.

Gendered substructure – In any organization there are social practices and arrangements that are influenced by gender. For example, workplace behaviour including the interaction between men and women and attitudes to work are based on gender specific assumptions.

Guilt – In criminal cases this needs to be established beyond reasonable doubt.

Hegemonic masculinity – Drawing on Gramsci's concept of hegemony this refers to a dominant form of masculinity which is used to organize **gender relations**. Hegemonic masculinity is the most highly valued form of masculinity towards which people orientate themselves. Crucially, it changes over time and there is no single hegemonic masculinity.

Heterosexist ideology – A set of attitudes and beliefs that promote heterosexuality (e.g. sexual relations between adult men and women) as the most acceptable and normal type of relationship. Homosexual and lesbian relationships are treated as inferior.

HM Inspectorate – These bodies carry out reviews of criminal justice agencies to ensure that their service delivery is efficient and effective. For example, there is an inspectorate for the police (Her Majesty's Inspectorate of Constabulary (HMIC), Her Majesty's Inspectorate of Probation (HMIP) and Her Majesty's Inspectorate of Prisons (HMIP).

Home Office – Government department responsible for the criminal justice system and law and order policies. In 2007 this department was changed with the creation of the Ministry of Justice, which assumed responsibility for probation, prisons and preventing reoffending.

Home Secretary – The minister in charge of policy at the Home Office.

Homophobic violence – This is violent crime motivated by negative feelings towards homosexual people. Like domestic violence, this can include emotional and psychological forms as well as physical harm.

Human rights – These are enshrined in various covenants and pieces of legislation, most notably the Human Rights Act 1998. The different articles making up the HRA rest on the premise that all people should be treated equally, fairly and with dignity. Our argument is that there needs to be a human rights framework that goes beyond legislation or the 'black letter law' perspective to consider wider debates about equality, justice and fairness, in particular citizenship.

Ideology – This is a set of ideas and beliefs that constitutes a coherent view of the social world and justifies particular courses of social actions, such as sexist **discrimination**.

Incarceration – The imprisonment of sentenced prisoners and persons awaiting trail.

Indeterminate sentence – A sentence that does not have a fixed period (e.g. a life sentence). This is in contrast to a determinate sentence.

Indictable offences – Crimes that are tried in the Crown Court.

Intermittent custody – A prison sentence which is spread over a longer period to ensure a prisoner can work in the week and go to prison at weekends.

Interpersonal violence – Crimes against the person, such as **domestic violence** and **homophobic violence**.

Judge – In the Crown Court this person sums up the court proceedings and provides direction relating to the necessary points of law.

Judicial diversity – Criminologists have shown over the years that the judiciary is dominated by men and that it is necessary for it to be more representative of the population it serves, thus including a more diverse population comprising a greater representation of women and minority ethnic groups.

Ladette – The behaviour of some girls is described as if they are adopting behavioural traits usually associated with boys, such as violence and aggression and heavy drinking.

Left realist criminology – A holistic explanation of crime that considers the complex causes of crime and solutions to offending behaviour.

Magistrate – This person passes sentence in the Magistrates' Courts.

Magistrates' Court – This is the lower court (i.e. the Crown Court is the higher one), which hears most criminal cases.

Marginalization – Some social groups, such as the **underclass**, are socially excluded and pushed to the edges of mainstream social life so that they do not experience the same rights as *included* individuals.

Masculinity/masculinities – Certain types of attitudes and behaviour are associated with men (e.g. masculinity), but it is recognized that there are many different types of masculinity that change over time and space. Hence masculinity needs to be seen in the plural (i.e. there are many masculinities). While masculinity is conventionally associated with men, women may adopt specific masculinities.

Mean girl – Rather like the **ladette**, this refers to aggression and substance misuse, drawing attention towards the cruelty of female offenders who are failing to conform with prevailing cultural expectations about what it is to be a girl.

Modernity – A set of ideas claiming that science and rational thought can be used by human beings to shape the external social world.

Moral panic – A reaction to a crime that is blown out of all proportion in comparison to its actual seriousness

Mothers in prison – This group of prisoners are particularly vulnerable and the right to private and family life (Article 8, Human Rights Act 1998) is not always fully observed.

New Public Management (NPM) (managerialism) – A method of public sector reform where there is an emphasis on economy, effectiveness and efficiency.

No-criming – A police practice where it is decided that an incident reported to them does not constitute a criminal offence.

Notifiable offences – These offences are those that are recorded by the police, including most indictable offences and triable either-way offences, also including a few summary offences.

Offence – Any behaviour which is prohibited by the criminal law.

Paedophilia – The sexually motivated abuse of children.

Pain – Victims of domestic violence experience physical and emotional suffering over an extended period.

Parole – The early release of prisoners from custody (i.e. prison).

Parole board – Takes decisions about whether, and when, to release prisoners.

Patriarchy – This word means the 'rule of the father' and radical feminists have adopted this idea to explain male dominance in social relations.

Plea – Defendants are able to say whether they are guilty of committing the offence with which they have been charged.

Pluralism – According to this perspective on **power**, power is distributed amongst a range of groups who compete in an open environment with each other to exert influence. It is contrasted with **elitism** in the sense that no particular groups dominate and that power is shared between many competing groups.

Police and policing – These two words are often used interchangeably but they relate to different things. The police is a specialist, bureaucratic organization that exercises legitimate force within a given territory to prevent crime and maintain the rule of law. Policing is a set of practices concerned with social control and surveillance that can be undertaken by a range of agencies (e.g. private security, individual citizens), not just the police.

Police culture – An outlook or world view which belongs specifically to police officers. It is usually connected with negative factors, such as sexism and racism, and tends to be concentrated amongst the rank and file. It is often described as something blocking effective police reform.

Policewomen – A word used to draw attention to the differential deployment and experiences of female police officers compared to their male counterparts.

Postmodernity and the postmodern – Challenges modernity and the values of scientific reason and rationality. The emphasis is on deconstructing social reality and recognizing the fragmentation of social life.

Power – In short, this is the capacity to effectively influence society and bring about change. Power can represent the interests of the many (**pluralism**) or the few (**elitism**) and for our purposes we show how power results in **discrimination** against women.

Probation – The activities performed by probation officers and the National Probation Service.

Psychosocial approaches – To understand masculinities it is necessary to consider psychic influences, in particular the irreducibility and rigidity of psychic identities. The psyche includes conscious and unconscious processes that are shaped by desire. Each person is engaged in splitting and projecting different parts of their personality, which may result in **interpersonal violence**.

Punitiveness – Policies that are influenced by ideologies that promote punishment as the most appropriate method of crime reduction. The greater the use of custodial penalties in any society, the more punitive it is.

Race – Usually this refers to the use of physical markers (i.e. the colour of a person's skin) to categorize people (e.g. white, black). In actual fact biological differences such as skin colour lack scientific credibility yet despite this race is treated as a real category, hence **racism**.

Racism – Some social groups are discriminated against because they are perceived to be not only different but inferior too. In other words, groups are arranged hierarchically, including dominant and subordinate groups. Racism can be seen at both an individual and an institutionalized level.

Radical criminology – According to this perspective there are dominant groups, such as men, who influence the activities of the criminal justice system. In doing this, the system systematically oppresses and disadvantages women.

Rape – A form of sexual violence involving unwanted penetration carried out by men against women and other men against their will. It is widely seen as an expression of individual, invariably male, power.

Rehabilitation – It is assumed by some criminologists that an offender can be reformed and eventually returned to normal life.

Remand – Depending on the seriousness of an offence, a suspect can be held in custody until the trial takes place.

Reparation – Some offenders are required to repair the damage they have done to their victim.

Respect agenda – Introduced by New Labour governments in the 2000s, this argues that the lack of respect for the values held by the decent and respectable majority, manifest in the form of crime and anti-social behaviour, pose a threat to civilized society.

Responsibilization – The **criminal justice system** cannot tackle crime and disorder on its own and it is necessary for more responsibility to be given to private and voluntary sector agencies, as well as individuals and communities. We are all in some way responsible for our own welfare and ensuring that we are not victimized.

Restorative justice – A offender may be required to meet with their victim in an attempt to right the wrong they have committed.

Retribution – A principle stating that criminals must be punished in order that they can appreciate that their actions are unlawful and wrong.

Search for equivalence – The view that men and women engage in crime in the same way and for the same reasons.

Secondary victimization – Following a person's initial victimization by an offender, some victims go on to experience further victimization at the hands of the criminal justice system. For example, insensitive cross-examination of rape victims by the defence.

Secret soundings – Part of the selection process used to appoint barristers and judges that involves informal, off-the-record communication to seek personal opinions about the suitability of a candidate.

Sentence(s) – These are passed by the courts and include fines, custodial or non-custodial (community-based) sentences.

Sexism – An ideology that treats men and women differently on the grounds of discriminatory assumptions.

Social class – A method of allocating people to socio-economic groups based on an individual's occupation.

Social divisions – The markers which make people different, including sex and **gender**, **social class**, **race** and **ethnicity**.

Social exclusion – A concept used to describe those people who are not able to participate in the social activities enjoyed by most people. Invariably it is used to describe the poorest members of society.

State – A complex idea that generally describes the more or less permanent legal and organizational framework which is there to control and manage society. Most crucially, the state defines the competencies and powers of its actors (e.g. judges) and agencies (e.g. the police).

State accountability – The activities of states need to be answerable to the wider community. In other words, the state cannot do what it wants without reference to legal principles like the HRA 1998.

Suicide and self-harm – These behaviours are prevalent in prisons, affecting women and men in different ways. It is our view that they both violate Article 2 of the HRA 1998, namely the right to life.

Summary offence – In addition to indictable and triable either-way offences, there are summary offences, which are only heard in Magistrates' Courts.

Surveillance – The mechanisms used to systematically observe and regulate places, people and things, such as closed circuit television (CCTV).

Suspect – An individual who is believed to be responsible for a criminal offence. A person remains a suspect until their guilt is proved beyond reasonable doubt.

The rights and needs of victims – In contrast to offenders who have the right to be presumed innocent until proven guilty beyond reasonable doubt, victims of crime do not have such formal rights. Indeed the status of victim is assumed by the state. Towards the end of the twentieth century there was talk about giving crime victims rights, but in practice victims have certain recognized needs for which there are available services.

Third Way – A political project set in motion which suggests that the distinction between right and left in politics is no longer tenable. It also claims that there is no alternative to capitalism, although the system needs some regulation.

Torture – The use of torture contravenes Article 7 of the HRA. In this book it is argued that **domestic violence** is a form of torture, thus adding to analyses that tend to see torture as something inflicted by the state and its agencies.

Triable either-way (T-E-W) – These offences may be tried either in the Crown Court or at a Magistrates' Court.

Underclass – The poorest and most deprived social groups, often alleged to be involved in criminal activity.

Victim – This is a person who has been affected by crime.

Victim precipitation – Early victimological research suggested that some victims of crime, especially of **interpersonal violence**, were to some degree responsible for their own victimization.

Victimization – The processes associated with the creation of a victim.

Victimology – The study of crime victims.

Vulnerability – Many offenders and victims are in a position of relative weakness, which means they are more susceptible to exploitation and discriminatory treatment.

Witness – A person who has either actually observed a crime being committed or who can provide information about an offence.

Women in prison – A population which expanded dramatically in the late 1990s and 2000s despite calls immediately prior to that period to restrict the imprisonment of women to the most violent. This population experience different needs to their male counterparts.

Youth Justice Board (YJB) – The agency overseeing youth justice policy and practice.

Youth Offending Team (YOT) – Teams set up to work exclusively with young people.

References

Acker, J. (1990) 'Hierarchies, Jobs, Bodies: A Theory of Gendered Organisations', *Gender and Society* 4(2): 139–58.

Acker, J. (1992) 'Gendering Organisational Theory', in A. Mills and P. Tancred (eds) *Gendering Organisational Analysis*. London: SAGE.

Adams, K. (2001) *Women in Senior Police Management*. Payneham, South Australia: Australasian Centre for Police Research.

Adler, S. (1975) *Sisters in Crime*. New York: McGraw-Hill.

Ainsworth, P. (2001) *Offender Profiling and Crime Analysis*. Cullompton: Willan Publishing.

Alder, C. and Worrall, A. (2004) 'A Contemporary Crisis?', in C. Alder and A. Worrall (eds) *Girls' Violence: Myths and Realities*, pp. 1–19. New York: SUNY.

Allen, J., Edmonds, S., Patterson, A. and Smith, D. (2006) *Policing and the Criminal Justice System – Confidence and Perceptions: Findings from the 2004–5 British Crime Survey*. Home Office Online Report 07/06. London: Home Office.

Amir, M. (1971) *Patterns of Forcible Rape*. Chicago, IL: University of Chicago Press.

Anderson, R., Brown, J. and Campbell, E. (1993) *Aspects of Sex Discrimination within the Police Service in England and Wales*. London: Home Office Police Research Group.

Appier, J. (1998) *The Sexual Politics of Law Enforcement and the LAPD*. Philadelphia, PA: Temple University Press.

Ashworth, A. (2003) *The Criminal Process* (3rd edn). Oxford: Oxford University Press.

Asthana, A. and Bright, M. (2004) 'Suicides Rise as Weekend Jail Fails Women', *Observer* 11 August.

Audit Commission (1996) *Misspent Youth*. London: Audit Commission.

Audit Commission (2004) *Youth Justice 2004: A Review of the Reformed Youth Justice System*. Wetherby: Audit Commission Publications.

Bachrach, P. and Baratz, M. (1970) *Power and Poverty*. New York: Oxford University Press.

Balfour, G. (2000) 'Feminist Therapy with Women in Prison: Working under the Hegemony of Correctionalism', in K. Hannah-Moffat, and M. Shaw (eds) *An Ideal Prison? Critical Essays on Women's Imprisonment in Canada*, pp. 94–102. Halifax: Fernwood Press.

Baron, J.N. and Davis-Blake, A. (1986) 'The Structure of Opportunity: How Far Promotion Ladders Vary Within and Among Organisations', *Administrative Science Quarterly*, 31: 248–73.

Bartlett, K.T. (1990) 'Feminist Legal Methods', *Harvard Law Review* 103: 829–88.

Bauman, Z. (1998) *Work, Consumerism and the New Poor*. Buckingham: Open University Press.

BAWP (2003) *Gender Agenda Force Survey Result*. London: British Association of Women Police.

Bayley, D.H. (1994) *Police for the Future*. New York: Oxford University Press.

Bayley, D.H. (2002) 'Policing Hate: What Can Be Done?', *Policing and Society* 12(2): 83–91.

Bean, P. (2004) *Drugs and Crime* (2nd edn). Cullompton: Willan Publishing.

Beck, U. (1992) *Risk Society*. London. SAGE.

Beirne, P. and J.W. Messerschmidt (2005) *Criminology* (4th edn). Los Angeles, CA: Roxbury.

Belknap, J. and Shelley, J.K. (1992) 'The New Lone Ranger: Policewomen on Patrol', *American Journal of Police* 12: 47–75.

Berk, S. and Loseke, D. (1981) '"Handling" Family Violence: Situational Determinants of Police Arrest in Domestic Disturbances', *Law & Society Review* 15(2): 317–46.

Bibi, N., Clegg, R. and Pinto, R. (2005) *Police Service Strength, England and Wales 31 March 2005*. Home Office Statistical Bulletin 12/05. London: Home Office.

Bielby, W.T. and Baron, J.N. (1987) 'Men and Women at Work: Sex Segregation and Statistical Discrimination', *American Journal of Sociology* 91: 759–99.

Bland, N., Mundy, G., Russell, J. and Tuffin, R. (1999) *Career Progression of Ethnic Minority Police Officers*, Police Research Series Paper 107. London: Home Office.

Bloch, F. and Rao, V. (2002) 'Terror as a Bargaining Instrument: A Case Study of Dowry Violence in Rural India', *The American Economic Review* 92(1): 1029–43.

Bloch, P. and Anderson, D. (1973) *Policewomen on Patrol: Major Findings: First Report*. Washington, DC: Police Foundation.

Bottoms, A.E. (1977) 'Reflections on the Renaissance of Dangerousness', *Howard Journal of Penology and Crime Prevention* 16: 70–96.

Bourlet, A. (1990) *Police Intervention in Marital Violence*. Milton Keynes: Open University Press.

Bowling, B. and Foster, J. (2002) 'Policing and the Police', in M. Maguire, R. Reiner and R. Morgan (eds) *The Oxford Handbook of Criminology* (3rd edn). Oxford: Clarendon Press.

Bowling, B. and Phillips, C. (2002) *Racism, Crime and Justice*. Harlow: Longman.

Bowling, B., Phillips, C., Campbell, A. and Docking, M. (2004) *Policing and Human Rights: Eliminating Discrimination, Xenophobia, Intolerance and the Abuse of Power from Police Work*, Identities, Conflict and Cohesion Programme Paper Number 4. Geneva: United Nations Research Institute for Social Development.

Boyd, M., Mulvihill, M. and Myles, J. (1991) 'Gender, Power and Post-industrialism', *Canadian Review of Sociology and Anthropology* 28: 407–36.

Brookman, F. and Maguire, M. (2003) *Reducing Homicide: A Review of the Possibilities*, Home Office Online Report 01/03. London: Home Office.

Brown, J. (1997) 'Equal Opportunities and the Police in England and Wales, Past, Present and Future Possibilities', in P. Francis, P. Davies and V. Jupp (eds) *Policing Futures*. Macmillan: London.

Brown, J. (1998) 'Aspects of Discriminatory Treatment of Women Police Officers Serving in Forces in England and Wales', *British Journal of Criminology* 38(2): 265–83.

Brown, J. (2003) 'Women Leaders: A Catalyst for Change', in R. Adlam and P. Villiers (eds) *Police Leadership in the Twenty-First Century: Philosophy, Doctrine and Developments*. Winchester: Waterside Press.

Brown, J. and Heidensohn, F. (2000) *Gender and Policing*. London: Macmillan.

Brown, S. (2005) *Understanding Youth and Crime: Listening to Youth*. Maidenhead: Open University Press.

BSIA (2001) 'Interesting Facts and Figures in the UK Security Industry' available at www.bsia.co.uk/industry.html

Bullock, K. and Tilley, N. (2002) *Shootings, Gangs and Violent Incidents in Manchester: Developing a Crime Reduction Strategy*, Home Office Research Series Paper 13. London: Home Office.

Bunting, M. (2007) 'This Equality Road Map Must Now Apply to Men', *Guardian* 24 July.

Burke, M.E. (1993) *Coming out of the Blue*. London: Cassell.

Burney, E. (2002) 'Talking Tough, Acting Coy: What Happened to the Anti-social Behaviour Order?', *The Howard Journal* 41(5): 469–84.

Burney, E. (2005) *Making People Behave: Anti-social Behaviour, Policy and Politics*. Cullompton: Willan Publishing.

Burton, C. (1992) 'Merit and Gender: Organisations and the Mobilisation of Masculine Bias', in A. Mills and P. Tancred (eds) *Gendering Organisational Analysis*. London: SAGE.

Butler, T. and Watt, P. (2007) *Understanding Social Inequality*. London: SAGE.

Byrne, C. and Trew, K. (2005) 'Crime Orientation, Social Relations and Improvement in Crime: Patterns Emerging From Offenders' Accounts', *Howard Journal* 44(2): 185–205.

Caddle, D. and Crisp, D. (1997) *Imprisoned Women and Mothers*, Home Office Research Study 162. London: Home Office.

Cain, M. (1973) *Society and the Policeman's Role*. London: Routledge.

Cain, M. (1990) 'Towards Transgression: New Directions in Feminist Criminology', *International Journal of the Sociology of Law* 18(1): 1–18.

Campbell, A. (1991) *The Girls in the Gang* (2nd edn). Cambridge, MA: Blackwell.

Campbell, B. (1993) *Goliath: Britain's Dangerous Places*. London: Methuen.

Carlen, P. (1983) *Women's Imprisonment*. London: Routledge and Kegan Paul.

Carlen, P. (ed.) (2002) *Women and Punishment: the Struggle for Justice*. Cullompton: Willan Publishing.

Carlen, P. and Worrall, A. (1987) *Gender, Crime and Justice*. Milton Keynes: Open University Press.

Carlen, P. and Worrall, A. (eds) (2004) *Analysing Women's Imprisonment*. Cullompton: Willan Publishing.

Carlson, B., McNutt, L. and Choi, D. (2003) 'Childhood and Adult Abuse Among Women in Primary Health Care: Effects on Mental Health', *Journal of Interpersonal Violence* 18(8): 924–41.

Carter P. (2003) *Managing Offenders, Reducing Crime: A New Approach*. London: Cabinet Office.

Cassen, R. and Kingdon, G. (2007) *Tackling Low Educational Achievement*. York: Joseph Rowntree Foundation.

Chakrabarti, S. (2005) 'Rights and Rhetoric: The Politics of Asylum and Human Rights Culture in the United Kingdom', in L. Clements and P.A. Thomas (eds) *Human Rights Act: A Success Story?* Oxford: Blackwell Publishing.

Chambers, G. and Miller, A. (1983) *Investigating Rape*. Edinburgh: HMSO.

Chan, J.B.L. (1997) *Changing Police Culture: Policing in a Multicultural Society*. Cambridge: Cambridge University Press.

Chan, J. (2003) 'Police and New Technologies', in T. Newburn (ed.) *Handbook of Policing*. Cullompton: Willan Publishing.

Charlesworth, H. (1994) 'What are Women's International Human Rights?', in R. Cook (ed.) *Human Rights for Women: National and International Perspectives*. Philadelphia, PA: University of Pennsylvania Press.

Chesney-Lind, M. (1980) 'Rediscovering Lileth: Misogyny and the "New Female Criminality"', in C. Taylor Griffiths and M. Nance (eds) *The Female Offenders*. New York: Simon Fraser University.

Chesney-Lind, M. (1989) 'Girls' Crime and Woman's Place: Toward a Feminist Model of Female Delinquency', *Crime & Delinquency* 35(10): 5–29.

Chesney-Lind, M. (2004) 'Girls and Violence: Is the Gender Gap Closing? National Electronic Network on Violence Against Women' www.vawnet.org/DomesticViolence/Research/VAWnetDocs/ARGirlsViolence.php

Chesney-Lind, M. (2006) 'Patriarchy, Crime, and Justice: Feminist Criminology in an Era of Backlash', *Feminist Criminology* 1(1): 6–26.

Chesney-Lind, M. and Belknap, J. (2004) 'Trends in Delinquent Girls' Aggression and Violent Behavior: A Review of the Evidence', in M. Putallaz and P. Bierman (eds) *Aggression, Antisocial Behavior and Violence Among Girls: A Development Perspective*, pp. 203–22. New York: Guilford.

Chesney-Lind, M. and Hagedorn, J.M. (eds) (1999) *Female Gangs in America: Essays on Gender and Gangs*. Chicago, IL: Lakeview Press.

Chesney-Lind, M. and Irwin, K., (2004) 'From Badness to Mean-ness: Popular Constructions of Contemporary Girlhood', in A. Harris (ed.) *All About the Girl: Culture, Power and Identity*, pp. 45–56. New York: Routledge.

Chesney-Lind, M. and Shelden, R.G. (1998) *Girls, Delinquency and Juvenile Justice*. Belmont, CA: Wadsworth.

Chigwada, R. (1999) *Black Women's Experiences of Criminal Justice*. Winchester: Waterside Press.

Choongh, S. (1997) *Policing as Social Discipline*. Oxford: Oxford University Press.

Choongh, S. (1999) *Policing as Social Discipline* (2nd edn). Oxford: Oxford University Press.

Clarke, J. and Newman, J. (1997) *The Managerial State. Power, Politics and Ideology in the Remaking of Social Welfare*. London: SAGE.

Clements, L. and Young, J. (1999) 'Human Rights: Changing the Culture', *Journal of Law and Society* 26: 1–26.

Cockburn, C. (1991) *In the Way of Women: Men's Resistance to Sex Equality in Organizations*. London: Macmillan.

Cohen, S. (1998) 'Intellectual Scepticism and Political Commitment: The Case of Radical Criminology', in P. Walton and J. Young (eds) *The New Criminology Revisited*. London: Macmillan.

Cohen, S. (2001) *States of Denial: Knowing About Atrocities and Suffering*. Cambridge: Polity Press.

Cohen, S. (2006) 'Neither Honesty nor Hypocrisy: The Legal Reconstruction of Torture', in T. Newburn and P. Rock (eds) *The Politics of Crime Control Essays in Honour of David Downes*. Oxford: Oxford University Press.

Cohn, S. (1985) *The Feminization of Clerical Labor in Great Britain*. Philadelphia, PA: Temple University Press.

Coleman, C. and Moynihan, J. (1996) *Understanding Crime Data: Haunted by the Dark Figure*. Milton Keynes: Open University Press.

Coleman, M. and Reed, E. (2007) 'Homicide', in K. Coleman, K. Jansson, P. Kaiza and E. Reed (eds) *Homicides, Firearm Offences and Intimate Violence 2005–2007*, Home Office Statistical Bulletin 02/07. London: Home Office.

Colgan, F. and Ledwith, S. (1996) 'Women as Organisational Change Agents', in S. Ledwith and F. Colgan (eds) *Women in Organisations: Challenging Gender Politics*. London: Macmillan.

Collier, R. (1998) *Masculinities, Crime and Criminology: Men, Heterosexuality and the Criminal(ised) Other*. London: SAGE.

Collison, M. (1996) 'In Search of the High Life: Drugs, Crime, Masculinities and Consumption', *British Journal of Criminology* 36(3): 428–44.

Comack, E. (1996) *Women in Trouble*. Halifax: Fernwood Press.

Comack, E. (1999) 'New Possibilities for a Feminism "in" Criminology? From Dualism to Diversity', *Canadian Journal of Criminology* 4(2): 161.

Connell, R.W. (1987) *Gender and Power: Society, the Person, and Sexual Politics*. Stanford, CA: Stanford University Press.

Connell, R.W. (1995) *Masculinities*. Berkeley, CA: University of California Press.

Connell, R.W. (2000) *The Men and the Boys*. Sydney: Allen and Unwin.

Connell, R.W. (2002) *Gender*. Cambridge: Polity Press.

Connell, R.W. and Messerschmidt, J. (2005) 'Hegemonic Masculinity: Rethinking the Concept', *Gender and Society* 19(6): 829–59.

Cook, D. (2006) *Criminal and Social Justice*. London: SAGE.

Cook, P.W. (1997) *Abused Men: The Hidden Side of Domestic Violence*. Westport, CT: Greenwood.

Cook, R. (1993) 'Women's International Human Rights Law: The Way Forward', *Human Rights Quarterly* 15: 230–61.

Cook, R. (1994a) 'Women's International Human Rights Law: The Way Forward', in R. Cook, (ed.) *Human Rights of Women: National and International Perspectives*. Philadelphia, PA: Pennsylvania Press.

Cook, R. (ed.) (1994b) *Human Rights for Women: National and International Perspectives*. Philadelphia, PA: University of Pennsylvania Press.

Coomaraswamy, R. (1999) 'Reinventing International Law: Women's Rights as Human Rights in the International Community', in P. Van Ness (ed.) *Debating Human Rights: Critical Essays from the United States and Asia*, pp. 167–83. London: Routledge.

Coomaraswamy, R. and Kois, L. (1999) 'Violence Against Women', *Women and International Human Rights* 1: 177–217.

Cope, N. (2003) 'Crime Analysis: Principles and Practice', in T. Newburn (ed.) *Handbook of Policing*. Cullompton: Willan Publishing.

Copelon, R. (1994) 'Intimate Teror: Understanding Domestic Violence as Torture', in Cook, R. (ed.) (1994) *Human Rights of Women: National and International Perspectives*. Philadelphia, PA: Pennsylvania Press.

Costigan, R. and Thomas, P. (2005) 'The Human Rights Act: A View from Below', in L. Clements and P.A. Thomas (eds) *Human Rights Act: A Success Story?* Oxford: Blackwell Publishing.

Council of Europe (2002) Parliamentary Assembly of the Council of Europe (2002) Recommendation on Domestic Violence, 1582. Adopted 27 September 2002 in UNIFEM (2003) 'Not a Minute More: Ending Violence Against Women'. New York: UNIFEM.

Crime, Social Control and Human Rights: Downes, D. Rock P., Chinkin, C. and Gearty, C. (2007) *Crime, Social Control and Human Rights: From Moral Panics to States of Denial*. Cullompton: Willan Publishing.

Crisp, D. and Stanko, B. (2001) 'Monitoring Costs and Evaluating Needs', in J. Taylor-Browne (ed.) *What Works in Domestic Violence? A Comprehensive Guide for Professionals*. London: Whiting and Birch.

Cromack, V. (1995) 'The Policing of Domestic Violence: An Empirical Study', *Policing and Society* 5: 185–99.

Crowther, C. (2000) 'Thinking About the Underclass: Towards a Political Economy of Policing', *Theoretical Criminology* 4(2): 149–67.

Crowther, C. (2007) *An Introduction to Criminology and Criminal Justice*. London: Palgrave.

D'Cruze, S. (ed.) (2000) *Everyday Violence in Britain 1850–1950: Gender and Class*. London: Longman.

Dahl, R.A. (1958) 'A Critique of the Ruling Elite Model', *American Political Science Review* 52(1): 463–69.

Daly, K. (1989) 'Rethinking Judicial Paternalism: Gender, Work–Family Relations, and Sentencing', *Gender & Society* 3(1): 9–36.

Daly, K. (1994) *Gender, Crime and Punishment*. New Haven, CT: Yale University Press.

Daly, K. and Wilson, M. (1988) *Homicide*. New York: Aldine De Gruyter.

Davies, A. (1998) *The Restructuring of Police Forces: Implications for Command Resilience*. Pangbourne: Police Superintendent's Association of England and Wales.

Davies, H., Nutley, S. and Smith, P. (eds) (2000) *What Works?: Evidence-based Policy and Practice in Public Services*. Bristol: Policy Press.

Davies, M., Croall, H. and Tyrer, J. (2005) *Criminal Justice: An Introduction to the Criminal Justice System in England and Wales* (3rd edn). Harlow: Pearson Longman.

Davies, P., Francis, P. and Greer, C. (2007) *Victims, Crime and Society*. London: SAGE.

Davis, R. and Willams, G. (2003) 'Reform of the Judicial Appointments Process: Gender and the Bench of the High Court of Australia', *Melbourne University Law Review* 27: 910–63.

DeKeseredy, W. and Schwartz, M. (1998, February) 'Measuring the Extent of Woman Abuse in Intimate Heterosexual Relationships: A Critique of the Conflict Tactics Scales' available at www.vawnet.org/DomesticViolence/Research/VAWnetDocs/AR_ctscrit.php

DeKeseredy, W., Sanders, D., Schwartz, M. and Alvi, S. (1997) 'The Meanings and Motives for Women's Use of Violence in Canadian College Dating Relationships', *Sociological Spectrum* 17: 199–222.

Department for Constitutional Affairs (2006) *Review of the Implementation of the Human Rights Act*. London: Department of Constitutional Affairs.

Department of Health (2002) *Women's Mental Health: Into the Mainstream – Strategic Development of Mental Health Care for Women* London: Department of Health.

DETR (1999) *Performance Indicators for 2000/2001. A Joint Consultation Document Produced by DETR and the Audit Commission on Best Value and Local Authority Performance Indicators for 2000/2001*. Wetherby: DETR Free Literature.

Diamond, P. (ed.) (2007) *Public Matters: the Renewal of the Public Realm*. London: Methuen Politicos.

Dingwall, G. (2005) *Alcohol and Crime*. Cullompton: Willan Publishing.

Dixon, M., Reed, H., Rogers, B. and Stone, L. (2006) *Crime Share: The Unequal Impact of Crime*. London: IPPR.

Dobash, R.E. and Dobash, R.P. (1992) *Women, Violence and Social Change*. London: Routledge.

Dobash, R.E., Dobash, R.P., Cavanagh, K. and Lewis, R. (2004) 'Not an Ordinary Killer – Just an Ordinary Guy: When Men Murder and Intimate Woman Partner', *Violence Against Women, An International and Interdisciplinary Journal* 10: 577–605.

Dobash, R.P. and Dobash, R.E. (1979) *Violence Against Wives*. New York: The Free Press.

Dobash, R.P. and Dobash, R.E. (2001) 'Violence Against Women: A Review of Recent Anglo–American Research', *Journal of Conflict and Violence Research* 3: 55-22.

Dobash, R.P. and Dobash, R.E. (2004) 'Women's Violence to Men in Intimate Relationships', *British Journal of Criminology* 44(3): 324–49.

Dorling, D. (2005) 'Prime Suspect: Murder in Britain', in P. Hillyard, C. Pantazis, S. Tombs, D. Gordan and D. Dorlin *Criminal Obsessions: Why Harm Matters More than Crime*. London: Crime and Society Foundation.

Downes, D. Rock, P., Chinkin, C. and Gearty, C. (2007) *Crime, Social Control and Human Rights: From Moral Panics to States of Denial*. Cullompton: Willan Publishing.

Dyer, C. (2004) 'Inquest Juries Blame Suicides on Jails, Law Lords Rule', *Guardian* 12 March 2004.

Eaton, M. (1986) *Justice for Women? Family, Court and Social Control*. Milton Keynes: Open University Press.

Eaton, M. (1993) *Women After Prison*. Buckingham: Open University Press.

Edwards, S. (1989) *Policing Domestic Violence: Women Law and the State*. London: SAGE.

Edwards, S. (2007) 'Female Genital Mutilation: Violence Against Girls and Women as a Particular Social Group', *Denning Law Journal*, 18: 271–8.

England, P. (1989) 'A Feminist Critique of Rational-choice Theories: Implications for Sociology', *The American Sociologist* 20: 14–28.

Equal Opportunities Commission (2004) *Long Hours Culture is Bad for Britain*. London: Equal Opportunities Commission.

Equal Opportunities Commission (2007) *Sex and Power: Who Runs Britain?* London: Equal Opportunities Commission.

Ericson, R. and Haggerty, K. (1997) *Policing the Risk Society*. Oxford: Clarendon Press.

Eurostat (2005) *European Social Statistics*. Luxembourg: Office for Official Publications of the European Communities.

Falconer, Lord (2005) *Increasing Judicial Diversity: The Next Steps* available at www.dca.gov.uk/speeches/2005.

Faragher, T. (1985) 'The Police Response to Violence Against Women in the Home', in J. Pahl, (ed.) *Private Violence and Public Policy*. London: Routledge and Kegan Paul.

Farrall, S. (2002) *Rethinking What Works with Offenders*. Cullompton: Willan Publishing.

Farrell, G. and Buckley, A. (1999) 'Evaluation of a Police Domestic Violence Unit using Repeat Victimization as a Performance Indicator', *Howard Journal of Criminal Justice and Crime Prevention* 38(1): 42–53.

Farrington, D.P. (1994) 'Human Development and Criminal Careers', in M. Maguire, R. Morgan and R. Reiner (eds) *The Oxford Handbook of Criminology*. Oxford: Oxford University Press.

Farrington, D.P. and Morris, A.M. (1983) 'Sex, Sentencing and Reconviction', *British Journal of Criminology* 30(4): 449–75.

Farrington, D.P., Coid, J.W., Harnett, L., Joliffe, D., Sorteriou, N., Turner, R. and West, D.J. (2006) *Criminal Careers Up To Age 50 and Life Success Up To 48*, Home Office Research Study No. 299. London: Home Office.

Faulkner, D. (2007) 'Prospects for Progress in Penal Reform', *Criminology and Criminal Justice* 7(2): 135–52.

Fawcett Society (2004) *Commission on Women and the Criminal Justice System*. London: Fawcett Society.

Fawcett Society (2006) *Justice and Equality*. London: Fawcett Society.

Fawcett Society (2007) *Women and Justice: Third Annual Review of the Commission on Women and the Criminal Justice System*. London: Fawcett Society.

Feeley, M. and Simon, J. (1994) 'Actuarial Justice: The Emerging New Criminal Law', in D. Nelken (ed.) *The Futures of Criminology*. London: SAGE.

Feinman, C. (1980) *Women in the Criminal Justice System*. New York: Praeger.

Feinman, C. (1986) 'Women in Law Enforcement' in C. Feinman (ed.) *Women in the Criminal Justice System* (2nd edn). New York: Praeger.

Ferguson, K. (1984) *The Feminist Case Against Bureaucracy*. Philadelphia, PA: Temple University Press.

Ferraro, K. (1989) 'The Legal Response to Woman Battering in the US', in J. Hanmer J. Radford and E. Stanko (eds) *Women, Policing and Male Violence*. London: Routledge.

Fielding, N. (1988) *Joining Forces: Police Training, Socialisation and Occupational Competence*. London: Routledge.

Fielding, N. (1994) 'Cop Canteen culture', in T. Newburn and E. Stanko (eds) *Just Boys Doing the Business; Men, Masculinity and Crime*. London: Routledge.

Finney, A. (2006) *Domestic Violence, Sexual Assault and Stalking: Findings from the 2004–5 British Crime Survey*, Home Office Online Study 12/06. London: Home Office.

Fionda, J. (2005) *Devils and Changes: Youth Policy and Crime*. Oxford: Hart.

Fitzgerald Report (1989) *Report of a Commission of Inquiry Pursuant to Orders in Council: Commission of Inquiry into Possible Illegal Activities and Associated Police Misconduct*. Brisbane: Queensland Government Printer.

Fitzpatrick, B., Seago, P., Walker, C. and Wall, D. (2001) 'The Courts: New Court Management and Old Court Ideologies', in M. Ryan, S.P. Savage and D.S. Wall, *Policy Networks in Criminal Justice*. Basingstroke: Palgrave.

Fitzpatrick, J. (1994) 'The Use of International Rights Norms to Combat Violence Against Women', in R. Cook (ed.) *Human Rights for Women: National and International Perspectives*. Philadelphia, PA: University of Pennsylvania Press.

Fleisher, M.C.S. (1998) *Dead End Kids: Gang Girls and the Boys They Know*. Madison, WI: Wisconsin University Press.

Flood-Page, C. Campbell, S., Harrington, V. and Miller, J. (2000) *Youth Crime: Findings from the 1998/1999 Youth Lifestyles Survey*. London: Home Office.

Foster, J., Newburn, T. and Souhami, A. (2005) *Assessing the Impact of the Stephen Lawrence Inquiry*, Home Office Research Study 294. London: Home Office.

France, A. (2007) *Understanding Youth in Late Modernity*. Milton Keynes: Open University Press.

Francis, B., Barry, J., Bowater, R., Miller, N., Soothill, K. and Ackerley, E. (2004) *Using Homicide Data to Assist Murder Investigations*, Home Office Online Report 26/04. London: Home Office.

Gadd, D. (2000) 'Masculinities, Violence and Defended Social Subjects', *Theoretical Criminology* 4(4): 429–49.

Gadd, D. (2002) 'Masculinities and Violence Against Female Partners', *Social and Legal Studies* 11(1): 61–80.

Gadd, D. (2003) 'Reading Between the Lines: Subjectivity and Men's Violence', *Men and Masculinites* 5(4): 33–354.

Gadd, D. (2006) 'The Role of Recognition in the Desistance Process: a Case Study of a Far Right Activist', *Theoretical Criminology* 10(2): 179–202.

Gadd, D. and Farrall, S. (2004) 'Criminal Careers, Desistance and Subjectivity: Interpreting Men's Narrative of Change', *Theoretical Criminology* 8(2): 123–56.

Gadd, D., Farrall, S., Lombard, N. and Dallimore, D. (2002) *Domestic Abuse Against Men in Scotland*. Edinburgh: Scottish Executive.

Gadd, D. and Jefferson, T. (2007) *Psychosocial Criminology: An Introduction*. London: SAGE.

Garland, D. (2001) *The Culture of Control: Crime and Social Order in Contemporary Society*. Oxford: Oxford University Press.

Garside, R. (2006) *Right for the Wrong Reasons: Making Sense of Criminal Justice Failure*. London: Crime and Society Foundation.

Gelsthorpe, L. (1989) *Sexism and the Female Offender*. Aldershot: Gower.

Gelsthorpe, L. (2006) 'Counterblast: Women and Criminal Justice: Saying it Again, Again and Again', *The Howard Journal* 45(4): 421–4.

Gelsthorpe, L. and Morris, A. (eds) (1990) *Feminist Perspectives in Criminology*. Buckingham: Open University Press.

Gelsthorpe, L. and Padfield, N. (eds) (2003) *Exercising Discretion: Decision Making in the Criminal Justice System and Beyond*. Cullompton: Willan Publishing.

George, M. and Yarwood, D. (2004) *Male Domestic Violence Victims Survey 2001: Main Findings* available at http://dewar4research.org/DOCS/mdv.pdf (last accessed 10 January 2007)

Giddens, A. (1999) *The Third Way*. Cambridge: Polity.

Giddens, A. (2007) *Over to You, Mr Brown*. Cambridge: Polity Press.

Gilligan, C. (1982) *In a Different Voice: Psychological Theory and Women's Development*. Cambridge, MA: Harvard University Press.

Golding, J. (1996) 'Sexual Assault History and Women's Reproductive and Sexual Health', *Psychology of Women Quarterly* 20: 101–21.

Goldman, S. (1979) 'Should There be Affirmative Action for the Judiciary?', *Judicature* 62: 489.

Goldson, B. (2002) *Vulnerable Inside: Children in Secure and Penal Settings*. The Children's Society.

Goldson, B. and Jamieson, J. (2002) 'Youth Crime, the "Parenting Deficit" and State Intervention: A Contextual Critique', *Youth Justice* 2(2): 82–99.

Goodey, J. (1997) 'Boys Don't Cry: Masculinity, Fear of Crime and Fearlessness', *British Journal of Criminology* 37: 401–18.

Goodey, J. (2005) *Victims and Victimology: Research, Policy and Practice*. London: Longman.

Grace, S. (1995) *Policing Domestic Violence in the 1990s*, Home Office Research Study No. 139. London: HMSO.

Grace, S., Lloyd, C. and Smith, L. (1992) *Rape: From Recording to Conviction*, Research and Planning Unit Paper 71. London: Home Office.

Grady, A. (2002) 'Female-on-Male Domestic Abuse: Uncommon or Ignored', in C. Hoyle and R. Young (eds) *New Visions of Crime*. Portland, Oregon: Hart.

Graham, J. and Bowling, B. (1995) *Young People and Crime*. Home Office Research Study 145. London: Home Office.

Graham, K. and Wells, S. (2003) '"Somebody's Gonna Get Their Head Kicked in Tonight!": Aggression Among Young Males in Bars – A Question of Values', *British Journal of Criminology* 43: 546–66.

Graham, R. (2006) 'Male Rape and the Careful Construction of the Male Victim', *Social and Legal Studies* 15: 187–208.

Gramsci, A. (1971) *Selection from the Prison Notebooks*. London: Lawrence and Wishart.

Grant, I. and Smith, L. (1991) 'Gender Representation in the Canadian Judiciary', in *Appointing Judges: Philosophy, Politics and Practice*. Ontario: Ontario Law Reform Commission.

Graycar, R. and Morgan, J. (2002) *The Hidden Gender of Law* (2nd edn). Sydney: Federation Press.

Gregory, J. and Lees, S. (1999) *Policing Sexual Assault*. London: Routledge.

Grennan, S.A. (1987) 'Findings on the Role of Officer Gender in Violent Encounters with Citizens', *Journal of Police Science and Administration* 15: 78–85.

Griffith, J. (1997) *The Politics of the Judiciary* (5th edn). London: Fontana Press.

Hadfield, P. (2007) *Bar Wars: Contesting the Night in Contemporary British Cities*. Oxford: Oxford University Press.

Hale, B. (2001) Equality and the Judiciary: Why Should we Want More Women Judges?', *Public Law*, 489.

Halford, S., Savage, M. and Witz, A. (1997) *Gender, Career and Organisations: Current Developments in Policing, Nursing and Local Government*. London: Macmillan.

Hall, E. (1993) 'Smiling, Deferring, and Flirting: Doing Gender by Giving "Good Service"', *Work and Occupations*, 20(4): 452–71.

Hall, S. (1997) 'Visceral Cultures and Criminal Practices', *Theoretical Criminology* 1(4): 453–78.

Hall, S. (2002) 'Daubing the Drudges of Fury: Men, Violence and the Piety of the "Hegemonic Masculinity" Thesis', *Theoretical Criminology* 6(1): 35–61.

Hall, S. and Winlow, S. (2003) 'Rehabilitating Leviathan: Reflections on the State, Economic Regulation and Violence Reduction', *Theoretical Criminology* 7(2):

Hall, S., Critcher, C., Jefferson, T., Clarke, J. and Roberts, B. (1978) *Policing the Crisis: Mugging, the State and Law and Order*. London: Macmillan.

Halliday, F. (2007) 'The Fates of Solidarity and Abuse' in D. Downes, P. Rock, C. Chinkin and C. Gearty *Crime, Social Control and Human Rights: From Moral Panics to States of Denial*. Cullompton: Willan Publishing.

Halliday Report (2001) *Making Punishments Work: Report of a Review of the Sentencing Framework for England and Wales*. London: Home Office.

Hallsworth, S. (2005) *Street Crime*. Cullompton: Willan Publishing.

Hallsworth, S. and Young, T. (2004) 'Getting Real About Gangs', *Criminal Justice Matters* 55: 12–13.

Hanmer, J. and Maynard, M. (eds) (1987) *Women, Violence and Social Control*. London: Macmillan.

Hanmer, J. and Saunders, S. (1990) *Women, Violence and Crime Prevention: A Study of Changes in Police Policy and Practices in West Yorkshire*, Violence, Abuse and Gender Relations Study Unit Research Paper 1. Bradford: Bradford University.

Hanmer, J. and Saunders, S. (1991) 'Policing Violence against Women: Implementing Policy Changes', paper presented to the British Criminology Conference, York, July.

Hannah-Moffat, K. (2002) in Carlen, P. (ed.) *Women and Punishment: the Struggle for Justice*. Cullompton: Willan Publishing.

Harper, G. and Chitty, C. (2005) *The Impact of Corrections on Re-offending: A Review of What Works*. Home Office Research Study 291. London: Home Office.

Harper, G. Man, L-H., Taylor, S. and Niven, S. (2005) 'Factors associated with offending', in G. Harper and C. Chitty (2005) *The Impact of Corrections on Re-offending: A Review of What Works*. Home Office Research Study 291. London: Home Office.

Harrington, V. and Mayhew, P. (2001) *Mobile Phone Theft*, Home Office Research Study 235. London: Home Office.

Harris, A. (1977) 'Sex and Theories of Deviance' *American Sociological Review* 42(1): 44–71.

Harris, J. and Grace, S. (1999) *A Question of Evidence? Investigating and Prosecuting Rape in the 1990s*. London: Home Office.

Hart, B. (1993) 'Battered Women and the Criminal Justice System', *American Behavioral Science* 36: 624–38.

Hay, C. (1999) *The Political Economy of New Labour: Labouring Under False Pretences?* Manchester: Manchester University Press.

Hayman, S. (2006) 'Reforming the Prison: a Canadian Tale', in F. Heidensohn, (ed.) *Gender and Justice: New Concepts and Approaches.* Cullompton: Willan Publishing.

Hearn, J. (1998) *The Violences of Men.* London: SAGE.

Hearn, J. (2003) '"Just Men Doing Crime" (and Criminology)', *Criminal Justice Matters* 53 (Autumn): 12–13.

Hearn, J. and Parkin, W. (1987) *'Sex' at 'Work': The Power and Paradox of Organization Sexuality.* New York: St. Martin's Press.

Hearn, J. and Whitehead, A. (2006) 'Collateral Damage: Men's Domestic Violence to Women Seen Through Men's Relations With Men', *Probation Journal* 53(1): 38–56.

Hearn, J., Sheppard, D.L., Tancred-Sheriff, P. and Burrell, G. (eds) (1989) *Gendering Organizational Analysis.* London: SAGE.

Hedderman, C. (2004) 'Why are More Women being Sentenced to Custody?' in G. McIvor (ed.) *Women who Offend.* London: Jessica Kingsley.

Heidensohn, F. (1985) *Women and Crime.* London: Macmillan.

Heidensohn, F. (1992) *Women in Control: The Role of Women in Law Enforcement.* Oxford: Oxford University Press.

Heidensohn, F. (1994) 'From Being to Knowing: Some Issues in the Study of Gender in Contemporary Society', *Women and Criminal Justice* 6: 13–37.

Heidensohn, F. (1996) *Women and Crime* (2nd edn) London: Macmillan.

Heidensohn, F. (2000) *Sexual Politics and Social Control.* Buckingham: Open University Press.

Heidensohn, F. (2003) 'Gender and Policing', in T. Newburn (ed.) *The Handbook of Policing.* Cullompton: Willan Publishing.

Heidensohn, F. (ed.) (2006) *Gender and Justice: New Concepts and Approaches.* Cullompton: Willan Publishing.

Heidensohn, F. and Rafter, N. (eds) (1999) *International Feminist Perspectives in Criminology: Engendering a Discipline.* Milton Keynes: Open University Press.

Herek, G. and Berrill, K.T. (eds) (1992) *Hate Crimes: Confronting Violence Against Lesbians and Gay Men.* London: SAGE.

HM Chief Inspector of Prisons (1990) *Suicide and Self-harm in Prison Service Establishments in England & Wales.* London: HMSO.

HM Chief Inspector of Prisons (1997) *Women in Prison: A Thematic Review.* London: Home Office.

HM Chief Inspector of Prisons (1999) *Suicide is Everyone's Concern: A Thematic Review.* London: Home Office.

HM Chief Inspector of Prisons (2003) Northern Ireland Prison Service, *Report of a full Announced Inspection of HM Prison Maghaberry,* 13–17 May 2002.

HM Chief Inspector of Prisons (2005) Annual Report of Prisons for England & Wales, 2003–4, 26 January.

HMCPSI and HMIC (2002) *A Report on the Joint Inspection into the Investigation and Prosecution of Cases involving Allegations of Rape.* London: HMCPSI and HMIC.

HM Crown Prosecution Inspectorate (HMCPSI) (2007) *Without Consent.* HMIC.

HM Inspectorate of Prisons (2004) *Expectations: Criteria for Assessing the Conditions in Prisons and the Treatment of Prisoners.* London: HMSO.

HM Inspectorate of Probation (2006a) *An Independent Review of a Serious Further Offence Case: Anthony Rice*. London: Home Office.

HM Inspectorate of Probation (2006b) *An Independent Review of a Serious Further Offence Case: Damien Hanson and Elliott White*. London: Home Office.

Hester, M. (2000) 'Child Protection and Domestic Violence', in J. Hamner and C. Itzin *Home Truths about Domestic Violence: Feminist Influences on Policy and Practice*. London: Routledge.

Hester, M.L., Kelly, L. and Radford, J. (1996) *Women, Violence and Male Power*. Buckingham and Philadelphia: Open University Press.

Hill, A. and Hellmore, E. (2002) 'Mean Girls', *Observer* 2002.

Hill, M. (ed.) (1993) *New Agendas in the Study of the Policy Process*. London: Harvester Wheatsheaf.

Hillyard, P., Sim, J., Tombs, S. and Whyte, D. (2004) 'Leaving a Stain Upon the Silence: Contemporary Criminology and the Politics of Dissent', *British Journal of Criminology* 44(3): 369–90.

Hird, C. (2006) 'Overview of Violent Crime', in K. Coleman, C. Hird and D. Povey (eds) *Violent Crime Overview: Homicide and Gun Crime in England and Wales 2004/05*, Home Office Statistical Bulletin 02/06. London: HMSO.

Hobbs, D. (1995) *Bad Business: Contemporary Professional Crime, Culture and Change*. Oxford: Oxford University Press.

Hobbs, D., Hadfield, P., Lister, S. and Winlow, S. (2003) *Bouncers: Violence and Governance in the Night-time Economy*. Oxford: Oxford University Press.

Hobbs, D., Winlow, S., Hadfield, P. and Lister, S. (2005) 'Violent Hypocrisy: Governance and the Night-time Economy', *European Journal of Criminology* 2(2): 161–83.

Hogarth, T., Hasluck, C., Pierre, G., Winterbotham, M. and Vivian, D. (2001) *Work–Life Balance 2000: Baseline Study of Work–Life Balance Practices in Great Britain*, Summary Report. London: Institute for Employment Research and IFF Research.

Holdaway, S. (1983) *Inside the British Police*. Oxford: Basil Blackwell.

Homant, R.J. and Kennedy, D.B. (1985) 'Police Perceptions of Spouse Abuse: A Comparison of Male and Female Officers', *Journal of Criminal Justice* 13: 29–47.

Home Office (1986) *Domestic Violence – Guidance to the Police*, Circular 69/86. London: HMSO.

Home Office (1990) *Domestic Violence – Guidance to the Police*, Circular 60/90. London: HMSO.

Home Office (1997) *No More Excuses: A New Approach to Tackling Youth Crime in England and Wales*. London: Home Office.

Home Office (1998) *The Crime and Disorder Act: Community Safety and the Reduction and Prevention of Crime – A Conceptual Framework for Training and the Development of a Professional Discipline*. London: Home Office.

Home Office (2000a) *Government's Strategy for Women Offenders*. London: Home Office.

Home Office (2000b) *Domestic Violence – Guidance to the Police*, Circular 19/2000. London: HMSO.

Home Office (2001) *A Review of the Victim's Charter*. London: HMSO.

Home Office (2003) *Safety and Justice: The Government's Proposal on Domestic Violence*. London: Home Office.

Home Office (2004a) *Statistics on Women and the Criminal Justice System 2003: A Home Office Publication Under Section 95 of the Criminal Justice System*. London: Home Office.

Home Office (2004b) *Building Communities, Beating Crime: A Better Police Service for the 21st Century*. London: HMSO.

Home Office, (2004c) *Women's Offending Reduction Programme*. London: Home Office.

Home Office (2005a) *National Policing Plan 2003–2006*. London: Home Office.

Home Office (2005b) *Rebuilding Lives: Supporting Victims of Crime*, Cm 6705. London: Home Office.

Home Office (2005c) *Domestic Violence: A National Report*. London: Home Office.

Home Office (2006a) *Respect Action Plan*. London: Home Office.

Home Office (2006b) *Respect Academy 2006*. London: Home Office.

Home Office (2006c) *Statistics on Race and the Criminal Justice System: A Home Office Publication of Section 95 of the Criminal Justice Act 1991*. London: HMSO.

Home Office (2006d) *Statistics on Women and the Criminal Justice System 2005/05: A Home Office Publication Under Section 95 of the Criminal Justice System*. London: Home Office.

Home Office (2006e) *Rebalancing the Criminal Justice System in Favour of the Law-abiding Majority: Cutting Crime, Reducing Reoffending and Protecting the Public*. London: Home Office.

Home Office (2007) *Corston Report: A Review of Women with Particular Vulnerabilities in the Criminal Justice System*. London: Home Office.

Home Office (2007a)

Home Office (2007b)

Home Office Review of Sex Offences (2000a) *Setting the Boundaries: Reforming the Law on Sex Offences* (Volume 1). London: Home Office Communication Directorate.

Home Office Review of Sex Offences (2000b) *Setting the Boundaries: Reforming the Law on Sex Offences* (Volume 2). London: Home Office Communication Directorate.

Hood, R. (1992) *Race and Sentencing*. Oxford: Clarendon Press.

Hood-Williams, C. (2001) 'Gender, Masculinities and Crime: Form Structures to Psyches', *Theoretical Criminology* 5(1): 37–60.

Hopkins Burke, R. (2005) *An Introduction to Criminological Theory* (2nd edn). Cullompton: Willan Publishing.

Hopkins Burke, R. and Morrill, R. (2004) 'Human Rights v. Community Rights: The Case of the Anti-social Behaviour Order', in R. Hopkins Burke (ed.) *Hard Cop, Soft Cop: Dilemmas and Debates in Contemporary Policing*. Cullompton: Willan Publishing.

Horne, R. and Hall, S. (1995) 'Anelpis: a preliminary expedition into a world without hope or potential', *Parallax: A Journal of Metadiscursive Theory and Cultural Practices* 1(1): 81–92.

Hough, M. (2004) 'Modernisation, Scientific Rationalism and the Crime Reduction Programme', *Criminal Justice* 4(3): 239–53.

Houldcroft, L. (2002) 'Bullying Girls who Make Lives a Misery, *The Journal* 6: 16–34.

Howard League for Penal Reform (1997) *Lost Inside: The Imprisonment of Teenage Girls*, Report of the Howard League Inquiry into the use of Prison Custody for Girls Aged Under 18. London: Howard League.

Howard League for Penal Reform (2002) submission to the UN Committee on the Rights of the Child, *Children in Prison – Barred Rights*. London: Howard League.

Hoyle, C. and Zedner, L. (2007) 'Victims, Victimisation and the Criminal Justice System', in M. Magurie, R. Margan and R. Reiner (eds.) *Oxford Handbook of Criminology* (4th edn) Oxford: Oxford University Press.

Hoyle, C. and Young, R. (2003) 'Restorative Justice, Victims and the Police', in T. Newburn (ed.) *Handbook of Policing*. Cullompton: Willan Publishing.

Hudson, B. (2003) *Justice in the Risk Society: Challenging and Re-affirming Justice in Late Modernity*. London: SAGE.

Hudson, R. (1986) 'Producing an Industrial Wasteland: Capital, Labour and the State in the North East of England', in R. Martin and B. Rowthorn (eds) *The Geography of Deindustrialisation*. London: Macmillan.

Hughes, G. (2007) *The Politics of Crime and Community*. Basingstoke: Palgrave.

Hughes, G. and Muncie, J. (2002) 'Modes of Youth Governance: Political Rationalities, Criminalisation and Resistance', in J. Muncie, G. Hughes and E. McLaughlin (eds) *Youth Justice: Critical Readings*. Milton Keynes: Open University Press.

Human Rights Watch (2006) *World Report: Events of 2005*. New York: United States.

Humphreys, C. and Thiara, R. (2002) *Routes to Safety: Protection Issues Facing Abused Women and Children and the Role of Outreach Services*. Bristol: Women's Aid Federation of England.

Immarigeon, R. and Chesney-Lind, M. (1992) *Women's Prisons: Overcrowded and Overused*. San Francisco, CA: National Council on Crime and Delinquency.

Innes, M. (2003) *Investigating Murder: Detective Work and the Police Response to Criminal Homicide*. Oxford: Clarendon Press.

Jackall, R. (1988) *Moral Mazes: The World of Corporate Managers*. New York: Oxford University Press.

Jackson, C. (2006a) '"Wild" Girls? An Exploration of "Ladette" Cultures in Secondary Schools', *Gender and Education* 18(4): 339–60.

Jackson, C. (2006b) *'Lads' and 'Ladettes' in School: Gender and a Fear of Failure*. Maidenhead: Open University Press.

Jamieson, J. (2005) 'New Labour, Youth Justice and the Question of "Respect"', *Youth Justice* 5: 180–93.

Jamieson, J., McIvor, G. and Murray, C. (1999) *Understanding Offending Among Young People*. Edinburgh: HMSO.

Jansson, K. (2007) 'Domestic Violence, Sexual Assault and Stalking – the 2005–6 British Crime Survey', in K. Coleman, K. Jansson, P. Kaiza and E. Reed (eds) *Homicides, Firearm Offences and Intimate Violence 2005–2007*, Home Office Statistical Bulletin 02/07. London: Home Office.

Jefferson, T. (1990) *The Case Against Paramilitary Policing Considered*. Milton Keynes: Open University Press.

Jefferson, T. (1992) 'Wheelin and Stealin', *Achilles Heel* 13 (Summer).

Jefferson, T. (1996a) 'Introduction', *British Journal of Criminology* 36(3): 337–47.

Jefferson, T. (1996b) 'From "Little Fairy Boy" to the "Complete Destroyer": Subjectivity and Transformation in the Life of Mike Tyson', in M. Mac an Ghaill (ed.) *Understanding Masculinities: Social Relations and Cultural Arenas*. Buckingham: Open University Press.

Jefferson, T. (1997) 'Masculinities and Crimes', in M. Maguire, R. Morgan and R. Reiner (eds) *The Oxford Handbook of Criminology* (2nd edn). Oxford: Oxford University Press.

Jefferson, T. (1998) 'Muscle, "Hard Men" and "Iron" Mike Tyson: Reflections on Desire, Anxiety and Embodiment of Masculinity', *Body and Society* 4(1): 77–98.

Jenkins, C. (2000) 'Gender Just', *Police Review* 108: 22–3.

Jessop, B. (2000) 'From the KWNS to the SWPR', in G. Lewis, S. Gerwitz and J. Clarke (eds) *Rethinking Social Policy*, pp. 171–84. London: SAGE.

Jessop, B. (2003) *From Thatcherism to New Labour: Neo-Liberalism, Workfarism, and Labour Market Regulation*. Lancaster: Department of Sociology, University of Lancaster. Available at www.comp.lancs.ac.uk/sociology/soc131rj.pdf

Jewkes, Y. (2004) *Media and Crime*. London: SAGE.

Jewkes, Y. (2005) 'Men Behind Bars: "Doing Masculinity as an Adaptation to Imprisonment', *Men and Masculinities* 8(1): 44–63.

Jewkes, Y. and Johnson, H. (2006) *Prison Readings: A Critical Introduction to Prisons and Imprisonment*. Cullompton: Willan Publishing.

Johnson, J., Haider, F., Ellis, K., Hay, D. and Lindow, S. (2003) 'The Prevalence of Domestic Violence in Pregnant Women', *British Journal of Gynaecology* 100: 272–5.

Johnston, L. (2000) *Policing Britain*. Harlow: Longman.

Joint Committee on Human Rights (2002) *The Case for a Human Rights Commission*, Sixth Report, HL, (2002-03 67), HC (2002-03) 489, para 9.

Joint Committee on Human Rights (2003) *Inquiry into Human Rights and Deaths in Custody*, written evidence from inquest, 15 December 2003.

Kallen, E. (2004) *Social Inequality and Social Injustice: A Human Rights Perspective*. Basingstoke: Palgrave Macmillan.

Karmen, A. (2004) *Crime Victims: An Introduction to Victimology* (5th edn). Wadsworth: Thompson.

Kelly, L. (2002) *A Research Review on the Reporting, Investigation and Prosecution of Rape Cases*. London: HM Crown Prosecution Service Inspectorate and HM Inspectorate of Constabulary.

Kelly, L. and Regan, L. (2001) *Rape: The Forgotten Issue? A European Research and Networking Project*. London: University of North London Child and Woman Abuse Studies Unit.

Kelly, L., Lovett, J., Regan, L. (2005) *A Gap or Chasm? Attrition in Reported Rape Cases*, Home Office Research Study 293. London: Home Office.

Kemshall, H. (2003) *Understanding Risk in Criminal Justice*. Buckingham: Open University Press.

Kendall, K. (2000) 'Psy-ence Fiction: Governing Female Prisons through the Psychological Sciences', in K. Hannah-Moffat and M. Shaw (eds) *An Ideal Prison? Critical Essays on Women's Imprisonment in Canada*, pp. 94–102. Halifax: Fernwood Press.

Krug, E., Dahlberg, L., Mercy, J., Zwi, A. and Lozano, R et al. (2002) *World Report on Violence and Health*. Geneva: World Health Organization.

Kruttschnitt, C. (1984) 'Sex and Criminal Court Dispositions', *Journal of Research in Crime and Delinquency* 21: 213–32.

Lea, J. (2002) *Crime and Modernity*. London: SAGE.

Lea, S.J., Lanvers, U. and Shaw, S. (2003) 'Attrition in Rape Cases: Developing a Profile and Identifying Relevant Factors', *British Journal of Criminology* 43: 583–99.

Lees, S. and Gregory, J. (1993) *Rape and Sexual Assault: A Study of Attrition*. London: Islington Council.

Leidner, R. (1991) 'Selling Hamburgers and Selling Insurance: Gender Work and Identity in Interactive Service Jobs', *Gender and Society* 5(2): 154–77.

Lester, A. and Clapinska, L. (2005) 'An Equality and Human Rights Commission Worthy of the Name', in L. Clements and P.A. Thomas *Human Rights Act: A Success Story?* Oxford: Blackwell Publishing.

Levi, M. with Maguire, M. (2002) 'Violent Crime', in M. Maguire, R. Morgan and R. Reiner (eds) *The Oxford Handbook of Criminology* (3rd edn). Oxford: Oxford University Press.

Liebling, A. (1992) *Suicides in Prison*. London: Routledge.

Liebling, A. (1994) 'Suicide amongst Women Prisoners', *Howard Journal of Criminal Justice* 33(1): 1–9.

Liebling, A. (1995) 'Vulnerability and Prison Suicide', *British Journal of Criminology* 35(2): 173–87.

Linden, R. (1983) 'Women in Policing – A Study of Lower Mainland Royal Canadian Mounted Police Detachments', *Canadian Police College Journal* 7: 212–29.

Long, M. (2003) 'Leadership and Performance Management', in T. Newburn (ed.) *Handbook of Policing*. Cullompton: Willan Publishing.

Long, M. (2004) 'Naming, Shaming and the Politics of Blaming. Police Middle Management Perceptions of the Impact of Best Value', Unpublished Phd thesis, University of East London.

Loveday, B. (2000) 'The Crime and Disorder Act 1998 and Policing', *The Police Journal* 73(3).

Lowthian, J. (2002) 'Women's Prison in England: Barriers to Reform', in P. Carlen, (ed.) *Women and Punishment: the Struggle for Justice*. Cullompton: Willan Publishing.

Lukes, S. (1974) *Power*. London: Macmillan.

Lukes, S. (1986) *Power: Readings in Social and Political Theory*. Oxford: Basil Blackwell.

Lunnenborg, P.W. (1989) *Women Police Officer: Current Career Profiles*. Springfield, IL: Thomas.

Lyon, J. (2004) 'High Price to Pay for Jailing Women', *Observer* 18 July 2004.

Mac an Ghaill, M. (1994) *The Making of Men: Masculinities, Sexualities and Schooling*. Buckingham: Open University Press.

McConville, M., Sanders, A. and Leng, R. (1991) *The Case for the Prosecution*. London: Routledge.

McGlynn, C. (1998) *The Woman Lawyer: Making the Difference*. London: Butterworth.

McRobbie, A. (2004) 'Notes on Postfeminism and Popular Culture: Bridget Jones and the New Gender Regime', in A. Harris (ed.) *All About the Girl: Culture, Power and Identity*, pp. 3–14. New York: Routledge.

McVeigh, T. (2002) 'Girls are Now Bigger Bullies than Boys: Charity says Increase in "Girl-to-girl" Cruelty Blights Lives and is in Danger of Escalating out of Control', 10 November 2002.

McWilliams, M. and McKiernan, J. (1993) *Bringing it Out in the Open: Domestic Violence in Northern Ireland*. Belfast: HMSO.

Maguire, M. (2002) 'Crime Statistics: The "Data Explosion" and its Implications', in M. Maguire, R. Morgan and R. Reiner (eds) *The Oxford Handbook of Criminology* (3rd edn). Oxford: Oxford University Press.

Maguire, M. and John, T. (2006) 'Intelligence Led Policing, Managerialism and Community Engagement: Competing Priorities and the Role of the National Intelligence Model in the UK', *Policing and Society* 16(1): 67–85.

Malleson, K. (1999) *The New Judiciary: The Effects of Expansion and Activism*. London: Ashgate.

Malleson, K. (2002) 'Judicial Appointments: Another Nail in the Coffin?', *New Law Journal* 152 (7052).

Malleson, K. (2003) 'Justifying Gender Equality on the Bench: Why Difference Won't Do', *Feminist Legal Studies* 11: 1–24.

Malleson, K. and Banda, F. (2000) 'Factors Affecting the Decision to Apply for Silk and Judicial Office', Lord Chancellor's Department Research Series 2/00.

Malleson, K. and Russell, P. (2006) *Appointing Judges in an Age of Judicial Power: Critical Perspectives From Around the World*.

Manning, P. (1977) *Police Work*. Cambridge, MA: MIT Press.

Manning, P. (1989) 'Occupational Culture' in W.G. Bailey (ed.) *The Encyclopaedia of Police Science*. London: Garland.

Martin, S.E. and Jurik, N. (1996) *Doing Justice, Doing Gender*. London: SAGE.

Martin, G. (2006) *Understanding Terrorism* (2nd edn). London: SAGE.

Martin, P.Y. (1993) 'Feminist Practice in Organisations: Implications for Management', in Fagenson E.A. (ed.) *Women in Management: Trends, Issues and Challenges in Managerial Diversity*. London: SAGE.

Maruna, S. (2001) *Making Good: How Ex-convicts Change and Rebuild their Lives*. Washington, DC: American Psychological Association.

Mason, B. (2006) 'A Gendered Irish Experiment: Grounds for Optimism?', in F. Heidensohn (ed) *Gender and Justice: New Concepts and Approaches*. Cullompton: Willan Publishing.

Mathieson, T. (2000) *Prison on Trial* (2nd edn) Winchester: Waterside Press.

Matravers, A. (1997) 'Women and the Sexual Abuse of Children', *Forensic Update* 5(1): 9–13.

Matravers, A. (2001) 'Breaking the Silence', *Guardian* 15 February 2001.

Mawby, R. (ed.) (1999) *Policing Across the World: Issue for the Twenty-first Century*. London: UCL Press.

Mawby, R. (2001) *Burglary*. Cullompton: Willan Publishing.

Mawby, R. and Walklate, S. (1994) *Critical Victimology, International Perspectives*. London: SAGE.

Mendelsohn, B. (1937) 'Methods to be used by Counsel for the Defense in the Researches made into the Personality of the Criminal', *Revue de Droit Penal et de Criminologie*. August–October.

Mendelsohn, B. (1956) 'Une Nouvelle Branche de la Science Bio-psycho-sociale: Victimologie', *Revue Internationale De Criminologie et de Police Technique* 10: 95–109.

Menkel-Meadow, C. (1985) 'Portia in a Different Voice: Speculations on a Women's Lawyering Process', *Berkeley Women's Law Journal* 39(1): 39–63.

Menkel-Meadow, C. (1986) 'The Comparative Sociology of Women Lawyers: The "Feminisation" of the Legal Profession', *Osgoode Hall Law Journal* 24: 897–910.

Menkel-Meadow, C. (1987) 'Excluded Voices: New Voices in the Legal Profession, Making New Voices in the Law', *University of Miami Law Review* 42(7): 29–53.

Menkel-Meadow, C. (1988) 'Feminist Legal Theory, Critical Legal Studies and Legal Education or the "Fem Crits" go to Law School', *Journal of Legal Education* 38(1): 61–85.

Messerschmidt, J.W. (1993) *Masculinities and Crime: Critique and Reconceptualization of Theory*. Lanham, MD: Rowman & Littlefield.

Messerschmidt, J.W. (1997) *Crime as Structured Action: Gender, Race, Class, and Crime in the Making*. Thousand Oaks, CA: SAGE.

Messerschmidt, J.W. (2000) *Nine Lives: Adolescent Masculinities, the Body, and Violence*. Boulder, CO: Westview.

Messerschmidt, J.W. (2004) *Flesh and Blood: Adolescent Gender Diversity and Violence*. Lanham, MD: Rowman & Littlefield.

Messerschmidt, J.W. (2005) 'Masculinites and Crime: Beyond a Dualist Criminology', in C. Renzetti, L. Goodstein and S. Miller (eds) *Masculinities, Crime and Criminal Justice: Original Feminist Readings*. Los Angeles, CA: Roxbury.

Miller, J. (2001) *One of the Guys: Girls, Gangs and Gender*. Oxford: Oxford University Press.

Miller, S. (2005) *Victims as Offenders: Women's Use of Violence in Relationships*. New Brunswick, NJ: Rutgers University Press.

Miller, S.L. (1999) *Gender and Community Policing: Walking the Talk*. Boston, MA: Northeastern University Press.

Mills, A. and Tancred-Sheriff, P. (1992) *Gendering Organisational Analysis*. London: SAGE.

Mirrlees-Black, C. (1999) *Domestic Violence: Findings from a New British Crime Survey Self-Completion Questionnaire*, Home Office Research Study 191. London: Home Office.

Mitchell, J. (1971) *Woman's Estate*. Harmondsworth: Penguin.

Monaghan, L.F. (2004) 'Doorwork and Legal Risk: Observations from an Embodied Ethnography', *Social and Legal Studies* 13(4): 453–80.

Mooney, J. (1993) *The Hidden Figure: Domestic Violence in North London*. London: Islington Council.

Morley, R. and Mullender, A. (1994) *Preventing Domestic Violence to Women*, Police Research Group Crime Prevention Series Paper No. 48. London: HMSO.

Morris, A. (1987) *Women, Crime and Criminal Justice*. London: Blackwell.

Moulds, E.F. (1981) 'Chivalry and Paternalism: Disparities of Treatment in the Criminal Justice System', *Western Political Science Quarterly* 31: 416–40.

Mullender, A. (1996) *Rethinking Domestic Violence*. London: Routledge.

Myhill, A. and Allen, J. (2002a) *Rape and Sexual Assault of Women: Findings from the British Crime Survey*, Findings 159. London: Home Office.

Myhill, A. and Allen, J. (2002b) *Rape and Sexual Assault of Women: The Extent and Nature of the Problem. Findings from the British Crime Survey*. Home Office Research Study 237. London: Home Office.

NACRO (2005) *Making a Difference: NACRO Annual Review*. London: NACRO.

Naffeine, N. (1997) *Feminism and Criminology*. Cambridge: Polity Press.

Nagel, I. (1980) 'Sex Differences in the Processing of Criminal Defendants', in A. Morris and L. Gelsthorpe (eds) *Women and Crime*. Cambridge: Cambridge Institute of Criminology.

National Probation Service (2005) *Human Resources Workforce Profile Report* (Issue 2). London: Home Office.

Nelken, D. (ed.) (1994) *The Futures of Criminology*. London: SAGE.

Newburn, T. (2002) 'Modernisation, New Labour and Criminal Justice Policy', *Criminal Justice Matters* No 46.

Newburn, T. (2003) *Handbook of Policing*. Cullompton: Willan Publishing.

Newburn, T. and Stanko, E. (eds) (1994) *Just Boys Doing Business: Men, Masculinities and Crime*. London: Routledge.

Nicholas, S., Povey, D., Walker, A. and Kershaw, C. (2005) *Crime in England and Wales 2004/05: Home Office Statistics Bulletin*. London: Home Office.

Nichols, N.A. (1993) 'Whatever Happened to Rosie the Riveter?', *Harvard Business Review* July/Aug (54): 62.

Nickel, J (1992) *Making Sense of Human Rights: Philosophical Reflections on the Universal Declaration of Human Rights*. Berkeley, CA: University of California Press.

NOMS (2005) *Prison Population and Accommodation Briefing for 9th December 2005*. London: NOMS Estate Planning and Development Unit.

Norrie, A. (2001) 'A Criminal Justice, Judicial Interpretation, Legal Right: on Being Sceptical about the Human Rights Act 1998', in T. Campbell, K.D. Ewing and A. Tomkins (eds) *Sceptical Essays on Human Rights*. Oxford: Oxford University Press.

O'Donnell, I. (2004) 'Prison Rape in Context', *British Journal of Criminology* 44: 241–55.

Office of National Statistics (1999) *Substance Abuse Among Prisoners*. London: Office of National Statistics

Owers, A. (2004) 'Prison Inspection and the Protection of Human Rights', *European Human Rights Law Review* 2: 108–17.

Packer, H. (1968) *The Limits of Criminal Sanctions*. Stanford, CA: Stanford University Press.

Padfield, N. and Maruna, S. (2006) 'The Revolving Door at the Prison Gate', *Criminology and Criminal Justice* 329.

Pearson, G. (1983) *Hooligan: A History of Respectable Fears*. London: Macmillan.

Pease, K. (1998) *Repeat Victimisation: Taking Stock*. Crime Detection and Prevention Series Paper 90. London: Home Office.

Phillips, C. and Brown, D. (1998) *Entry into the Criminal Justice System: A Survey of Police Arrests and their Outcome*. London: Home Office.

Phoenix, J. (2002) 'Youth Prostitution Policy Reform: New Discourse, Same Old Story', in P. Carlen (ed.) *Women and Punishment: the Struggle for Justice*. Cullompton: Willan Publishing.

Pitts, J. (2003) 'Changing Youth Justice', *Youth Justice* 3(1): 5–20.

Plotnikoff, J. and Woolfson, R. (1998) *Policing Domestic Violence: Effective Organizational Structures*. London: Home Office.

Police Regulations (2003) Statutory Instrument 2003 No. 527 available at www.opsi.gov.uk/si/si2003/20030527.htm

Pollack, S. (2000) 'Dependency Discourse as Social Control', in K. Hannah-Moffat and M. Shaw (eds) *An Ideal Prison? Critical Essays on Women's Imprisonment in Canada*, pp. 94–102. Halifax: Fernwood Press.

Pollak, O. (1950) *The Criminality of Women*. Philadelphia, PA: University of Pennsylvania Press.

Pollard, C. (2000) 'Victims and the Criminal Justice System: A New Vision', *Criminal Law Review* 5.

Povey, D. (ed.) (2004) *Crime in England and Wales 2002/03: Supplementary Volume I: Homicide and Gun Crime*. London: Home Office.

Pratt, J. (2007) *Penal Populism*. London: Routledge.

Pryce, K. (1979) *Endless Pressure*. Harmondsworth: Penguin.

Rackley, E. (2006) 'Judicial Diversity, the Woman Judge and Fairy Tale Endings', *Legal Studies* 27(1): 74–94.

Radford, J. and Stanko, E. (eds) (1989) *Women, Policing and Male Violence*. London: Routledge.

Radford, J. and Stanko, E. (1991) 'Violence against Women and Children: The Contradictions of Crime Control under Patriarchy', in K. Stenson and D. Cowell (ed.) *The Politics of Crime Control*. London: SAGE.

Radford, J., Harne, L. and Trotter, J. (2006) 'Disabled Women and Domestic Violence as Violent Crime', *Practice* 18(4): 233–46.

Radford, L. and Gill, A. (2006) 'Losing the Plot? Researching Community Safety Partnership Work against Domestic Violence', *Howard Journal of Criminal* 45(4): 369–87.

Radford, L. and Tsutsumi, K. (2004) 'Globalization and Violence against Women-Inequalities in Risks, Responsibilities and Blame in the UK and Japan', *Women's Studies International Forum* 27: 1–12.

Raine, J.W. (2001) 'Modernizing Courts or Courting Modernization?', *Criminal Justice* 1(1): 105–28.

Raine, J. (2002) 'Modernisation and Criminal Justice', in D. Ward, J. Scott and M. Lacey (eds) *Probation: Working for Justice*. Oxford: Oxford University Press.

Rake, K. (2005) *Whither Feminism*. London: Fawcett Society.

Reed, J. and Lyne, M. (1997) 'The Quality of Healthcare in Prison: Results of a Year's Programme of Semi Structured Inspections', *British Medical Journal* 315: 1420–4.

Reilly, J., Muldoon, O. and Byrne, C. (2004) 'Young Men as Perpetrators and Victims of Violence in Northern Ireland: A Qualitative Analysis', *Journal of Social Issues* 60(3): 469–84.

Reiner, R. (1978) *The Blue-Coated Worker*. Cambridge: Cambridge University Press.

Reiner, R. (1991) *Chief Constables*. Oxford: Oxford University Press.

Reiner, R. (1992)*The Politics of the Police* (2nd edn). Brighton: Wheatsheaf.

Reiner, R. (2000) *The Politics of the Police* (3rd edn). Oxford: Oxford University Press.

Reiner, R. (2007) *Law and Order: An Honest Citizen's Guide to Crime and Control*. Cambridge: Cambridge University Press.

Reskin, B.F. and Hartmann, H. (1986) *Women's Work, Men's Work: Sex Segregation on the Job*. Washington: National Academy Press.

Reskin, B.F. and Roos, P. (1990) *Gender Queues, Job Queues: Explaining Women's Inroads into Male Occupations*. Philadelphia, PA: Temple University Press.

Rhodes, R.A.W. (1997) *Understanding Governance*. Buckingham: Open University Press.

Rifkin, J. (1984) 'Mediation from a Feminist Perspective: Promise and Problems', *Law and Inequality* 2: 21–2.

Ringrose, J. (2006) 'A New Universal Mean Girl: Examining the Discursive Construction and Social Regulation of a New Feminine Pathology', *Feminism and Psychology* 16(4): 405–24.

Roberts, J.V. (1996) 'Sexual Assaults in Canada: Recent Statistical Trends', *Queens Law Journal* 21: 395–421.

Roberts, J.V. and Hough, M. (2002) *Changing Attitudes to Punishment: Public Opinion, Crime and Justice*. Cullompton: Willan Publishing.

Rock, P. (1994) 'The Social Organisation of British Criminology', in M. Maguire, R. Morgan and R. Reiner (eds) *The Oxford Handbook of Criminology*. Oxford: Oxford University Press.

Rock, P. (2007) 'New Labour Policies for Victims', *Criminal Justice Matters* 67: 38–9.

Roth, K. (1994) 'Domestic Violence as an International Human Rights Issue', in R. Cook, (ed.) *Human Rights of Women: National and International Perspectives*. Philadelphia, PA: Pennsylvania Press.

Rowe, M. (2004) *Policing, Race and Racism*. Cullompton: Willan Publishing.

Royal College of Psychiatrists (2004) *Troubled Inside: Responding to the Mental Health Needs of Children and Young People in Prison*. London: Prison Reform Trust.

Ruggerio, V. (1996) *Organised and Corporate Crime in Europe*. Aldershot: Dartmouth.

Rutherford, S. (2001) 'Are you Going Home Already?: The Long Hours Culture, Women Managers and Patriarchal Closure', *Time and Society*, 10(2/3): 259–76.

Sanders, A. (1993) 'Controlling the Discretion of the Individual Officer', in R. Reiner and S. Spencer (eds) *Accountable Policing: Effectiveness, Empowerment and Equity*. London: IPPR.

Sanders, A. and Young, R. (2003) 'Police Powers', in T. Newburn (ed.) *Handbook of Policing*. Cullompton: Willan Publishing.

Scarman, Lord (1981) *The Brixton Disorders 10–12 April, Report of an Inquiry by the Rt. Honourable Lord Scarman*, Cmnd 8427. London: HMSO.

Scarry, E. (1985) *The Body in Pain: The Making and Unmaking of the World*. New York: Oxford University Press.

Schafer, S. (1968) *The Victim and his Criminal: A Study into Functional Responsibility*. New York: Random House.

Schechter, S. (1982) *Women and Male Violence*. Cambridge MA: Southend Press.

Scraton, P. and Moore, L. (2004) *The Hurt Inside: The Imprisonment of Women and Girls in Northern Ireland*. Belfast: Northern Ireland Human Rights Commission, Northern Ireland.

Sedley, S. (2005) 'The Rocks or the Open Sea? Where is the Human Rights Act Heading?', in L. Clements and P.A. Thomas, *Human Rights Act: A Success Story?* Oxford: Blackwell Publishing.

Segal, L. (1999) *Why Feminism?* London: Polity Press.

Senior, P. (2005) 'Are You Thinking What I'm Thinking', *British Journal of Community Justice* 3(3): 1–4.

Senior, P., Crowther-Dowey, C. and Long, M. (2007) *Understanding Modernisation in Criminal Justice.* Maidenhead: Open University Press.

Sherman, L. (1975) 'Evaluation of Policewomen on Patrol in a Suburban Police Department', *Journal of Police Science and Administration* 3: 434–8.

Silvestri, M. (2003) *Women In Charge: Policing, Gender and Leadership.* Cullompton: Willan Publishing.

Silvestri, M. (2006) '"Doing Time": Becaming a Police Leader', *International Journal of Police Science and Management.* Vol. 8, No: 4: 266–81.

Sim, J. (1990) *Medical Power in Prisons: the Prison Medical Service in England 1774–1989.* Milton Keynes: Open University Press.

Simon, R. (1975) *Women and Crime.* Lexington: London.

Simpson, M., Shildrick, T. and MacDonald, R. (eds) (2007) *Drugs in Britain: Supply, Consumption and Control.* Basingstoke: Palgrave Macmillan.

Simpson, S. (1989) 'Feminist Theory, Crime, and Justice', *Criminology*, 27: 605–31.

Smart, C. (1977) *Women, Crime and Criminology.* London: Routledge and Kegan Paul.

Smart, C. (1989) *Feminism and the Power of the Law.* London: Routledge.

Smith, C. and Allen, J. (2004) *Violent Crime in England and Wales*, Home Office Online Report 18/04. London: Home Office.

Smith, D.J. and Gray, J. (1983) 'The Police in Action', in D.J. Smith *Police and People in London.* London: Policy Studies Institute.

Smith, G. (2002) 'Reasonable Suspicion: Time for a Re-evaluation', *International Journal of the Sociology of Law* 30: 1–16.

Smith, L.J.F. (1989) *Concerns About Rape*, Home Office Research Study No. 106. London: HMSO.

Smith, R. (2003) *Youth Justice: Ideas, Policy and Practice.* Cullompton: Willan Publishing.

Smith, R. (2007) *Youth Justice: Ideas, Policy and Practice* (2nd edn). Cullompton: Willan Publishing.

Snider, L. (2003) 'Constituting the Punishable Woman: Atavistic Man Incarcerates Postmodern Woman', *British Journal of Criminology* 43(2): 354–78.

Social Exclusion Unit (2002) *Reducing Re-offending by Ex-Prisoners.* London: Cabinet Office.

Social Work Services and Prisons Inspectorate for Scotland (1998) *Women Offenders – A Safer Way: A Review of Community Disposals and the Use of Custody for Women Offenders in Scotland in 1998.* Scottish Executive Office.

South, N. (1998) 'Late-Modern Criminology: "Late" as in "Dead" or "Modern" as in "New"?', in D. Owen, *After Sociology.* London: SAGE.

Spalek, B. (2006) *Crime Victims: Theory, Policy and Practice.* Basingstoke: Palgrave.

Spencer, S. and Bynoe, I. (1998) *A Human Rights Commission, the Options for Britain and Northern Ireland.* London: Institute of Public Policy Research.

Spillar, K. (1999) 'A Testimony of Katherine Spillar: Police Use of Excessive Force: Taking Gender into Account' National Centre for Women and Policing: available at www.feminist.org/police/kstestim.html

Squires, P. and Stephen, D. (2005) *Rougher Justice: Anti-Social Behaviour and Young People*. Cullompton: Willan Publishing.

Stanko, E. (1985) *Intimate Intrusions: Women's Experiences of Male Violence*. London: Routledge.

Stanko, E. (1989) 'Missing the Mark: Policing Battering', in J. Hanmer, J. Radford and E. Stanko (eds) *Women, Policing and Male Violence*. London: Routledge.

Stanko, E. (1990) *Everyday Violence*. London: Virago.

Stanko, E. (1995) 'Policing Domestic Violence: Dilemmas and Contradictions', *Australian and New Zealand Journal of Criminology* Special Supplement: 31–44.

Stanko, E. (1998) 'Making the Invisible Visible in Criminology: A Personal Journey', in S. Holdaway and P. Rock (eds) *Thinking about Criminology*. London: UCL Press.

Stanko, B. (2002) *Taking Stock: What Do We Know About Interpersonal Violence* (ESRC Violence Research Programme). London: Royal Holloway University London.

Stanko, B., O'Bierne, M. and Zafutto, G. (2002) *Taking Stock: What Do We Know About Interpersonal Violence*, The ESRC Violent Research Programme. London: HMSO.

Steffensmeier, D.J. (1980) 'Sex Differences in Patterns of Adult Crime, 1965–1977', *Social Forces* 58: 1080–108.

Steffensmeier, D. and Herbert, C. (1999) 'Women and Men Policymakers: Does the Judge's Gender Affect the Sentencing of Criminal Defendants', *Social Forces* 77: 1163.

Steffensmeier, D.J. and Steffensmeier, R.H. (1980) 'Trends in Female Delinquency: An Examination of Arrest, Juvenile Court, Self-report and Field Data', *Criminology* 18: 62–85.

Steffensmeier, D.J., Schwartz, J., Zhong, H. and Ackerman, J. (2005) 'An Assessment of Recent Trends in Girls' Violence using Diverse Longitudinal Sources', *Criminology* 43: 355–406.

Stenson, K., Travers, M. and Crowther, C. (1999) *The Police and Inter-ethnic Conflict: Report Commissioned by the Metropolitan Police*. Buckingham: Social Policy Research Group: Buckinghamshire Chilterns University College.

Stets, J. and Straus, M. (1990) 'Gender Differences in Reporting Marital Violence and its Medical and Psychological Consequences', in M. Straus and R. Gelles (eds) *Physical Violence in American Families*. New Brunswick, NJ. Transaction.

Stewart, A. and Madden, K. (1997) 'Police Officers' Judgements of Blame in ... the Impact of Legal and Extralegal Factors', *Law and Human Behaviour* 4: 81–99.

Stone, R., Kemp, T. and Weldon, G. (1994) 'Part-time Working and Job Sharing in the Police Service', Police Research Series Paper 7. London: Home Office.

Straw, J. and Boateng, P. (1996) *Bringing Rights Home: Labour's Plan to Incorporate the European Convention on Human Rights into UK Law*. London: The Labour Party.

Stubbs, J. (ed.) (1994) *Women, Male Violence and the Law*. Sydney: Institute of Criminology.

Sutton, R. and Farrall, S. (2004) 'Gender, Socially Desirable Responding and the Fear of Crime', *British Journal of Criminology* 45: 212–24.

Taft, J. (2004) 'Girl Power Politics: Pop-culture Barriers and Organizational Resistance' in A. Harris (ed.) *All About the Girl: Culture, Power and Identity, pp. 69–78*. New York: Routledge.

Taylor, S. and Tyler, M. (2000) 'Emotional Labour and Sexual Difference in the Airline Industry', *Work, Employment and Society* 14(1): 77–95.

Temkin, J. (1987) *Rape and the Legal Process*. London: Routledge and Kegan Paul.

Temkin, J. (1997) 'Plus Ca Change: Reporting Rape in the 1990s', *British Journal of Criminology* 37: 507–27.

Temkin, J. (2000) 'Literature Review: Rape and Sexual Assault', in *Setting the Boundaries*. London: Home Office.

Thomas, T. (2005) *Sex Crime: Sex Offending and Society*. Cullompton: Willan Publishing.

Thompson, M., Arias, I., Basile, K. and Desai, S. (2002) 'The Association between Childhood Physical and Sexual Victimization and Health Problems in Adulthood', *Journal of Interpersonal Violence* 17(10): 1115–29.

Thornton, M. (1996) *Dissonance and Distrust: Women in the Legal Profession*. Melbourne: Oxford University Press.

Tilley, N. (ed) (2005) *Handbook of Crime Prevention and Community Safety*. Cullompton: Willan Publishing.

Travers, M. (2007) *The New Bureaucracy: Quality Assurance and is Critics*. Bristol: Policy Press.

Tuffin, R. and Baladi, Y. (2001) *Flexible Working Practices in the Police Service*, Home Office Police Research Paper No. 147. London: Home Office.

UNIFEM (2003) *Not a Minute More: Ending Violence Against Women*. New York: UNIFEM.

United Nations (1955) *Standard Minimum Rules for the Treatment of Prisoners*. Office of the High Commissioner for Human Rights.

United Nations (1993) *Declaration on the Elimination of Violence Against Women*. United Nations.

United Nations (1995) *Platform for Action*, Report of the Fourth World Conference on Women, Beijing, September (UN Publication, E96.IV.13). New York: United Nations.

United Nations (1999) *Declaration on the Right and Responsibility of Individuals, Groups and Organs of Society to Promote and Protect Universally Recognised Human Rights and Fundamental Freedoms*, Office of the United Nations High Commissioner for Human Rights. United Nations.

United Nations (2002) *Optional Protocol to the Convention against Torture and Other Cruel, Inhuman or Degrading Treatment or Punishment*. Office of the United Nations High Commissioner for Human Rights. United Nations.

UNPFA (United Nations Population Fund) (2005) *Violence against Women*, available at: www.unfpa.org.swp/factsheets.

Visher, C. (1983) 'Gender, Police Arrest Decisions, and Notions of Chivalry', *Criminology* 21: 5–28.

Von Hentig, H. (1948) *The Criminal and His Victim*. New Haven, CT: Yale University Press.

Waaland, P. and Keeley, S. (1985) 'Police Decision Making in Wife Abuse: The Impact of Legal and Extralegal Factors', *Law and Human Behavior* 9: 355–66.

Waddington, P.A.J. (1999) *Policing Citizens*. London: UCL Press.

Wadham, J. and Modi, K. (2004) 'Policing and the Human Rights Act', in R. Hopkins Burke (ed.) *Hard Cop, Soft Cop: Dilemmas and Debates in Contemporary Policing*. Cullompton: Willan Publishing.

Waiton, S. (2001) *Scared of the Kids?: Curfews, Crime and the Regulation of Young People*. Sheffield: Sheffield Hallam University.

Walby, S. (2004) *The Cost of Domestic Violence*. London: Women and Equality Unit Department of Trade and Industry.

Walby, S. and Allen, J. (2004) *Domestic Violence, Sexual Assault and Stalking: Findings from the British Crime Survey*, Home Office Research Study 276. London: Home Office.

Walker, A., Kershaw, C. and Nicholas, S. (2006) *Crime in England and Wales 2005–6*, Home Office Statistical Bulletin 12/06. London: Home Office.

Walker, L.E. (1979) *The Battered Woman*. New York: Harper & Row.

Walklate, S. (1989) *Victimology: The Victim and the Criminal Justice Process.* London: Unwin Hyman.

Walklate, S. (1993a) 'Sexing Sheehy: Towards a Gendered Agenda for Policing', *Masculinity and Crime: Issues in Theory and Practice Conference Report,* Brunel University 14–15 September.

Walklate, S. (1993b) 'Policing by Women, with Women, for Women', *Policing* 9 (Summer): 101–15.

Walklate, S. (1996) 'Equal Opportunities and the Future of Policing', in F. Leishman, B. Loveday and S. Savage (eds) *Core Issues in Policing.* London: Longman.

Walklate, S. (2001) *Gender, Crime and Criminal Justice.* Cullompton: Willan Publishing.

Walklate, S. (2004) *Gender, Crime and Criminal Justice* (2nd edn). Cullompton: Willan Publishing.

Wallace, H. (1998) *Victimology: Legal, Social and Psychological Perspectives.* Boston, MA: Allyn and Bacon.

Walsh, C. (2003) 'Dispersal of Rights: A Critical Comment on Specified Provisions of The Anti-Social Behaviour Bill', *Youth Justice* 3(2): 104–11.

Walters, R. (2003) 'New Modes of Governance and the Commodification of Criminological Knowledge', *Social and Legal Studies – An International Journal* 12(1): 5–26.

Watson, J. (2007) *Where are All the Women?* London: Equal Opportunities Commission.

Watts, C. and Zimmerman, C. (2002) 'Violence Against Women: Global Scope and Magnitude', *The Lancet* 359, April 6.

Webster, C. (2007) *Understanding Race and Crime.* Milton Keynes: Open University Press.

Wedderburn, D. et al. (2000) *Justice for Women: The Need for Reform.* London: Prison Reform Trust.

West, D. and Farrington, D.P. (1977) *The Delinquent Way of Life: The Third Report of the Cambridge Study in Delinquent Behaviour.* London: Heinemann.

Whitehead, A. (2005) 'Man to Man Violence: How Masculinity May Work as Dynamic Risk Factor', *Howard Journal of Criminal Justice* 44(4): 411–22.

Whitehead, C.M.E., Stockdale, J.E., and Razzu, G. (2003) *The Economic and Social Costs of Anti-Social Behaviour: A Review.* London: London School of Economics.

Wiles, P. (1999) 'The Contribution of Research to Policy', speech given at the Centre for Criminal Justice Studies (ISTD), AGM, November.

Williams, B. (2003) 'Where do Victims of Crime Fit in?', *British Journal of Community Justice* 2(2): 1–10.

Williams, B. and Canton, R. (2005) 'Victim of Crime, Offenders and Communities', *British Journal of Community Justice* 3(2): 1–8.

Williamson, E. (2000) *Domestic Violence and Health: The Response of the Medical Profession.* Bristol: Policy Press.

Winlow, S. (2001) *Badfellas.* Oxford: Berg.

Winlow, S. and Hall, S. (2006) *Violent Night: Urban Leisure and Contemporary Culture.* Oxford: Berg.

Wolfgang, M.E. (1958) *Patterns of Criminal Homicide.* Philadelphia, PA: University of Pennsylvania Press.

Women's Advisory Council to the Los Angeles Police Commission (1993) *A Blueprint for Implementing Gender Equality in the Los Angeles Police Department.* Los Angeles, CA: Los Angeles Police Department.

Women and Equality Unit (2002) *Equality and Diversity: Making it Happen*. London: Women and Equality Unit.

Wood, J.R.T. (1997) *Final Report of the Royal Commission into the New South Wales Police Service*.

Woodiwiss (2005) *Human Rights*. Oxon: Routledge.

World Heath Organization (2002) *World Report on Violence and Health*. Geneva: WHO.

Worrall, A. (2002) 'Rendering them Punishable', in P. Carlen (ed.) *Women and Punishment: The Struggle for Justice*. Cullompton: Willan Publishing.

Worrall, A. (2004) 'Twisted Sisters, Ladettes, and the New Penology: the Social Construction of "Violent Girls"', in C. Alder and A. Worrall (eds) *Girls' Violence: Myths and Realities,* pp. 41–60. New York: SUNY.

Wykes, M. and Welsh, K. (2007) *Violence, Gender and Justice*. London: SAGE.

Yar, M. (2006) *Cybercrime and Society*. London: SAGE.

Yodanis, C.L., Godenzi, A. and Stanko, E. (2000) 'The Benefits of Studying Costs: A Review and Agenda for Studies on the Economic Costs of Violence Against Women', *Policy Studies* 21(3): 236–76.

Young, J. (1986) 'The Failure of Criminology: The Need for a Radical Realism', in R. Matthews and J. Young (eds) *Confronting Crime*. London: SAGE.

Young, J. (2007) *The Vertigo of Late Modernity*. London: SAGE.

Young, M. (1991) *An Inside Job*. Oxford: Clarendon Press.

Zedner, L. (1994) 'Victims', in M. Maguire, R. Morgan and R. Reiner (eds) *The Oxford Handbook of Criminology*. Oxford: Oxford University Press.

Zedner, L. (2002) 'Victims', in M. Maguire, R. Morgan and R. Reiner (eds) *The Oxford Handbook of Criminology* (3rd edn). Oxford: Oxford University Press.

Index

NOTE: Page numbers in **bold** type refer to glossary definitions.

judiciary, 145, 168, 173–4, 182–4
  see also courts
juvenile delinquency *see* anti-social
  behaviour; mean girls

Kallen, E., 11, 13–14, 96, 106
Karmen, A., 114, 123
Kelly, L., 91
Kennedy, D.B., 170
Kruttschnitt, C., 34

ladette, 27–8, **221**
  see also mean girls
latent conflict, 155
Lees, S., 89, 90
left realist criminology, **221**
legal profession, 144–5, 168, 173–4,
  182–4, 185
Lester, A., 15
Liebling, A., 18, 40
lifestyle, and victimization, 120, 123, 124, 126
Lowthian, J., 36, 40, 46
Lukes, S., 154–5
Lyon, J., 18, 36, 43

Macpherson Inquiry, 150, 158
magistrates, **221**
magistrates' courts, **221**
Maguire, M., 119, 120
Mahmod, Banaz, 95
male criminal justice workers, 140–7
male offenders, 192–3
  and human rights, 5, 53, 69–77, 79
male offending, 54–9, 77–8
  compared with female, 26–8, 30–1
  and masculinities, 59–68
male prisoners, 26, 58–9, 72, 116
male rape, 115–16, 122
male victims, 6, 85, 112–20, 194
  criminal justice response to, 120–3
  of domestic violence, 29–30, 114–15, 122–3
  human rights of, 125–33
  masculinities, 124
  men's victim-offender status, 124–5
male violence
  and human rights, 76
  see also domestic violence
Malleson, K., 173–4, 183
managerialism *see* New Public Management
manhood, 68
marginalization, 53, 63, 72–6, 131, **221**
Martin, D., 156

masculinity/ies, **221**
  and ASB, 126
  in criminology, 10
  and human rights, 5, 53, 69–77, 79
  and male victimization, 124
  and policing, 149–52
  theorizations of, 59–68, 78
  see also cult of masculinity;
    hegemonic masculinity
Mason, B., 47
Mathiesen, T., 18, 37
Matravers, A., 29
Mawby, R., 19
mean girls, 28–9, 30–3, **221**
media, 28, 206, 209, 210
men
  criminalization of, 56–7
  perspectives on, 59–60, 78
    psychosocial approach, 65–7
    sociological approach, 60–5, 68
  writing on criminality and, 69
  see also gender balance in organizations;
    male offenders; male victims;
    masculinities
Mendelsohn, B., 92, 123
mental health problems, 17, 18, 35
merit, 184
Messerschmidt, J.W., 63, 64–5, 68
Middleton case, 41, 49–50
Miller, J., 31
Miller, S.L., 171
Mirrlees-Black, C., 114
Mitchell, J., 61
modernity, **221**
modernization, 156–7, 196–201
Monaghan, L.F., 152
Monckton Enquiry, 208
monopolization of perception, and
  coercion, 100
Mooney, J., 94
Moore, L., 40–1, 42–3, 44–5
moral panics, 210, **221**
moral perspective, 91
Morgan, R., 205, 211
Morley, R., 94
Morrill, R., 132
Morris, A.M., 34
mother and baby units, 42, 43
mothers in prison, 37, 42–3, **221**
mugging, 113
Mullender, A., 94
Muncie, J., 128

murder, 118–20
Myhill, A, 86

NACRO, 147
Narey, M., 144
National Centre of Women Police
    (NCWP), 172
National Offender Management Service
    (NOMS), 142–4
National Probation Directorate (NPD), 143
natural rights, 11
Nelken, D., 19
Netherlands, women prisoners in, 43
New Public Management (NPM),
    196–201, **221**
Newburn, T., 148
Newman, Sir K., 88
Nicholas, S., 85
Nichols, N.A., 171
night-time economy, 124, 126, 152
no-criming, 90, 91, **221**
Northern Ireland Human Rights Commission,
    15, 18, 40
notifiable offences, 56, **221**

O'Donnell, I., 116
offences, **221**
offences against property, 112–13
offender behaviour programmes, 58
offenders, 17–18, 20–1
    see also female offenders; male offenders
offending see female offending; male
    offending; search for equivalence
omnipotence, and coercion, 101
Optional Protocol to the Convention against
    Torture, 38
organizational cultures
    and gendered working of power, 158–9
    see also police culture
organizations
    gender balance in, 167–75
    gendered, 175–84
Owers, A., 17

Packer, H., 75
paedophilia, **222**
pain, 98–102, **222**
para-professionals, 147
parenting contracts, 131
parenting orders, 131
parole, **222**
Parole Board, 146, **222**

parole hearings, 209–10
part-time work, 179–81
patriarchy, 60, **222**
Patten Commission, 74–5
penal populism, 203–6, 210
performance management, 196–201
physical torture, 98, 99
Pitts, J., 199
plea, **222**
Plotnikoff, J., 95
pluralism, 154, **222**
pluralization of policing, 152
police, **222**
    approach to justice, 206
    career progression, 141, 172–3,
        177–8, 180–1
    gender composition, 140–2
    and human rights of marginalized
        men, 72–6
    and policing, 148–9
    response to ASB, 129, 130
    response to victims, 202
        of domestic violence, 88–90, 93–5, 122–3
        male victims, 122
    and risk assessment, 211
Police Community Support Officers
    (PCSOs), 130
police culture, 88, 94, 149–52, 158–9, **222**
Police Performance Assessment Framework
    (PPAF), 197
police violence, 149, 171, 172
policewomen, 141, 149, 150, 151, 170, 171–3,
    177–81, 186, **222**
policing, 148–9, **222**
    benefits of gender balance for, 170
    gender and styles of, 171–3
    privatization of, 148–9, 212
policy see criminal justice policy;
    government policy
political rights, 12, 71, 96
Pollack, O., 26
postmodern, 62, **222**
power, 153–9, **222**
Prashar, Baroness U., 183
prison service, 142–3, 200–1
prisoners
    human rights of, 17–18
    see also female prisoners; male prisoners
prisons
    expanding population, 204–5
    penal populism, 203–6, 210
    and rehabilitation, 206–7